ALSO BY RORY NUGENT

The Search for the Pink-Headed Duck

Drums Along the Congo

DOWN
at the
DOCKS

DOWN
at the
DOCKS

Rory Nugent

PANTHEON BOOKS, NEW YORK

All rights reserved. Published in the United States by Pantheon
Books, a division of Random House, Inc., New York, and in
Canada by Random House of Canada Limited, Toronto.

Pantheon Books and colophon are registered trademarks
of Random House, Inc.

ISBN-13: 978-1-61523-517-9

Printed in the United States of America

TO
ELIZABETH

CONTENTS

One Hard by the Water's Edge   3

Two Good as Gone   55

Three Pink   105

Four Mr. Jinx   148

Five Whalebone   188

Six Perfect Wreck   241

Acknowledgments   289

DOWN
at the
DOCKS

One

HARD BY THE WATER'S EDGE

SWORD CURSES AND PROMISES TO smack the next person who enters the Harborside Cafe and says, Good morning. There's a nor'easter moving into the neighborhood, and he calls it a freakin' horror show sure to punish fishermen for being fishermen from here to Timbuktu. Good morning, my ass. Anyone worth saluting and still alive on the docks knows there be bad in the air. He warns: If you aren't eyeball-to-eyeball with a nasty blow, it'll bite you awful hard. Hell, it will eat you whole.

The weatherman on the late-night news described the storm as a minor disturbance sure to dissipate by morning. Don't forget the sunblock, he reminded viewers, before signing off. Sword studied the maps and radar imagery on TV and went to bed expecting to wake a few hours later to clear skies and smooth sailing. His seabag was packed for a twelve- to fourteen-day fishing trip aboard the *Ocean-C,* an offshore dragger rigged for catching scallops. She had been iced, fueled and provisioned the day before, her gear checked, tweaked and greased, and her crew was prepared to leave for the fishing grounds off Georges Bank at slack tide, around five this morning.

Sword awoke at three a.m., eager to begin the hunt. But, Christ Almighty, he says, he wasn't out of bed ten minutes before his marine radio started yapping. The unit automatically responds to storm alerts issued by the National Weather Service, and he listened to a bulletin about a major depression forming off the Jersey coast and tracking northward. The wind was expected to clock speeds over 60 knots, with waves building into twenty-five-foot monsters. The news got him swearing something fierce. After a bit, though, he remembers going all quiet-like, thinking hard, truly, wondering about how much a feller misses between one snore and his last.

He taps a forefinger on the sea-green Formica countertop and says he's bothered, way-so, by the possibility that he could someday end up dead in bed. While others might welcome such a peaceful exit, he ain't one of them. It would deny him his right to fight. Just as bad, it'd mean betrayal. He reasons: A bunk be a feller's hurricane hole. No matter what it be blowing or what direction shit be flying, a pillow done always put a muffler on the howl.

Sword pauses (three count) and says, Another big fact, this: there's nothing much safe. The newspaper be full of stories about hims and hers and way-bad conclusions. You get babies smothered by their mother's breasts. Honeymooners electrocuted in the bubble bath. And, sure-sure, there always be family dogs eating families.

He digs into what's left of his $3.29 Harborside Cafe Breakfast Plate Special: two eggs, spuds, links or bacon, toast and coffee. I scan the eatery hoping to raise Fatima, Keeper of the Coffeepot and heiress to the cafe. The place is nearly empty today and there's no sign of Fatima. The coffeepot is dry; dirty dishes clutter tabletops; meal checks sit untended by the register, which carries a note taped to its side: *Please return the Jimmy Fund jar.* Off to the left, along the north wall, decorated with dozens of pictures of local fishing boats, a fluorescent lightbulb flickers, its ballast shot and humming the problem.

Leaning backward on the stool, Sword issues a low, one-note whistle, and says, Listen to this, will-ya? He lists some reasons why: Because he just thought of it. Because it happened to him, so you know it be awful-like real. And because he loved her some way-lots.

The *Magnificence,* he repeats three times. That was her name, the boat, it was, and it fit her right and tight. He was one of eight aboard during her last voyage and says everyone was feeling lucky. The weather was finest-kind. Warm. Flat seas. A big sky showing more stars than anybody knows what to do with. Better yet, they were six days out and had bagged nearly six tons of scallop meat. With that treasure in the hold, and more coming up in every tow, he remembers dreaming about the payday ahead: wads of presidents ain't nobody knows shit about, except how smooth, all silky-like, they feel slipping in and out of a pocket.

He stops to raise his coffee mug and makes a toast. To the *Magnificence,* he says, and swallows. Solid her, he adds, and only needing a coat of paint to look young again. Christ, her Cat always purred, never a sputter or a cough; feed her diesel and she'd go as she gulped. Every inch was built in oak or ash. Hardly a splice in her. Tell-ya, they don't make trees like that no more and, no sir, they don't make boats like the *Magnificence* no more. Look around today and it all be steel. Steel. Everywhere steel.

He twists his neck, left-right, to see if anyone's listening. We're the only ones at the counter, but he keeps his voice low, saying, While trouble was cooking, he was off-watch, asleep in his bunk, until the bilge alarm sounded. He says that noise is something you neverever, no, want to hear again. It cuts right through you, a knife-like ripping out gut and brain. He reckons several seconds went missing before he put one and one together and realized, holy shit, there be all sorts of twos. Maybe a false alarm. Maybe not.

Again, Sword looses a low, one-note whistle and this time says, Screw answers. At sea, only dead fellers got the time to wait for them things. He remembers running out of the fo'c'sle like some sort of big-shot king, not caring about nobody or nothing but his his own royal ass. Once he saw the emergency gear in place, his mates still aboard, he says the king-feller died and he rejoined the crew. When the skipper yelled, Launch the raft, he was all aye-aye, cap'n-boss-sir.

There was no saving her, the *Magnificence,* he says, and says it again. Only a million pumps could've kept her afloat. Her shaft be gone, along with the prop. Slid right through the stuffing box and from the amount of water coming in, the stuffing box might've disappeared, too-like. No sir, he can't say how such a thing happened and can only guess it be another mystery of the sea. The place got lots of them, he adds. All he knows for certain is how speedy-like disaster arrived: from Dreamland to Mayday took less than one minute. If that bilge alarm wasn't—

Fatima cuts him off, breezing through the kitchen doors, her voice booming: Hey, Sailor, what will it be? Without waiting, she answers, The usual, of course: Breakfast Plate Special. Scrambled. Wheat. Joe first.

As she heads to the coffee stand, she asks Sword, How's the food, mister?

Cosmic, he replies, and bites into some cold toast.

Yous, too, the same, she says, and winks.

Sword and I watch as she prepares the Bunn-O-Matic drip coffeemaker. The instant hot water exits a nozzle she strokes the unit's chromed dome and turns our way. Don't-ya hate f——ing storms?

Killers, Sword pipes. A mess of trouble. He labels himself a storm victim unjustly detained on shore. You know the saying, he adds: The lower the barometer, the taller the trouble.

Fatima wiggles a hand as if defending herself against a no-see-um and moves to the picture window set into the cafe's south wall. It overlooks New Bedford Harbor, a working waterfront servicing fish, fishermen and America's largest fishing fleet and is half the reason one sign outside the restaurant says, in large red letters, GOOD FOOD & VIEW. With her face tight to the glass, her breath condensing on its surface, she gives the elements a piece of her mind. Damn, damn-ya, weather. Hate-ya, like-bad. Okay, she concludes, grabbing a fish tote filled with dirty dishes, and heads for the kitchen. Back soonest, she purrs in passing.

It's dead calm outside. Near the channel, dinghies nuzzle mother ships they usually trail. Flags droop on their halyards, and the exhaust from boat engines charging batteries flattens as it exits each stack, forming oily pancakes which curl heavenward at the edges. The water is flat, not a line to be seen, the harbor a chalkboard ready to record the coming action. Nimbostratus clouds dim the outdoor light and appear stuck in place; gray and featureless, they wait for wind and a drop in atmospheric pressure before dumping their loads.

Sword bends over an empty sugar packet featuring a stylized portrait of Poseidon. The god wears a crown of sea horses over flowing locks of eels and a beard formed by octopi. His cheeks are puffed, his mouth blowing a gale, and one hand grips a trident with a demasted square-rigger impaled on the center tine. Sword pokes the water god in the puss and calls him a fuckin' murderer. Killed millions, him. Got the *Magnificence,* too. Took her, he did, in one gulp. No manners, all beast, him.

For three years, Sword says, the *Magnificence* was his home, nearly; she was his true love, for sure. She's the one who always brought up the day. So, at the end, he felt there was a heap of reasons the size of Everest to sit with her and say, Thanks, plus more. But, damn, she was sinking too fast for anything polite.

Raising his right hand like a Scout taking a pledge, Sword swears he jumped off the boat with only seconds to spare before he would've drowned, sucked under and down with the hull. He remembers the life raft drifting only a few yards from the wreck when the cry went out: She's gone, she's gone. True, this, he adds: Poseidon didn't burp up nothing. There was no oil slick. No flotsam. No trace of her. Not a thing to mark her grave.

I wait for more and end up staring at all the tattoos exposed by his cut-off T-shirt. Arms on arms, he once explained, referring to the arsenal needled into his skin from knuckles to pits. The grenade, knives and various-caliber bullets are drawn full size; the tank, chopper, artillery pieces and assorted handguns and rifles are inked to scale. Above the weaponry, circling his neck and appearing strangely animate whenever he twists, stretches or strains, there's a serpent's tail done up in hot colors: raspberry spikes atop fire-orange armor-plated skin. Near each spike a tiny land mine in mid-explosion sprays red ink in three directions. There's more under his T-shirt, including a map of Vietnam running the full length of his spine and marked with a skull and crossbones in places where he saw action.

Much of the artwork was done in Thailand during R&R breaks from a war he doesn't talk about, unless asked; he believes most people don't want to know a damn thing about Nam, and he wishes he were one of them. On his wiry frame— five foot ten, about 160 pounds—and with his mousy looks up top, the tattoos keep strangers at a distance, always guessing, unsure what's inside the package with all the labels saying *Caution, Highly Explosive.* This suits him just fine. He says he hates people he doesn't know breathing on him and he loves to ride elevators alone.

Back to now, Sword announces. He explains that he got fetched up, snagged in memories of the shipwreck, and got lost as he tried to track the *Magnificence's* course to the bottom. Go deep and it gets some way-black, he reports. He grabs his coffee mug and, *whap,* sets it atop the empty sugar packet. Bottom's up, he tells Poseidon.

Fatima steps out of the kitchen. Damn-damn, she says, and

brakes, her Dr. Scholl's sandals raising a squeak as they drag
across the waxed linoleum. She cocks her head to one side,
burying her left shoulder under frizzy black hair as big as can be,
and taps her right temple with a pencil. Forgot. Forgot all about
your order, Sailor. Believe me, you: nothing is steering the right
way today.

She turns, retraces her steps into the kitchen and yells the
breakfast order to her mom, Marie, who handles the cooking
chores. Marie's response is immediate: the sound of eggs breaking followed by the noise of a fork whipping them into a froth.
As the toaster engages, Marie says something in Portuguese
which sparks a mother-daughter argument. Although he has no
idea what they're jabbering about, his Portuguese limited to
boat terms, Sword whispers that he's rooting for Marie. Of
course, he likes Fatima, a friend for ages, but he loves Marie, his
ardor stoked every time he bites into one of her specials. He
says he'd kill for her fava beans.

There are now only two other customers in the cafe and
they rise from their table with the racket of ten: lots of chair
dragging punctuated by grunts from men looking like they've
worked all night and still have tons to do. They shuffle toward
the door, and Sword hails them: Aren't you fellers off that blue,
big-ass clammer that pulled in from Virginia yesterday?

The shorter of the two, a man with a pie-face and nut-
colored hair in a pageboy cut, shakes his head no. He points to
his T-shirt and says, This, us. The T-shirt is emblazoned with an
illustration of a beaver equipped with a dick longer than its tail.
In its buckteeth, there's a log with writing on it: I'M FROM
CANADA. SHOW ME YOUR BEAVER.

His partner is more talkative and introduces the duo as truckers out of Sydney, Nova Scotia, where the ferry to Newfoundland docks. They arrived with a load of frozen lobster and crab
meat and they're leaving with a mixed cargo of fresh ground-

fish. Round-trip, it's a twenty-eight-hour marathon, and since they co-own the rig, get paid by the mile and haul perishables, they're always in a rush. Today, however, the driver says it's balls to the wall for them. They want to stay ahead of the storm, which is expected to race up the coast and smack the Maritimes, and if there's anything he hates more as a driver than troopers and Mounties, it has to be storms.

The truckers exit the cafe and make their way to an eighteen-wheeler parked behind a nearby fish house. Sword labels them fellers a vanishing species, rare as cod these days. Noting that only three trucks now service the cross-border trade, down from a fleet of thirty during the 1980s, he thinks it won't be long before fishing in both Canada and America turns into mission fuckin' impossible. Because he believes feds, regs and quotas are killing the industry, he wonders who will be the first to disappear from the scene after the truckers go belly-up. Will it be fish or fishermen?

He drains his coffee mug, crumples the empty sugar packet into a wad and sends it into a fish tote used to bus tables. There's a problem, he cautions, standing to pat the outside of his pant pockets. He's broke. Not a penny on him. See, he left home in the dark a dutiful crewman, at the boat before five a.m. and hoping the storm alert was wrong. But the weather fax aboard the *Ocean-C* only confirmed the worst, mapping out a whopper of a storm and forcing the skipper to postpone the trip.

Got cheese to spare, Sailor?

I empty a pocket and do a count: twenty-eight dollars.

Pony got to eat, too, he says, and points to Alexander Hamilton.

The pony could be dope or his car. Either way, ten bucks won't take him far, and the greenback is his.

I watch through a window as he opens the door to his car, a dinged but smooth-running late-1960s Bel Air. He tosses his seabag into the back seat, while a shiny metal briefcase stays up front with him for use as an elbow rest. The engine starts and unleashes a sound from an earlier time in America, before a Chevy weighed more than a computer. He's hooked on old machines and surrounds himself with familiar items from his youth, products minted in the 1950s and 1960s. He doubts he'll ever buy a computer before they're issued with full schematics of their innards. He insists on being able to repair anything he uses and says he's not the kind of man who relies on others for help. All he asks for is a map so he can troubleshoot on his own and find his way from A to Z to A. After his discharge from the army, he said, he returned to civilian life without a map and got lost way-way-bad. The navigational aids which had guided him as a kid and a teen had been screwed with, either turned off or cut free of their moorings and sent drifting into the shallows they had once warned him to avoid. The result, he said, was shipwreck, thousands of vets on the rocks.

Sword sees me watching him through the cafe window and snaps a salute before leaving the parking lot. The first time we met, back in 1987, I wanted to smack him with a chair, a bottle, anything except my fist, willing to inflict but not share any pain. It happened at the National, a bar hard by the docks and a favorite hangout for local fishermen, their guests and visiting members of other seafaring tribes. It's the kind of joint where the decor comes and goes, dropped off one day by a liquor distributor and stolen the next by an opportunist wanting to spruce up his pad or to barter on the street corner for a nickel bag. The lighting is dungeonesque and this suits the clientele, making it a bit easier to shoot up, snort, swallow or inhale drugs without attracting others wanting a free bump.

Sword was juiced, off-balance and way off-key, staggering from table to table while singing along with the juke. It was late afternoon, around four p.m., and business was slack. Two barflies on stools slouched over highballs, and a crew of four fishermen stood at the pool table analyzing spin and angles.

Toward the end of one sing-along, Sword found new entertain-
ment, focusing on me sitting alone at a corner table. Who the
fuck are you, asshole?

Hi, there.

Dickhead, you get out-a-here, he squalled, his breath a nox-
ious mix of Marlboros, house rye, beer and Slim Jims. The gang
at the pool table urged him on. Sword responded by raising the
temperature, starting to poke me. Git-get out. His finger started
landing harder and harder, until, dammit, he was throwing jabs.
At the same time, his mouth pressed his case for trouble: Try it,
Dickhead. C'mon, take a shot . . .

I had only recently set anchor in New Bedford and didn't
want any trouble. Besides, in part, Sword wasn't out of line. He
and his clan of ill-mannered watermen owned the New Bedford
docks. This was their turf. Their bar. Their waterfront. Their
freaking salt air. The whole damn place: it belonged to them.
They'd inherited it and maintained every stick, brick and boat. If
an outsider wanted entry into this part of town, he had to earn
those rights, and only the sea can punch that sort of entry ticket.

I was from away, a strange, unknown fish drinking at his
watering hole. Perhaps I was an amateur or worse, someone
who carried a clipboard or a badge. Those types, as well as most
other outsiders, are scorned around the docks and considered
fair game. Anything goes, from mugging to murder. If cops
were to get involved after the fact, it'd be no big deal. Lying
comes easy along the waterfront.

I figured it was neither the time nor the place to introduce
myself and flash my seaman's ticket, all dues paid in full, plus
some. Instead I told the bartender to give the jacked-up fisherman wearing war paint a double on me. After paying for the
drink, along with a hefty tip, I walked backward through the
front door.

Slowly, word trickled out about the bald guy hanging out at
the docks, and fishermen lost the wild look they normally

flashed, dogs around raw meat, when an outsider approached. I heard some of the talk: Him, that new feller, lives in one of the mills by the estuary. Made his bones the old way aboard freighters and canvas fliers. Sailed solo, him, like lots across the Atlantic. Lost a boat, too. Five days in the drink alone, him . . .

Sword later dragged me to the National. He paid for every round and insisted the booze shouldn't be confused with an apology of any kind. Hell, no, he don't apologize, not ever for nothing. People can take him or leave him and whatever they decide is okay by him. He only bought the booze as a gesture of a man who refuses to owe anything to anybody worth saying hell-o to in a bar. He raised his drink in one hand and extended the other to shake. Welcome to New Bedford, Dickhead.

In New Bedford, like every other commercial waterfront I ever sailed into or shipped out of, the docks bind a community separate from the city they edge. Seaward, its reach is boundless; inland, its perimeter stretches as far as the smell of low tide during a full moon in August. Within the waterfront district, old and new joust for attention, eighteenth-century brick neighboring Steel Space buildings, and Civil War facades parked next to polished aluminum storefronts. All of it, though, was built from money made from fish and fishing.

The sailors' part of town is chockablock with warehouses, fish houses, flophouses, cathouses, crack and powder houses, tenements, mill building after mill building, bars, low-slung shops, a few restaurants, trucks and truck depots, marine gear suppliers and manufacturers, boats in the water, boats out of the water, boats half in the water and rotting in place, boatyards, pieces of boats for sale and for free, fishing equipment of every kind for sale, new and used, and rope, some coiled and stacked eye-high and other lengths snaking through lots and hugging curbs. Byways of varying widths and lengths, shoulder-wide alleys to boulevards, crisscross the area, and only a few patches are lit at night. Deep shadows dog any stroller, and recessed doorways demand a cautious approach since they're often temporary squats for derelicts and doped-up fishermen unsure of the space they occupy or supposed to occupy.

Every footfall on the docks comes with the crack of a seashell or the pop of seaweed or the squish of oil, man-made and fish, along with the background sounds of wind, sand and wood on the move. As well, but less identifiable, are the disturbing echoes and thumps and raps, which seem to rise up out of the past as much as the here and now. They come from all directions and compel a walker to check his wallet and remain alert to what's behind him, seen and unseen. Many watermen never feel alone on the docks and sense the presence of dead sailors rejected by both heaven and hell, their waterlogged souls doomed to ride the currents until some tide washes them up onshore. Above it all, day and night and without a break, the ocean assumes countless voices, some friendly and some not.

The docks are insulated from landlubbers by a dark seam of willful sinning which runs through the place, by a lingua franca as salty as it is blue, by arcane rites and rituals no less impenetrable to outsiders than the Mafia's code and by the watermen's fidelity to the sea—its gods, traditions and myths—and to each other. Around the world, working waterfronts form a confederation of seafaring tribes connected by a common heritage and workplace. Each commune flies its own flag (the Jolly Roger for New Bedford) and operates as a free agent, adept at deceiving neighbors and immune to landlubbing arguments for participation in a greater good. Pecking orders and systems of justice vary from port to port, each derived from hundreds of years of precedent, with the mechanics known to battle-scarred veterans and few others.

The overall course a waterfront community steers is usually determined by its fleet and the cargo transiting its docks. In New Bedford, it has been fishing boats and fish since the beginning, the hunt shaping its character and the sea its teacher. At first, it was whales, and now the gear is out for what little is left in the ocean. Scallops are the port's biggest moneymaker and the main reason why New Bedford is the largest commercial fishing port in America, home to more than 250 boats and dozens of processors handling landings scratching the $300 million mark.

What planet you circling, Sailor? Fatima asks, entering the dining area and finding her only customer adrift. She delivers a Breakfast Plate Special and eyes her domain while pushing the small of her back into the counter lip and repeatedly bending and unbending her knees. She's itching like crazy, she says, the result of poison ivy on her back. She wishes the irritation came from rolling in the hay with Mr. Hunk, but, damn, she has been wishing for that ever since she can remember having a good-like naughty thought. She guesses the trouble came from Engine, her cat and so named because it purrs like a well-tuned outboard. The cat sleeps with her at night and spends its days outside, and she'll bet a million bucks Engine has been visiting the house behind hers, the one with a poison ivy patch the size of Texas, almost.

Finished rubbing her back, Fatima straightens her five-foot-one frame and labels the poison ivy a major drag. But it's nothing, she's quick to add, compared to the storm and her mom, Marie. Both are driving her off the edge. So nuts you can't believe it, she says. The storm chased away her customers and flipped on the loony switch inside Marie. Captains, her best tippers, are aboard their boats and preparing them for rough weather. Meanwhile, crewmen would've heard the storm alerts on their radios and stayed in bed, deep-sixing any plans for day work or boat chores. And, boy, oh, boy, bed is where she wants to be.

She throws a dish towel as if at the foul line, a two-hand overhead toss which sends the towel into the middle of the table by the picture window. If only she were a foot or more taller, she thinks, she could've made it as a pro. She wipes down the table and extends an invitation: Sit at this table, Sailor. Chairs beat stools any day. She sets silverware for three and yells to Marie: Ma, have some coffee with us.

Marie shouts back that there's plenty of work to do. A storm is coming and, she says, you can't be ready enough for a blow.

Fatima runs air over her bottom lip and rolls her eyes, brown as cane sugar and endowed with a liveliness most people only see in the faces of cartoon characters. She's in her late thirties, a divorce-court pro, no kids, and battling a waistline that keeps her in a one-piece bathing suit. From the shoulders up, she's instantly recognizable as the same person onstage and wearing a formal dress in the newspaper clipping (now yellowed and under glass in a frame hung over the Mixmaster) depicting the finalists in the 1978 Miss Teen Massachusetts Pageant. She placed fourth, becoming, as she says, a near-f——ing Miss. For months afterward, she prayed to her patron saint to make the top three girls pregnant or dead.

Again she tries to coax Marie out of the kitchen and this time elicits a rush of metallic sounds in response. Air streams over her bottom lip until the noise subsides. Believe me, you, she says, Ma's out where the buses don't run. She claims Marie has cleaned every pot and pan in the kitchen a zillion damn times since they opened the cafe at six a.m. and listened to a weather report. Walking to the coffee stand, she talks about an old form of weather prediction she heard about on the radio this morning. Yes sir, a big-head scientist was running on about stuff before plug-in this and that. People would watch a pond-like for signs of bubbles and scum, because low-pressure systems release all sorts of crap from the bottom. High pressure, ya-know, keeps the lid on things, but storms, my God, they bring the worst to the surface. No wonder they're called depressions.

She returns to the table with fresh cups of coffee and a whole new attitude, suddenly upbeat. Check 'em out, she says. Look at these honeys.

She holds out both hands, modeling her latest manicure, and together we admire the paint job. It's the work of a pro, each nail meticulously brushed in two shades of high-gloss green: dark near the cuticle and lighter, almost an aqua, above the half-moon. Atop all ten surfaces, floating smack-dab in the middle of an enameled sea, is a decal of a spouting sperm whale.

Marlene, she did them last night, Fatima reports, and keeps going, gathering speed until the words meld: Marlene, you must know her. A genius, that woman, truly. Owns Nails of Distinction by St. Anthony's. Bestintown. A trueartist, Marlene.

She takes a breath, then adds, Twenty bucks. That's all it cost. No tax. Wouldn't take a tip. Tell me, where else can you get this sort of good art for that sort of cheap?

Fatima winks and buffs the artwork on her white cotton blouse. She studies the shine and wonders what put the gloss on Sword this morning. For a guy who's usually quiet and as dull as baked beans at the breakfast counter, he was all yak-yak, she says. She didn't smell any booze on him and guesses he ate some uppers before heading to the *Ocean-C*.

Sword enjoys a slow dance, and for as long as I've known him, he has been hooked on opiates. The romance began in the army and he has seen fit to remain partnered to dope for life.

He's a fisherman, and fishermen will swallow anything around that gets them high, she says, and punctuates things with a dismissive flick of the wrist. Anyway, she's looking for some speed. It's for a friend, of course, wanting to lose weight. Back to Sword, she says. What was he yakking about?

Shipwreck. The last voyage of the *Magnificence*.

Insurance job, that, and cleaner than most, she says matter-of-factly and continues: The boat was old and she needed a new engine, the compression way-low. She was punked at the keel-son, too. And, hell, now, somebody had to pay for Captain Gold's new boat and it sure wasn't going to be that tightwad.

None of that was mentioned in Sword's tale, and I share some of his accident report.

Get out-a town, she instructs. The *Magnificence* didn't sink, she was sunk. Accident? That's what he calls work with a wrench? Listen up, Sailor: don't be buying into the crap fisher-men spew to insurance agents and judges at inquests.

She reaches for the Camel cigarettes in my shirt pocket and returns for the matches. Lighting up, she says, Greed killed the *Magnificence*. Gets a lot of boats one way or the other. If you're not greedy, you're not a fisherman, least not a good one.

One sandal falls to the linoleum, then the other. With both feet on a nearby chair, she homes in on fishermen, saying, They're so good at lying they believe their own gas as truth be told. Not nothing is ever their fault. If an overloaded boat rolls, they scream bad luck, rotten weather. When the fish finally dis-appear, they'll scream bloody murder and point a finger at the feds, oil companies, foreign boats, anybody and everybody but themselves.

She looses a cloud of smoke and sends it across the table, rounding lips the reddish purple of a Portuguese olive. The cloud thins and she speaks: Jesus, there was nothing accidental or one-in-a-million about that wreck. Ya-know, don't-ya, that the crew saved every pound of meat aboard, seven-like tons. They tied the bags to buoys and when they were picked up in the life raft, the rescue boat helped them salvage every bag. The scallops were worth a hundred grand and the insurance paid out five hundred and fifty grand for a boat not worth a second look. Add it all up and that trip was the best moneymaker in the history of the fleet. In a softer voice, she advises, Think about those facts, Sailor.

She sits and stares out the picture window, her mouth opening and closing in step to puffs on a cigarette and sips of coffee. I follow instructions and think about fishermen and their fish stories.

Each tale is processed for market consumption based on the talker's mood, audience, memory and the intoxicants circulating in his or her system. It's part of the reason why dockside stories change from day to day like the tide, sometimes expressed with a flood of emotion and minutiae and sometimes empty of most everything except self-polishing imagery, the alpha hunter tooting his prowess. However, in flood or ebb, out of the mouths of old-timers or greenhorns, the teller of a fish story rarely misses any opportunity to pledge honesty and plug his version of events as unvarnished fact. Swear-true, he'll often begin. No lie, he'll vow at any point. Honest to God, he'll testify at the end, and declare a willingness to do the same atop a stack of Bibles taller than Paul Bunyan or atop his mother's grave, the poor woman most likely still alive.

Half man and half fish, fishermen naturally find it difficult to separate their component parts. Each piece offers the individual a sense of identity, but instead of inducing a split personality, they appear perfectly matched, twin gears engaging the cogs of an air-breather's life at sea. Like their prey, fishermen tend to flop all over the place, hard to pin down, oily and extremely slippery. They're adept at making quick turns and equally liable to twist, snap and fight. And it's the fish in them that promotes the unctuous salesmanship which goes into transforming minnows into whales, piracy into heroism, frozen fillets into premium fresh cuts and cash payouts into unreported income.

At sea, no mariner steers a straight course. It's a zig for every zag caused by wind, wave and current. Similarly, like their boats and quarry, fishermen never follow a precise course in their storytelling. While landlubbers tend to keep their colors inside conventional lines, fishermen routinely change the colors, blur things and move the lines to accommodate their wandering. In their work, pinpoint accuracy isn't a necessary ingredient for success. They prowl opaque, black-green water and chase what they can't see with wide-mouthed nets, giant rakes weighing tons, hooks with multiple barbs and venturi pumps able to suck thirty-eight-pound rocks off the bottom and spit them out on deck. The only system of weights and measures they oblige is ancient, antedating the Greeks and universal among seafaring tribes; it pegs the value of a man's worth to his experience at sea, factoring in his instinct for the hunt and whether or not he can pull his own weight, plus more.

When it comes to the production and marketing of fish tales, Sword and Fatima are masters of the trade. Within that elite group, though, there are degrees of expertise, and Sword's position is at a rank far below Fatima's. He arrived comparatively late to the docks, and as a fisherman he has put in less than twenty years before the mast. Fatima, on the other hand, learned how to tie her shoes with bows as well as bowlines. While Sword had to learn how to fit in aboard a boat, Fatima arrived already part of the crew.

Fatima is the daughter of a fisherman, and her mother is the daughter of a fisherman; she's the grandchild of two fishermen, both of whom married daughters of fishermen. And she says it has been that way for more than a thousand years in her family. Three times she has married and divorced fishermen, and driven by some inner force which trumps experience and can't be denied, she has recently moved in with another fisherman. Fresh out of high school she crewed aboard scallop boats for four years, quitting when she decided to live beyond fifty-five with her fingers and toes intact and her body untwisted by the arthritis and damaged cartilage which plague most fishermen.

It's likely that she knew everyone aboard the *Magnificence,* and the chances are good that she's intimate with the facts related to the sinking. However, there's an equally good chance that she nurtures a grudge against somebody aboard that day.

Like most people doing business on the waterfront, she considers payback a lifelong pursuit. Once, she described herself as no f——ing angel, saying that to cross her was to cross the devil in her. If you do that, she warned, she'll bite and bite until there is nothing left to bite. At that point, she'll decide whether or not to douse the asshole's grave with Clorox to ensure that nothing pretty ever sprouts at the site.

Sword is the first in his family to work as a fisherman. His parents and grandparents toiled in the local textile mills, where he, too, was employed, after dropping out of high school in the middle of eleventh grade. His dad worked at the Berkshire Hathaway mill and told him about a job opening in the mechanics department, which he applied for and got. He said he loved fixing looms and he excelled; eighteen months into the job, he was promoted and started making more money than the old man. He felt he was set for life, the view ahead unobstructed all the way to the supervisor's chair, and he started looking for a house to buy. But he was forced to pack his bags in October 1966, when his draft notice came in the mail. He said the army taught him two things: how to kill real-like good and why he must never-ever-ever mistake shit for duty again.

He first came to the docks seeking refuge after his discharge from a VA hospital, where he'd spent more than one year as doctors tried to fix what a grenade had destroyed. The pieces were all there, but not much was connected, he said, and he demonstrated how the pounds of artificial ingredients sewn into his left side could spin the needle of a cheap compass. The army told him they used only top-grade stainless and titanium, but somebody lied, he said. The docks beckoned because that's where the dope was the cheapest and easiest to find. Because that's where nobody gave a shit if he sat around, nodded out or died. And because cops avoided the place. Over time, he became friendly with some fishermen and surprised himself when he accepted an offer to replace a no-show crewman aboard a day boat.

That first fishing trip lasted only eleven hours, but it unscrolled his future. Invoking Saul's journey to Damascus, he said a lightning bolt hit him halfway into the voyage and redirected his life. He described his encounter: It began-like when the net came up with enough fish to fill the deck. The captain was all happy and shouted, This is some good. And, boy, was he right. The sky had stars in it bigger than honeydew melons and it felt like you could touch them if you were only a couple of feet taller. It was some-clear, everything. And calm, too, the water gurgling under the stern same as some way-happy baby. The wind was just a whisper and it tickled your ear sweet as any lady speaking of love. Then, Jesus, a switch flipped on the juice. Some rush, that, the best. It was so good that choice be gone. Just had to have more and more. It done set the hook to the bone.

He cut back a bit on the dope, started obliging a daily regimen of physical therapy, bought books on knots and seamanship and began hunting for boat work. Without a blood relative in the fleet to vouch for him, Sword spent three years as a fishing temp, filling in at the last minute for missing crewmen. Finally, in 1982, he landed a steady gig aboard a scallop boat and was on his way to becoming a dock citizen. He says he knew he arrived the day he walked up to some fellers on the dock and they kept talking all easy and natural-like. Up to then, people usually treated him as an interruption in their life or rhythm, always pausing or changing the subject the moment he neared.

Sword quickly gained a reputation for his skills as a knifeman, able to fillet and shuck faster than most, and things gelled for him, his name suddenly solid on the docks in 1985. It hap-

pened at sea when a Coast Guard frigate ordered the scalloper
Audrey & Jake to stop for an inspection. The boarding party took
offense at the foul language greeting them and tried to make the
fishermen eat their words, demanding apologies and threatening to seize the boat for minor saftey violations. The fishermen only became more bellicose, unnerving one Coastie, who
jammed his weapon into the mate's gut. Sword reacted; in seconds, he'd disarmed two Coasties and had a gun aimed at the
officer in charge. He ordered them off the boat and threw their
weapons overboard. Apparently, since the charges against Sword
were later dropped, the Coasties had abused their power. And
because of him, headquarters overhauled procedures for boarding New Bedford fishing boats, doubling the number of officers
and banning live ammunition.

Fatima snuffs the last of the cigarette and breaks the silence,
saying, The *Magnificence* was sunk 'cause she was old. That was
her crime. Believe me, you: fishermen can't stand nothing old
around them. If it's female and old, she's the first to go when a
new model catches their eye. Boats and women, it's the same
send-off: See-ya. Owe-ya. Had some good times with-ya. And
we're still friends, right? Those words, she adds, are skips in the
brains of fishermen. Let me tell-ya, they're pros at forgetting
the important stuff.

With a sound part groan and part statement, she draws out
the *God* in *Gaawd-dammit* and grabs for the pack of butts. She
says she's trying to quit smoking. It's the reason she has been
wearing a nicotine patch for a week, but today, she declares, is a
patch-and-stick kind of day. Two tokes later, she issues a large
smoke ring. As the circle expands, she pokes a painted finger
with a whale on it through the center of the ring and announces,
Shamu does tricks.

Other smoke rings and tricks follow, all of them taught to her
by her dad, Manny Sousa. His best trick, though, is not part of
her repertoire. Manny earned his nickname, Captain 110-Proof,

but she can't handle the booze necessary to conjure the magic and has to describe the performance. He'd blow this way-awesome smoke ring, she says, and then swallow a triple brandy. Flicking his Bic, he'd burp into the flame and this way-wild-like blue flash would race through the middle of the smoke ring. It'd make anyone watching shout, Again, do it again, Manny. And he'd do it over and over until he passed out or got ugly-sick. His own freak show, Dad.

She stands at the picture window, hands on hips, her eyes on a trackless harbor, tabletop flat and licorice-colored. With her back to everything in the cafe, she talks about her dad and how she'd love to have one day beyond reach of the man. It'd help, she adds, if people would only shut up about him, like they care or something good like that. But they don't care and never did. Believe me, you: the only true thing anyone can say is he never came home. (Manny Sousa was reported missing at sea in 1976.) She doubts she'll ever know exactly what happened to him and she's positive she'll never search for answers. Gimme another Camel, she adds.

Fatima turns, squares her patch of poison ivy to a windowsill, bends her knees, and as she rubs the prickly spot, she repeats, Lost at sea. She then adds, Sounds mysterious, doesn't it? Christ, it almost sounds brave. But she doesn't know why. What she does know is how much lighter life became when she first heard those words—*Lost at sea*—applied to her dad. If that sounds mean, she says, she doesn't care. For her and Marie, the world became an easier place to live. Awake or asleep, we were better off without him.

She stops scratching her back and sits down. Softly, in a voice not meant to carry into the kitchen, Fatima tells a story from her youth. If there wasn't school, she begins, we—Ma, Nana, even the dog—had to be at the dock for Dad. Depending on the boat, there'd be five or six, maybe seven other families on the dock waving to the men as they cast off to go fishing. Two weeks later-like, we'd all be back at the dock waving them in. Coming and going, Ma and the other wives would empty a box of Kleenex, wiping and drying the leaks. And for years and years, she had it backward, way-so-wrong. Finally, in the fifth grade, when she says a girl starts discovering what has been hidden from her for so long, Ma set her straight. The tears were the real McCoy, all right, but the good tears, the ones pumped out by joy, happy thoughts and all, they flowed out of seeing Dad leave. The other tears came from the pain of seeing him return to the dock.

Fatima stirs sugar into her coffee and, noisily, she works the spoon until she creates a mini-whirlpool. She keeps at it while noting how rare it is these days for families to gather at the dock for any reason except memorial services. If anything explains this change in behavior, she says, it's because nobody gives a damn about a divorced Mr. and Mrs. Whatever. Twenty-five years ago, not many fishermen and certainly no Portuguese fishermen were getting divorced. It was a big-like sin back then.

She takes in a final lungful of cigarette smoke and crushes the butt in the ashtray, twisting it like a screw being driven into hardwood. There's no smoke ring as she exhales, just a steady stream exiting a small gap in lips wet with coffee. Suddenly, though, she opens wide. It's starting, she says. Thank God, the storm's here at last.

Outside, a plastic bag takes wing, sent aloft by a northeast breeze whispering of big things to come. The wind excites the water, stroking its surface until it quivers and raises ripples like so many goose bumps. The flags at the Coast Guard station shake free some of their creases and, as if choreographed, boats at anchor swing as one, each pointing her nose toward the eye of an approaching storm.

Fatima notes the wind direction and rolls up the welcome mat. Screw you, Nor'easter. Nothing good ever comes out of the northeast, she adds, just three days of crummy weather and a mom dressed in a life jacket, crazy as a loon. When she was a kid, her dad used to tell her that a northeast storm always blew in monsters and ghosts; they'd hitch rides on the spume and head for shore. Know what? she says. Her answer is handy: It might be one of the few things he ever told the truth about.

The first raindrops ploink the cafe's metal roof. While Fatima hates storms, she likes rain and hopes it starts teeming. In her experience, rain sends fishermen off their boats and away from their dockside chores and into the cafe for hot food and conversation. And for some reason she can't explain, the harder it rains, the better her tips. Anticipating a rush, she starts cleaning tabletops and tries yet again to coax Marie out of the kitchen. Take a breather, Ma. We'll be busy soon.

What sounded like a Portuguese radio program drifting out of the kitchen for the last few minutes turns out to be Marie. As if to answer her daughter, she sings louder, unleashing an untrained voice. Although she stumbles while climbing the scale and tears certain notes apart, she produces a commanding sound, intensely sad and genuine, a fado delivered true to its original form and intent.

Fatima shakes her head, disappointed. She hears these songs whenever there's a storm and can only associate the music with a mother temporarily out of order. Reluctantly, she agrees to translate Marie's lyrics. It's a down-in-the-dumps story, she instructs. There's this mister who Ma never wants to see again and she's afraid the wind will blow him through the door. All Ma's fados are about storms, unwanted men and the pain, ya-know, of having no control over them.

It starts pouring outside. At the same time, the wind starts cranking up the volume and drowns out Marie's singing. It also steals any smoke from boat stacks and clears the parking lot of litter. The water responds to the increased friction on its surface with wavelets, many topped in lines of white. Boats tug at their moorings, bucking with each header or lift. Flags snap smartly and rafts of garbage in the harbor pick up speed, sent southwest by wind and water.

Fatima stops wiping down the counter. One sandal clops loudly on the linoleum. A fist whacks the stool where Sword sat. Damn him, she huffs. That son-of-a-bitch skipped.

As she pulls in air for round two, I tell her Sword's tab is on me. He was broke and needed a few bucks.

Fatima extends one hand like a cop stopping traffic and says, Don't go there. She then rages, calling Sword a worm and worse and promising to squish him under her shoe. Better yet, a tire. That way she won't have to clean up any goo. She says this isn't the first, second or third time he has waltzed into the cafe and ordered a meal knowing he couldn't pay for a single home fry. In her opinion, a man should lose his balls for stiffing a waitress wrong. Them type shouldn't, not ever, reproduce, she adds.

Suddenly, the rain wants entry, knocking on the door as the wind gusts. Visibility out the windows drops to less than one mile, rendering the docks at the South Terminal into smudges of grays, blues and greens. Wavelets grow into troublemakers as they march down the harbor, slapping any boat hull they meet and exploding at the riprap. Without a barometer to reference, there's no telling where the wind will top out. At the moment, it's blowing a steady 30 knots and gusting hard enough to give voice to the building, making the roof rafters groan.

Fatima either doesn't notice or doesn't care anymore about the deteriorating weather conditions. She's caught up in her own wind, blowing a gale, incensed that someone would even think about stiffing her. And the fact that it's Sword, a man with three strikes against him, makes her blister. The guy's rich as all get-out, she says.

Rich? Sword? The two don't connect for me. He lives with La-Z-Boy furniture, a TV, a stereo and a fish tank on the second floor of an unremarkable triple-decker in a lousy part of town. He travels only by boat or old Chevrolet. His wife left him years ago for the driver of the Pepperidge Farm delivery truck after a no-contest divorce; she couldn't live with his tattoos anymore and wanted a steady, reliable partner to start a family with. He never hit Lotto. And when his mom died last year, a group of us chipped in to help cover the funeral expenses and clear the debt she'd racked up after crooks at Atlas Tack, where she'd worked for forty-two years, liquidated the pension fund and took the cash south of the border.

Fatima growls and lists Sword's revenue streams: military disability payments, his income from fishing aboard a good earner like the *Ocean-C,* and his money from standard waterfront work, like lumping (unloading fish), selling shack (ocean catch dressed during off-watch hours and sold at the back door of restaurants), and plain old jacking anything left unattended in the back of a truck. She puts a number to everything and adds them up on her order pad. The total comes to more than $50,000 a year, and it makes her gasp. Her breath returns: Holy Mother, that's twice what she makes working ten hours a day, six days a week. Suddenly, she loses any desire to run him over with a car; instead, she now wants his death to be slow and painful and decides a steak knife is the proper tool for the job. First, she says, she'll peel him, then cut him and mince the works.

While Sword may in fact earn north of $50,000 a year (his take from fishing is at least $35,000, plus Uncle Sam sends him nearly $800 a month), he's a junkie, a compulsive buyer of dope and more dope. He's also a fisherman and prone to conflate greed and need. From the early 1970s to the mid-1980s, more than half of all New Bedford fishermen were hooked on horse or coke, often both, or booze. According to a state health survey, there was a significant drop in the addiction rate by the mid-1990s, when 30 percent of the dock population was identified as users. At the time, Sword dismissed the state findings as wishful baloney. He said he didn't know nothing about percentages, what he knew was tonnage, and he claimed tons of fishermen were still junkies and tons and tons of powder were still coming through the port every year. If anything, he contended, usage was on the rise.

For him, certainly, intake was increasing. He explained: The hurting never stops growing. It'll hide in the haze and come on some-fierce from the left side. He showed where, rolling up his left pant leg to expose a shank riddled by scars from stitchwork. Sole to waist, he said, identifying the length of his pain-maker. In Vietnam, he added, he gave up on tomorrows, too many fellers were dying to think about the next day, the next patrol, the next list of KIAs. It's the reason why he lives for the moment and does business with his dealer, buying in bulk, within an hour of getting paid for a fishing trip. Afterward, there are bars, restaurants and whorehouses to visit. If he runs out of cheese before his next fishing trip, he said, it's no big deal. He just stays home, does dope and sleeps a lot.

Fatima doesn't blink. Listen up, she orders: Sword stiffed her three times and would've done it again if he hadn't found an easy mark to hit on. That sort of behavior is unacceptable, and the best way to deliver her message is through pain. People have to know what they're in for if they dare cheat her or even think about it.

She'd go on, gladly, but a high-pitched, eardrum-shattering noise coming out of the kitchen redirects her attention. She races to investigate and, seconds later, the bothersome sound disappears. Reversing roles, Fatima adopts the voice of a parent scolding a child caught playing with matches: You could've burned down the whole place. Stay away from the blender, you. The motor's a spark machine and you know it. So why, why did you turn it on?

Marie responds in Portuguese, the words flowing in an island dialect she learned growing up on São Miguel, in the Azores.

Fatima doesn't interrupt, nor does she stick around to listen, quick-stepping into the dining area while mumbling something about nut jobs wrapped in life jackets. She moves to the picture window and shifts gears, calmly using her forefinger to trace the paths of raindrops zigzagging down the outside of the glass. Leaving plenty of room between words, she says, Boy—oh—boy, it's—going—to—be——one——long——day.

She remains fixed on the relationship of gravity, time and place but extends her field of view. While storms warp things at the cafe, bending Marie out of shape until sun and moon reappear, she says, every day without exception is a long one for most folks around here. She calls New Bedford a rust bucket of a town that's sinking at the mooring. Going deeper and deeper into the muck all the time. Because of this, seconds pass as f——ing hours for a whole lot of folks, she says, adding, It's all slo-mo when you're hurting, and this city's hurting some-bad. Bleeding jobs like crazy.

For proof, she refers to a story in last week's paper detailing the shuttering of the city's largest clothing manufacturer. With-out any warning, the company closed its doors and put 640 peo-ple out of work. That raises the number of jobs lost in the local manufacturing sector over the past twenty-five years above the thirty-five-thousand mark. Soon, she predicts, the number will take another jump the wrong way. She heard that two stitch shops are about to go under, while at the rubber plant, where they make gaskets, wiper blades and gas masks, more layoffs will be announced in a day or two.

Fatima reaches for a cigarette and nearly spits out the smoke. Damn, she says, she needs a break from this city. Go on trips. Gulp fresh air. Stretch. She just has to figure out how to do it on the cheap. This town really-like started to get to her, being anchored here, that is, all the time, she says, a few days ago, while she was at Shaw's Supermarket. She was standing in the canned food aisle, checking out tins on sale and minding her own business. Next to her was a woman with three kids. The oldest child was about five. Mom was maybe twenty-one. The woman picked up a can of tomatoes and, my God, Fatima says, she started yelling for the world to hear, This is me. My f——ing life is this f——ing can. Her screaming set off the kids, all of them crying and looking scared as hell.

The woman held up the can so Fatima could see a large dent in its side, along with a pinched lid looking ready to pop open. Again, the woman erupted: This is me. My f——ing life. All f——ing wrong and useless. Fatima says store employees rushed to the scene and she hightailed it out of there and left the place empty-handed. Back home, she couldn't shake the weirdness she'd experienced and started thinking about all those people in town who really do see themselves as damaged goods, a bunch of dents, dings and missing wrappers.

Fatima takes two drags on the butt and says, Christ, she knows plenty who fit the bill. Of the twenty-seven girls in her homeroom class at the start of ninth grade, thirteen had become single moms by age seventeen. That's some bang-up rate, she notes, personalizing state statistics which put the pregnancy rate among city teenagers at or near the high line for the past fifty years. From 1979 to 2006, the dropout rate among local high school students never dipped below 40 percent. In this city of 100,000, some 18,000 were collecting state aid in 1990 and today, the one place busier than the unemployment office is the women's shelter.

Fatima shrugs, says, Sinking this town, and stares out the picture window. Because of the heavy rain and the spume sent flying off the top of harbor waves, most of what's clearly visible out the window are busted remnants of the old economic engine: empty mill buildings, rotten pieces of the old docks which used to service barges delivering cotton to the shoreside mills, and smokeless smokestacks, all of them once promising growth to everything in their shadows.

Enough, she harrumphs, and goes for the broom. Her mood now mirrors the ugly weather. She grumbles as she sweeps, her words clearly enunciated only when she's cursing Sword's existence. She keeps at it until a stack of frying pans crashes to the kitchen floor. Speeding to the scene, she yells at Marie: Pull it together, Ma. Take off the life jacket. Get real. Dad's not coming back. Marie answers in Portuguese. Fatima does the same. And so begins another round of battle on a stormy day.

I leave money to pay for two breakfasts, plus a double large tip. As I head for the door, a breeze at my back carries a message from Fatima: Have a good-un, Sailor.

Before the skies clear, the nor'easter dumps almost three inches of rain and puts the gust needle on the anemometer at home within a hairsbreadth of 70 knots. Two dozen New Bedford draggers were offshore when the unexpected storm hit. All of them remain on station, their work disrupted but never shut down. Pickers and cutters stand their normal watches, the gear engaged for all but a few hours during the worst of the blow. Because federal regulations now cap the number of days a boat can be at sea and make no accommodation for rotten weather, there isn't a captain willing to waste precious sea time by seeking shelter in Nova Scotia or Nantucket. Returning crewmen will undoubtedly curse those men in suits and ties and lab coats who write rules penalizing any skipper wanting to play it safe. And then they'll show off why they're cursing the jerks, revealing eggplant-colored skin, their bodies bruised by waves that sent them rail to rail like human pinballs.

Messy sea conditions persist for a day or two after any storm, further postponing fishing trips. Last night at the bar, Puffer, the skipper of Sword's boat, *Ocean-C,* said the regs make every second at sea count big, and he wasn't going to eat fuel and waste hours bucking the storm's slop. Sure, it screws up life. Plans are

shot to hell and you got to reschedule day care and deal with a
pissed-off ex. But it's nothing, he claimed, compared to losing
valuable fishing time. He explained: A rake stays down thirty to
forty minutes. An okay tow drops $600 to $800 of scallops on
deck. Hit gaffers and it's twice that, hopefully more.

Driving to the cafe for breakfast, I expect to meet Sword. He
had left a message on my phone machine saying breakfast was
his treat. Instead, I pull into the cafe parking lot as two EMTs
roll Sword into the back of an ambulance. He'll be fine, one of
the EMTs says, shutting the door to the bus, which heads to the
hospital without flashing any lights.

Inside the cafe, Fatima issues a greeting. Gimme a cigarette,
she says. She extracts one stick and drops the pack into a pocket
of her apron. She moves a bucket crowned in suds by the door,
near a mess of blood-soaked paper towels. Sword tripped or
maybe-like fainted on his way out, she says, lighting up. Hit his
head way-awful on the table. And, damn, Ma picks this day not
to show up.

Three fishermen off the *Costa Regal* stand at a table and hur-
riedly make sandwiches out of their Breakfast Plate Specials. As
they head for the door, napkin-wrapped food in their hands, one
crewman asks Fatima a favor: If the cops come, we weren't
here, okay? She nods. She understands why no fisherman wants
to be bothered by cops and why cops rarely get to interview wit-
nesses to accidents around the docks, minor or major, fender
bender to murder. If, by chance or by stupid mistake, a fisherman is rounded up, he'll usually feign amnesia. If that doesn't
work, he'll simply lie and try to keep to the lie. A good example
happened a few days ago, when a fisherman was walking by a
Coast Guard storage trailer as two men were stealing a generator. Kindly, he stopped to help them lift it into a truck. Later,
when picked up and confronted with the surveillance tape, he
broke down in tears and urged the cops to find the man in the
video. It could only be one person: his long-lost twin adopted

days after birth. He was released and remains free while cops investigate his story.

One cafe patron remains rooted to his chair: Captain Mack, owner of the *Atlantic-Sue,* a seventy-two-foot dragger, which, like Mack, is among the oldest workers in the fleet. He has been trying to sell the boat ever since a bad hip sent him into semiretirement last year, at age seventy-five. He has had plenty of offers, but so far no one will agree to his terms, which require the buyer to work the old woodie for ten years. Suitors crave her license and will pay dearly for it; nobody, though, wants to take on a wooden boat for longer than the few days needed to strip her of gear. When he first bought her, in the early 1960s, Mack made a deal with *Atlantic-Sue,* promising to take care of her if she did the same for him. Both sides, he said, remained faithful to the bargain. He kept her looking bright and she put food on the table, money in the bank and sent sixteen kids (three his own, plus those of crewmen) to college. Besides, he always figured when she dies, he dies and, dammit, he wants ten more years of living.

Mack pulls out a chair. Take a load off them stumps, he invites.

Mack's a large man. Two of me might fit inside his work clothes, which never vary: brown shirt tucked into brown pants. As a young family man in the 1950s and 1960s, he, like most captains, kept the boat at the dock during the Christmas season. He used the downtime to work as a UPS helper and decided brown was his color as well. His face, though, is the red of a weathered barn door, while his eyes are shaded inside deep sockets and could be some other color than gray. Creases form an intricate hatchwork on both his forehead and his pelican-like double chin. Some people say he looks like Alfred Hitchcock, and he's one of them.

I stop to pour two cups of coffee.

Mack welcomes the fresh brew and says, That big storm wasn't so big after all. A barker, sure, but no bite to it.

What happened to Sword?

Mack says he wouldn't know. He was eating. He offers up two strips of bacon and, hearing a refusal, he stacks one atop the other and sends them down the hatch. He says his doctor ordered him off the good stuff, like bacon, chocolate and butter, but that same doctor is fatter than he and twenty years younger. So, to hell with him.

Fatima comes alongside with a pot of coffee. Customers first, she says, and then she'll deal with the mess on the floor. Mack declines a topper, looks at his watch (seven-ten a.m.) and wonders about the action at this morning's fish auction. Because the storm disrupted normal business, there's a chance scallops might go up enough for him to unload some inventory. Most boats sell their catch to processors the day they make dock, but Mack often buys his own scallops and keeps them in storage at the flash-freeze plant.

It's some wacky business, this fishing is, Mack says. A few months ago, the main buyer for the Japanese market forgot to put paper in his fax machine. Without him buying one scallop, the price dropped nearly twenty cents minutes after the morning auction started. The next day, with the fax machine back on line, scallops went up seventeen cents, but that still left fishermen shortchanged because of one stupid mistake. On the happy side, he continues, the U.S. Navy placed an order for twenty tons of scallops last week and the price jumped twelve cents in less than one hour.

Breakfast is on the house, Fatima tells Mack, and sits at the table, deciding to have one more cigarette before dealing with the cleanup chores. Meanwhile, if the phone rings with another take-out order, she swears she'll kill the jerk. She wishes she could unplug the thing, but she's hoping the cafe's insurance agent and lawyer will open their offices early and return her calls. She's confident some ambulance chaser will have Sword suing her before he's out of the hospital. Also, she's expecting Marie to check in. For some reason, Marie isn't answering the phone at home, and it's making Fatima think the storm did more than the usual damage to her mom.

Mack says Marie is the reason he came to the cafe, the same as he does on this date every year.

Fatima gasps, then coughs up smoke from the Camel and manages to say, Today? Oh, Jesus.

Yes, ma'am, Mack replies. Manny went missing on this date. The *Atlantic-Sue* was fishing near Manny's boat when the distress call went out over the radio: Man overboard. Mack and his crew spent the day crisscrossing the search area, switching from rescue to recovery mode after a few hours. Mack recalls the water was fifty-some degrees and hypothermia would've done in anybody right fast.

Fatima blows smoke rings as she listens, but stops when Mack rises from the table to leave and surprises him with a kiss on the cheek. This way, she cues, grabbing his hand and leading him through the kitchen door. As she goes, she deftly slips the ten-dollar bill he put down near his plate back inside the pocket it came from.

Fatima reappears wearing rubber gloves and gets to work. The fresh coat of floor wax she applied before opening up this morning speeds the cleanup and she's done in minutes. Betcha, though, she says, the damn wax will cause trouble in court. Screw it, she'll worry about that when it happens; right now her big worry is Marie. Fatima knows she's at home, but can't recall one instance when her mother let the phone ring unanswered. Something has got-a-be wrong, she surmises. As two cars filled with customers pull into the parking lot, Fatima carries the cleaning supplies into the kitchen and speaks over her shoulder as she goes: Check on her, Sailor. Be a hon.

The Azores is the collective name for a group of nine main islands and numerous volcanic formations flying the Portuguese flag and located approximately eight hundred miles west of Lisbon. The shallows around the islands made the area a natural feeding ground for both whales and whalers, but by the early 1800s the whales were scarce, their population decimated by Yankee hunters. Even so, American whale ships continued to visit the islands to recruit sailors and to replenish stocks of food and water and wine. In 1808, Emmanuel Joseph became the first Azorean to call New Bedford home after debarking from the whaler *Sally* and refusing to go to sea again. Today, nearly thirty thousand city residents identify themselves as Portuguese-Americans on census forms.

Back in high school and involved in a class project inspired by the TV series *Roots,* Fatima went to the library and researched the Sousas, her paternal line. In a whaler's logbook from 1818, she found mention of a crewman named Manuel Sousa, who was recruited on São Miguel and set anchor in New Bedford. She reckoned it had to be Manny Number One, because her dad was a Manny, her grandad was a Manny, and she was told there'd always been at least one Manny in her family since whaling days. In contrast, there was no research necessary tracking the course of her mother's side (Freitas) to America. That happened in 1966, she said, when she and Marie left the Azores and traveled by cattle boat to Lisbon, where they boarded a plane for Boston.

Marie lives in the city's South End, off misnamed Pleasant Street, in a neighborhood where, from 1840 until recently, Portuguese islanders (Azoreans, Cape Verdeans and Madeirans) formed the majority. Rich Yankees lived on the hill, beyond the stink of the waterfront, and yielded this part of town, along with two other, unsavory districts, to blacks and immigrants.

Marie's house was built in 1851, a shingled, two-family job like most on the block, and from then to now, it has been owned by a Portuguese speaker. The Salchicharia on the corner opened in 1858, while the neighborhood's two other corner stores are now bodegas catering to the newly installed majority of Spanish speakers.

Fatima didn't lay eyes on the place until she was four, spending her early years with Marie and Marie's parents on São Miguel and wondering about her father. At the mention of the man, she said, her mom would cry and her grandparents would curse. Manny met Marie while he was visiting relatives on the island and, according to Fatima, he was twenty, way-handsome and a huge-like liar. On their first date, he told Marie he was in love; on their next date, he proposed marriage. Marie fell for it and gave herself to Manny, even believing his line that he had to return to America to arrange their wedding. Manny never answered any of Marie's letters; when she was five months pregnant, she finally explained her predicament to her family.

Back then, Fatima says, the Azores were more Catholic than the pope, and Marie was shunned by the community. Eventually bowing to family pressure, Manny made good on his original promise and sent money for Marie and Fatima's passage to America. Because Manny and Marie had a child born out of wedlock, no Portuguese parish would consecrate their vows of marriage; luckily, the monsignor at St. Anthony's, a Franco-Canadian, opened the church doors and blessed the couple's future happiness. For this reason Fatima was schooled at St. Anthony's instead of Immaculate Conception, the Portuguese bastion of grammar school education.

Fatima recalled her first few months in America as so-so awful good. With the family united, her dream had come true. There were plenty of kids in the neighborhood, and most spoke Portuguese. She had toys that weren't made out of old socks and hammered tin. And it was her first encounter with a household equipped with a television and a refrigerator, as well as indoor plumbing. At Gram's house on St. Mike's, she said, you had to go outside to pee or poop, in a hole over Gram's pig. Always, that pig was happy to see you coming and while you were sitting down to do your business, it'd shove its snout into your privates and grunt. God, she hated that pig. At the same time, she never wanted it to die or she'd be forced to eat it.

Marie found work as a stitcher at Lynx Manufacturing, joining thousands of other Portuguese speakers already employed in the local needle trades. By the mid-1960s, sewing machines had pretty much replaced looms in the old mills, and the city was on its way to becoming the nation's capital of needle work. The local specialty was midpriced garments; in the mid-1970s, city factories supplied more than half the men's suits sold over the counter, as well as three out of every five overcoats sold for both women and men. Lynx was a union shop and provided a steady income plus benefits, keeping afloat a fisherman's family with a drunk at the wheel.

Lynx went out of business in 1974, and it took Marie nearly a year to find a new job, this time at Triplet, making winter coats for sale at large chain stores. During that search for a job, Fatima said, her dad snapped like a saltine, going all crumbly and jagged-like. That's when a buffoon turned into a monster, vicious, a needing man relying on gin for a compass, and he started physically abusing Marie. The worst attacks came during storms, when all the boats were tied to the dock and when Manny felt himself excused from even trying to work. On those days, Fatima said, he'd be corked by noon, and as soon as Marie came home, he'd be seeing five of her and go at them all. To soften the blows, Marie took to wearing a life jacket, which came out most nights and during every storm.

At the time, nobody on the docks doubted that Manny Sousa

had gone missing, but the exact cause of his disappearance became a mystery with as many endings as fishermen telling the tale. According to the skipper of the boat, Manny arrived at the dock at three a.m., like the rest of the crew, but he was drunk and sent below to sleep it off. As the boat neared the Nantucket Lightship, it was Manny's watch, but no one could find him. In fact, neither the crew nor the captain could remember seeing him after he was sent to his bunk. Had he slipped off the boat while she was still tied to the dock? Or had he slipped off the boat while she was under way? Frantic, the captain made phone call after phone call via radio, asking people to look for Manny around his home and the docks. There were no sightings on land, and the skipper issued a distress call over Channel 16: Man overboard.

Afterward, finding no sign of Manny, the captain and the crew lied to the Coast Guard and just about everyone else, saying they saw Manny tumble over the rail as an odd wave hit and sent the boat rolling. Captain Mack also went on the record, swearing a rogue wave hit the *Atlantic-Sue* within seconds of the distress call. It was the only way the widow could collect on the boat's insurance policy without waiting seven or more years due to the lack of a body or testimony from eyewitnesses. Satisfied that an unpreventable accident had taken place, the Coast Guard speedily concluded its inquest and the insurance company surrendered the money, which Marie used to open the cafe.

Pinched by derelicts needing immediate repairs, and diagonally across the street from a home gutted by fire, Marie's tidy house stands out, a reminder of what the whole neighborhood looked like before the needle trades went into a nosedive in the early 1980s, then crashed ten years later. Her front yard, fairway smooth and uniform, resembles the picture on a bag of Scotts

Turf Builder, and the shingles appear freshly painted. Mr. Rezendes, the landlord and the occupant of the other half of the house, ran a landscaping business before he retired. He and Marie share chores tending the extra-large garden in the back, its grapes and fava beans reputed to rival the best grown in the Azores. Like Marie, he intends to die at this address.

Marie answers the doorbell dressed in a lemon-colored blouse and a black skirt hemmed below the knee. Her hair is in a bun and a gold crucifix hangs around her neck, the feet of Jesus a bit worn from her habit of fingering the charm while listening to cafe customers talk about what interests them. She leads the way to the kitchen, her home office, saying, House rule: no guest talks until their mouth is full. The cramped hallway, padded with coats and rain slickers, opens to a light-filled living room, inviting and comfortable. Pictures of Fatima, cooking magazines and bowls of candy crowd the end tables, while the walls feature a series of oil paintings depicting an imaginary fishing village, its men and women wearing smiles and ceremonial outfits as they mend nets and gut fish the size of manatees.

She puts water on to boil, lays out a plate of desserts—she makes them here for sale at the cafe—and talks about the change in weather, how sunshine makes her feel tip-top and banishes any memory of a storm. It's like magic, she says. After listening to my brief report of happenings at the cafe, she keys on Sword. His health is all that matters, and she promises to say prayers for him and make pots of fava beans to soothe any pain. She calls Captain Mack her angel, a real protector. Fatima, however, can clean up her own mess and do it alone. She declares today her holiday, but instead of working through it, this year she's celebrating with friends. They're off to Providence to shop and eat at a restaurant that just opened. At five, she's booked at St. Anthony's to begin a novena. After that, she'll soak fava beans for Sword and make more desserts.

Before I leave, she writes a note to Captain Mack, which she hands over for delivery. She'd hate to waste a stamp and insists my services are worth half a gallon of kale soup. In the hallway, as Marie backsteps to open the door, I end up in a corner, hard against her life jacket hanging on a wooden peg. An extra layer of foam is carefully sewn inside the original job, and behind the third buckle the material is doubled, forming a pocket holstering a small, black-handled pistol.

Smoke curls out of the stack of the *Atlantic-Sue,* signaling the whereabouts of Mack. He often visits the boat after checking the auction prices; he sits in the wheelhouse, the engine running, and listens to traffic over the VHF radio. Today, though, he spied some rust on the steel half-round capping the starboard rail and intends to wire-brush and paint it. If he's lucky, he says, a few of his old cronies will come aboard and help stretch a forty-minute job into an all-day affair.

Mack opens Marie's letter and smiles, flashing gold where the ivory was replaced after a winch handle went wild and took out several teeth. He says what beats him about Marie, such a nice lady, is how she managed to stay hooked to that shit, Manny Junior. He remembers him as a jerk you wanted to kick overboard, like a bottom rock, something dense and useless. And, boy, is he glad he had three girls and never had to deal with the disappointment and anger that Manny Senior had to shoulder. When the search was on for Manny Junior, he recalls, everyone blocked out the name of the missing man. It could've been the devil himself, he says, but still, you do your best. The next time—who knows?—it could be yourself. So no half measures, no bad habits to lose.

He slips Marie's note into a back pocket and finds—Holy Jesus, love-ya, Fatima—the ten-dollar bill he thought he left at the cafe. While the fish auction was flat, prices stable beginning to end, Mack reports, Fatima's name was buzzing. Mind you, he didn't see anything, but word's out, he adds, about her almost

clocking that man trying to leave without paying. She saw him
go for the door, yelled, and when he didn't stop, she threw an
apple a thousand miles an hour at the cheapskate. Lucky, really,
that he ducked, then stumbled. That shot of hers would've
ripped the bean right off the stalk. Some arm she got. Some
temper, too. The arm was the big surprise.

That afternoon different versions of the incident are the talk
of the docks. Some depict Fatima throwing a chair or a fish tote
at the speed of light, and a few claim Sword lost all his teeth or
half his brains through a large hole in his head. Like bread and
fresh fish, any story aired on the docks has a short shelf life, two
days at the most, but everyone agrees there's a message being
broadcast which no one should ever forget: when eating at the
Harborside Cafe, tip as if your life depended on it.

Sword stays out of sight after leaving the hospital with
stitches in his head. Oddly, Fatima won't say anything about
Sword; instead, she talks nonstop about the new car she's buying. She had to place a special order to get a two-tone paint job
the same as her nails on her new set of wheels. Every other day
Fatima delivers food to Sword, cooked specially for him by
Marie, but the chef says she's in the dark about the patient's
condition. Even Sword's dope dealer is wondering about him.
Where be my dude, dude?

Two weeks after hitting the floor, Sword responds to mes-
sages left on his answering machine. Been road-tripping, he
says. His lawyer—you know, the feller on TV with the ad and
the phone number SUE-4YOU—warned him about insurance
dicks with video cameras out to scuttle their case by catching
him acting normal. Instead of staying cooped up in his apartment, he went to Niagara Falls and then drove northeast to
Fundy National Park to watch twenty-six-foot tides at work.
He's used to three- to four-foot tidal flows and says when you
start multiplying stuff times seven or eight, all sorts of space

appears and disappears every twelve hours. While the ebb current unrolled a carpet of sand and mud almost as fast as he could walk, the flood tide sent him running for his life, his escape route puddling in minutes. He says he almost had to swim for shore—a panicky reminder, he added, that he was in salt water and dealing with the Big Boss. The river gods at Niagara Falls thundered and spewed spray, but they never tried to trick or kill him. He decamped once he ran out of dope.

He extends an invitation for dinner and says there's enough food in the fridge to feed China for a million years. He recommends parking away from his house and using the neighbors' yards as the best approach to his back door. He'd hate to have some insurance dick bug anyone he knew, 'cause them people be diseased worse than cops.

Sword lives in the North End and near Weld Square, a hub of sin offering more connections to illegal sex and drugs than any other public space in the city, county or region. Within shouting distance of the square, there's a Vietnam vets center, one of several in town that he has frequented since his discharge from a VA hospital. As he walked to a meeting one day, he saw a FOR RENT sign in the window of a triple-decker. It has been his home for years.

While Marie's neighborhood was forming, in the 1830s, the city expanding southward and marching toward the open sea, the North End of town remained farmland and home to the dump. Most of its shoreline bordered the estuary, all of it shallow and useless to New Bedford's moneymakers: deep-draft, oceangoing whale ships. However, starting in the mid-1840s, North End land values rose as speculators bet on a future which favored machines over ships, with looms instead of whales ringing the cash register. Wamsutta Mills opened its doors in 1846, and within months, it couldn't keep pace with orders for its extra-fine cotton goods. More mill buildings went up, and by the 1880s, Wamsutta was the world's largest manufacturer of sheeting and shirting. Equipped with three thousand looms, the complex spun out twenty-five million yards of fabric a year and employed more than two thousand workers.

During the same period, the whaling industry went from heyday to graveyard, but New Bedford's passage from a sailors' town to a smokestack city was complete. By 1920, the area was host to nearly seventy textile mills, employing thirty-five thousand people. To house them all, developers worked in cahoots with mill owners and built hundreds of triple-deckers. The design was cheap and easy to construct and could accommodate three generations of one family or upwards of twenty-five single people on each floor. Weld Square was in the middle of the building boom and prospered as a business district catering to factory workers. In the 1920s, it was one of the hottest and priciest city addresses; come the late 1980s, it was still hot, but not in a good way, the district blighted by fire-scorched storefronts and empty lots cleared because of arson. Drop by drop, the lifeblood of Weld Square drained as the mills closed one after the other, starting with Wamsutta in 1959.

As instructed, I enter Sword's house by the rear doorway. Spanish music leaks through the first-floor entryway, where a crew of Guatemalans live. They toil in fish houses as filleters, cleaners and packers, tedious, low-wage jobs with high accident rates. Ceaselessly polite, they maintain a low profile, and Sword likes them as neighbors because they're quiet; even so, he says, he has never met any of them Guats or knows how many live below him. The stairs are narrow and follow a tight spiral as they race upward on eleven-inch risers, the treads clacking and shifting underfoot. Ahead, Sword's back door, like his front entrance, is reinforced with a layer of metal sandwiched between sheets of plywood. The added security is common in the city's triple-deckers, as much protection against unannounced visits by cops as crooks.

The door opens to a kitchen smelling of shrimp simmering

in a sauce of green wine, paprika and garlic. Drinks are already poured. Here's to no fire ever-like in this tinderbox, he says, clinking glasses. He swallows, then adds: If the smoke and flames don't get you, running down them back stairs will. Fire is on his mind, he explains, because last week the triple-decker on the corner was torched by a crackhead getting high in the hallway. Demolition work on the hulk is due to begin in a few days.

Sword is dressed in jeans, sweatshirt and a baseball cap, which he lifts to display the hospital's work: eight stitches. While the wound looked like a killer at both the cafe and the hospital doorway, he says it be nothing like that, really, just a dent in the box. He happens to be a bleeder. Always has been. Christ, as a kid he'd enter the house with a scraped knee and his mom would think he had backed into a chain saw. In Nam, he remembers bleeding enough to almost drown in the red stuff. On the tape from security cameras at the hospital, he says, it shows him bleeding a river-like, way-bad. His lawyer thinks the tape makes their case a freakin' slam dunk, a big-like cheese deal.

Originally, he confides, the plan for the cafe was an easy payday, one-two-three: slip, sue and settle quick. He and his partners—Yes sir, there be two others—figured on scoring around six grand each, willing to take the insurance company's first offer and that'd be that. But when his head hit the table's edge, the blood gushing, he heard opportunity knocking and says he opened the door. Suddenly, he felt intense pain upstairs and downstairs, ankle, knee and noggin.

He pours himself another triple rye and turns to the stove. If Marie would have him, he'd marry her that day, he says, snuffing the flame under the shrimp Mozambique. He leads the way into the living room and points me toward an overstuffed chair next to the aquarium and in line with the TV. In this castle, it's his throne. For a bachelor fisherman, the place is remarkably neat, and none of the normal shipboard habits—wearing the same clammy outfit for days on end and rarely cleaning galley or fo'c'sle until the boat nears the dock—followed him home. The walls are bare and he swears he'll never hang a picture unless it shows him holding the winning ticket to a Powerball draw.

He goes to the kitchen to warm up some bread and asks me to put on some music. The sound of a radio tuned at a low volume beckons from inside a bedroom with no bed in it. A boom box sits on the floor, but there's no sign of CDs or tapes. Tight to one wall is a folding table like the kind used in prison and school lunchrooms. Its Formica top is laid out in a grid—two rows of four squares—marked by masking tape, with a manila envelope double-wrapped inside freezer bags atop each square. Off to the side, near some cardboard boxes on the floor, Sword's fancy metal case sits on an armless chair.

Loudly, the Allman Brothers play music in another room, and Sword finds me next to the lunch table. He looks surprised and curses himself for forgetting to lock the room. But, shit, it don't matter, he says. Look all you want. He doesn't have anything to hide, at least not in here. Indeed, what's in evidence are facts of his existence, all public records. He opens one manila envelope, which he dubs The Early Show, and spreads out some of its contents: birth certificate, baptismal papers, grammar school report cards and a sheet of heavy stock paper naming him Champion of the Holy Family Church Festival Bubble Gum Blowing Contest.

As a kid, he recalls, he dreamed of blowing bubbles that could carry him around the world. This was also the first dream he chased which tripped him up along the way. In fourth grade, he stole a helium tank from the church basement, thinking if he swallowed enough gas and then sent it into a bubble, he'd balloon and begin his journey. He was caught with it strapped to his bike and from then on, the nuns at school treated him like a doped-up thief. This inspired him to match action to expectation—Sure-sure, got way-serious about stealing and getting high. Glue. Pot. Crystal. Whatever. He says high school shop class turned him around and redirected a punk headed for the slammer on a course to a union card. He excelled at fixing machines, especially the looms the mills provided the school to train future mechanics. He was class star until he dropped out to work full tilt at the mill. But by the time he got out of the service, there was hardly a loom left in the city.

Sword doesn't open any other envelope and merely thumps his fist atop four more as he names them: Family World; High School Crap; Military Stuff; Fishing Life. He says the cardboard boxes on the floor are garbage cans which never get emptied. They contain receipts, pay stubs and anything else deemed useful during an IRS audit. He claims being a fisherman makes him target practice for the feds. To date, he swears to Almighty God, he has been audited a million freakin' times.

All eight manila envelopes fit inside his metal case and go with him every time he leaves New Bedford. It's travel insurance, he says, and reasons: If he dies at sea or in a car crash, the facts of his life will remain intact inside the buoyant, fire resistant and watertight case. It be proof—today, tomorrow, forever-like—that he has done things and been places and anyone who says he's just a junked-up fisherman is wrong. Hell, he gave up more than he ever got back.

He checks his watch and announces, Rice be done. Several forkfuls into the meal he wonders if Marie should be featured on the Food Network or some health-related cable TV show. He feels she's a perfect fit either way, but decides she should host a medical program. Honest, he says, feed this chow to a dead feller and he'd be awake and crying for more in seconds. He hates to think Marie might stop cooking for him and wants everyone he sees to tell her that he's alive only because of her generosity.

A little rye in your coffee? he asks, and fills half his mug with booze. Usually, he prefers to mix gin or vodka with his coffee, but the liquor store won't deliver and he's supposed to be too ill to walk. Well into his third cup of paint remover, he shares some of his plans for the insurance money coming his way. First, he wants to visit Lourdes and take a dip in magic water. After the cure, he plans on buying a way-big TV. He stops there, his eyebrows arching as the knob to his front door starts jiggling. A key works a lock, but the interior chain is engaged. Fatima announces herself. Open the door, she yells. She has food and good news: They cut the check. Open up . . .

My partner, Sword whispers, then screams, Hold your horses, Fatima. Come-n. But before he can answer the door, he must first solve a problem in the kitchen: there's one too many in the room for any business to get done. She'd freak if she saw you here, he adds, escorting me to the back door. Shhh, he admonishes, the stair treads clacking underfoot.

Several banking days later, Sword parks his car in the lot at Pier 1 and waves to me and Captain Mack, sitting on a bench by the office of the Mariner's Assitance Program, at the head of the wharf. It's eight-twenty a.m. and there's a crowd gathered to board the ferry to Cuttyhunk Island, which leaves on the hour from the dock. Sword toes a discarded foam cup as he moves toward us, a soccer forward dribbling downfield. With a mighty kick he sends the cup flying, and shouts, Goal! Fuck, we win.

Early bird ferry riders, mostly Harvard and MIT professors and their families headed to vacation homes, tighten ranks. Parents reach for children; shoulders bump shoulders; and every briefcase and purse goes snug to a hip. Sword notes the reaction he elicits and responds: You scare me, too.

He goes for the door handle to the Mariner's Assistance office, but it doesn't budge and won't open until nine a.m. at the earliest. It depends on how late any AA or NA meeting ran the night before, any overtime usually deducted from daylight business hours.

Sword moves to the bench and Captain Mack immediately signals discomfort, forcing air noisily through his nostrils. By my watch, it takes six seconds before Mack taps my knee, says, This package is addressed to you, and excuses himself: Got to see a man about a dog. Sword recommends a Labrador. Can't do better than a Lab, Cap'n. A pile of paws and all love between the ears. Mack maintains a brisk pace to his truck.

Again, Sword checks the door. Damn. He thought the place opened at seven and says it shows how often he has been here for help. Today, though, he needs some paperwork on the fisherman's pension plan, but he can't hang around much longer. There are a million and one things to do before he leaves for the airport in under an hour. Boston to Paris. Paris to Lourdes.

He takes another peek inside the office and this time returns to the bench complaining about people who pop their buttons while saying it's their job to help him. He heard that line all the time at the VA hospital and learned way-quick-like not to believe a word of it. Tell-ya this, he says: if he actually expected help from others, he'd be dead by now. There's only so much disappointment a feller can handle before putting a finger to the trigger.

Sword jumps up, seeing movement inside, but it's only the reflection in the window of ferry passengers boarding the boat. Taking a seat, he says he might keep going, chewing gum and blowing bubbles on plane after plane around the world. Oh, jeez, look at the time, he adds. Got to go. We shake hands and he promises to send a shitload of postcards pinpointing his travels.

Sword was last seen heading west on the interstate minutes after he pulled out of the Pier 1 parking lot. His fast fade was partially explained days later by a cop getting nowhere in his investigation of fraud and theft complaints leveled against Sword by his lawyer. In fact, while visiting the lawyer's office, he stole the insurance settlement check destined for an escrow account and cashed it before it was discovered missing. In addition to the cops, the lawyer also enlisted help from fishermen-clients, offering a hefty reward for information leading to the scofflaw's capture.

Sword's vanishing act doesn't generate much wind around the docks. Puffer, the skipper of the *Ocean-C,* says he expected more and better from his former deckhand, who he now considers a buckethead on the run and not worth thinking about. He doubts we'll ever see Sword again, unless, of course, the guy gets tired of running and wants some rest in jail. If there's anything to lure Sword back, Puffer can't see it. He lists what's missing: The guy has no family left here; no apartment (Sword gave his door key to his first-floor neighbors and told them to help themselves); and no job. Hell, Puffer adds, Sword knew he was getting bounced from the crew. He couldn't keep pace no more, too old and that bum leg didn't help none-neither. The guy had one trip left and he blew it off to run a scam. So screw Sword, Puffer says, and changes the subject to his new deckhand, a man in his twenties as good with a knife as Sword was in his prime.

No one is more positive in his thinking about Sword's whereabouts than Gill. He's an occasional fisherman, hanging out more than shipping out, and a low-level dealer, considered good for a bag or two between visits to a wholesaler. Gill says he's as sure as any man ever been sure of anything that Sword is dead as she goes. He has no proof and no idea where to start looking for a body. What he has is the inside scoop. He'll even offer two-to-one odds that Sword is now flat on his back inside some refrigerator. And since there's no next of kin to inherit the body and all the paperwork which goes with a found body, he's also willing to bet—this time his life—that Sword will burn twice: first, he'll be cremated and then he goes to hell.

Snake eyes, that's what killed him, Gill insists. There was a screwup at a powder house and some uncut junk was sold as regular product. Sword, doing some last-minute shopping before his trip, bought two bricks (two hundred bags) of the killer powder in packets stamped with two dice showing snake eyes and left town before word got out. Gill says three people overdosed, including Sword's dealer, and everyone in the trade believes Sword is victim number four.

At the Harborside Cafe, Marie doesn't talk about Sword and on those rare occasions when his name pops up in conversation, she closes the door. More coffee? she'll ask. And how's the family? Fatima, too, seeks distance. When she hears his name, she shakes her head as if an ear infection is killing her or denies ever knowing the man. Sword who? What? She prefers to talk about her new car and says the two-tone paint job was worth the wait, its value verified when she drove to Marlene's shop, Nails of Distinction, and watched her friend turn green. After dragooning customers to rearrange the parking lot, moving the HANDI-CAP ONLY sign, she now moors it next to the front door so she can eye her new love all day long through the cafe windows.

But ten days later, she starts parking the car in the back of the cafe. Oh, sure, she says, she's still way-so in love, only the temperature dropped a bit. The car is now another piece of her life that she adores yet worries about more than she gets to enjoy. Like Ma. Like her boyfriend. Like her Johnny-on-the-side (Shh about him for now). And like her bank account. The chill came on several nights ago, after someone tried to steal the car while it was parked in her driveway and ruined the driver's-side lock. In this stinking, sinking city, she figures, people now have to be bad just to keep things right with the landlord and Ma Bell. If it's valuable, she's hiding it.

Until she found a garage to rent, she slept with an egg timer and got up every twenty minutes to check on the car. In the morning, she awoke feeling like a hard-boiled egg, with nothing much jiggling inside the shell for hours afterward. If that wasn't bad enough, last night, dear God, she didn't get a wink of sleep, her body and her brain going numb when she sat at her desk and got a good look at her future: three years of biweekly car payments, monthly garage rent, quarterly insurance premiums, yearly taxes, plus-plus all the usual: gas, oil, windshield cleaner.

The way she adds up her bills: her debt could sink a battleship. She admits to going hog wild when ordering the car, but she was hallucinating, she says, seeing a big chunk of cheese floating her way. With it, she imagined paying off most of the car on day one and freeing herself to act on her dreams. To travel. Get the hell out of town. Visit the desert. Go to Florida. See new stuff. But, damn-damn-dammit, here she is. Stuck. In debt up to her eyeballs. If she goes on vacation, she'll miss work. If she doesn't work, she can't afford the car.

She'd love to blame someone else for digging the hole she's in, and does, too, but, really, mostly-like, she says, it's her own fault. She knows, oh, baby, she knows and has said it over and over a million times since she learned English: Never trust a fisherman. She calls it lesson one around the docks. Lesson two, she adds: Big fish eat small fish. Number three: Take the bait, never the hook. Four: Be ready to wiggle. And now, she says, there's lesson number five: Make Sword extinct.

She doesn't believe for one lousy second that snake eyes killed Sword. She insists there was one thing that the dope was smart about, and that was dope; he always took a taste—a dot on the tongue—to measure the cut before firing up and driving home the spike. She's also convinced that he'd never go to Lourdes. She has known Sword for more than twenty years and if he prayed to any god it was Poseidon. She says the nuns at school

beat the living Jesus out of him. And if there was an iota of religion left in him, it was blasted straight to hell in Vietnam.

Believe me, you, she says, Sword left the hospital a total
wreck; the sea is what saved him. She feels the loss of his job
aboard the *Ocean-C* made him flip out and turn stupid and, boy,
she's pissed at Puffer for not telling her his plans to axe Sword.
Her guess: Sword is camped somewhere near salt water and
fishing boats. He'll be back, she predicts. At this point, there's so
much fish in him he'll have to return to where he was spawned.

Four customers walk into the cafe and Fatima tells them to
sit anywhere they please. She grabs four mugs off the shelf by
the Mixmaster and under the framed newspaper clipping of a
youthful beauty queen and her court. With two mugs in each
hand, she sends her arms up, then out and down, drawing a
large zero in the air. Forget him, she says. Best forget until some
storm blows him through the door. And then get out of the way.
She'll be ready to fire and plans to use every bullet in the gun.

Four specials, all scrambled, with wheat, she shouts to Marie
after taking breakfast orders, and disappears behind the kitchen
door.

Two

GOOD AS
GONE

MAKO'S FAITH IN HIS BOAT and the sea comes out of the tradition and religion he was born into, the son of a fisherman. He affirmed it all for himself as a teenager, when he signed a lifelong contract to toil at sea. Like his ancestors, he invested everything in a future of mining the ocean's resources, betting the wad on his own ability to develop the skills needed to deliver the goods in ever-increasing amounts. Before entering the contract, he was told—and had every reason to believe——not only that his faith was well placed, but that it fit precisely inside the context of a larger communal deal which constituted the American Promise, valuing sweat over pedigree, push over pull. Put in the hours and reap the rewards; the harder you work, the bigger your piece of the pie, the sky's the limit.

For two hundred years, this was the common arrangement in the engine room powering the nation. Mako never thought to question the compact. The terms were straightforward, no fine print or lawyerly mumbo jumbo involved. It had worked as advertised from the start. Certainly, his dad had no complaints, and his grandfather couldn't imagine anything else. And it was the same deal all his friends accepted. Like previous generations, he and his pals assumed the system was sound, the integrity of the machine guaranteed. Plus, one look around told

him that the same deal held true coast-to-coast. It had built New
Bedford, Detroit and Los Angeles, and it had been documented
in his high school textbooks.

For Mako and other fishermen his age (forty-six) and older,
the contract they signed as teens was broken the day Washington dispatched the sheriff to manage the fishery and establish
law and order among the unregulated tribes operating at
the nation's fringe. Previously, the government had taken on the
forestry and mining sectors and, at last, the fishery was in the
crosshairs. By the early 1990s, federal agents, abetted by environmental groups working the judicial system, had closed vast
swaths of the North Atlantic to fishermen, the oceanic plain
suddenly bounded by the laws of the land. They also began putting limits on just about every aspect of the commercial fishing
business. In the process, the deals fishermen considered invio-
late were deemed null and void. When fishermen complained,
they were summarily dismissed by the media, the courts and
bureaucracy as cranks and crooks deserving neither sympathy
nor compensation.

The feds viewed the ocean as a communal warehouse and
accused fishermen of robbing the place blind, a bunch of pirates
swiping the nation's inheritance and trashing the bottom as they
went about their rapacious business. Lawmen and their agents
took inventory after inventory, and each time the results were
the same: not only were certain species, like cod and sole,
approaching the vanishing point, but the entire marine eco-
structure had been undermined and was threatening to collapse
in near-apocalyptic ways. The survey data inspired countless
reports by the media, greenies and academics which depicted
fishermen wearing black hats, a greedy and unconscionable lot,
and the reason why things had gone so terribly wrong at sea.
Out of all that ink and commentary a guilty verdict was shaped,
debate closed on appeals from fishermen.

While no cure for a sick ocean was handy, further research

necessary, the lawmen sought to remediate things through rules
and regulations, quotas for landings, caps on fishing time and
crew size, and by slapping electronic bracelets on boats and
foisting mountains of paperwork on boat owners, captains
and fish processors. As far as the sheriff's department was concerned, fishermen were agents of their own demise and lucky
they weren't behind bars. Citing the newly established law of
the sea, lawmen reminded fishermen that old attitudes and old
ways of fishing were dead and gone, and were now criminalized. Any sign of its lingering spirit would be arrested, then
fined and jailed. In the modern American construct, there was
no room for any industry operating under a frontier mentality;
those days were over.

Mako, of course, believes he has been royally screwed and
wrongly convicted by a bunch of landlubbers who don't know
jack about the sea, what lives in it or lives off it. Besides, no one
asked him if they could rip up the old contract. To him, a deal's
a deal, live with it and fuck anyone messing with the terms;
growing up on the docks, he was taught that bargain busters
usually got what they deserved: a knife or marlinespike in the
back or gut. And what really pisses him off, he says, is how the
feds, the greenies and the lab coats twisted themselves into
heroes, champions of the ocean and protectors of the future, by
demonizing fishermen. He feels that is not only wrongheaded
but insane, way-so far beyond retarded.

In fact, he believes any talk which makes fishermen into a
bigger problem than pollution is just plain crazy. It's the landlubbers, he insists, and all their cars and sewage and factories
and garbage that are killing the sea. They're the ones raising the
water temperature and killing the coral, changing the acidity
and screwing up the stocks. So go after them and let fishermen
do their job. He says he winces every time he sees fishermen
mentioned in the media, because they're always shown as gang-
sters, killers all—until, that is, they die in a storm or get rescued

by fearless Coasties. Then, dammit, fishermen come across as uneducated dopes who should've stayed in school or never should've left the rehab clinic.

This makes him wonder what he's supposed to do. Bend over and say, Here's the Vaseline, boys? To hell with that. He'll fight for his rights until he drops. He'll wiggle through their traps. He'll end-run their stupid laws. For every rule and reg, there's a countertactic. For each inspection at sea by Coasties, there are dozens of secret hiding places on a fishing boat. For every fishery agent, there's a good lie. And for every Coastie on watch, there are two or three pirates at work.

But-but-but, he motors, a few years ago there were six pirates for every Coastie. The old gang is just that, old, he adds. And most are exhausted, tired of losing to greenies and lab coats, tired of talking to people who only pretend to listen. He, however, is in for the long count. And since what impels him is reaction, not revolution, he'll do his fighting alone. He says the solo act is the only way to assure himself of never surrendering. He steers wide of trade groups and fishery councils, which didn't exist until the sheriff appeared, and he sees them as either tools in the hands of the feds or fronts for corporate fleet owners. While he'd love to hear the hometown team cheering his position, all he hears are lawmen and industry big shots jerking each other off.

He rises from his office chair, a seat on the cap log running alongside his lobster boat, the *Amy-C,* and turns to rap his knuckles twice on her wood. It's you and me baby, he says, and climbs aboard to fetch a pack of butts from behind the wheel. She's an old-timer, constructed in the 1940s out of materials stolen from government stockpiles at local shipyards building PT boats and barges for the navy. Some of her original fittings show gouges made with a cold chisel to obliterate federal serial numbers. These days she's in rough shape, her innards slowly

rotting inside a thin skin of fiberglass, which Mako applied several years ago. The leaking had gone out of control, her pumps
cycling twenty-four hours a day, and other than the fiberglass,
he didn't know what to do without it costing him an arm and a
leg. As it is, he blows much of the money he makes as captain of
an offshore scalloper on her and her business.

If the *Amy-C* stays afloat for three more years, he expects
to make enough money from lobstering to buy a new, fuel-
efficient and fast boat. Three years ago he said the exact same
thing. But he's a fisherman and easily forgets what has been put
astern. What matters is his next outing at sea. The next big fish.
The next record haul. He understands the ocean as pitiless,
utterly arbitrary and a place where nature, not man, makes the
rules. As such, it's a wide open hunting ground to those willing
to break their backs and risk their necks, and, God willing, he
intends to empty it of every salable product before he dies. After
all, commercial fishing is a business in which greed is cloaked in
promise.

Perhaps inspired by the sun breaking through the tail end of
a cumulus cloud riding a fair, southwesterly breeze, or maybe it
comes out of the nicotine from his first cigarette in more than
five minutes, Mako stretches for the sky. He's a big man, six foot
five, thick in all the right places, his shoulders barely squeezing
through hatchways. An athlete in profile, he casts a shadow considered among the largest anywhere on the waterfront. He has
plenty of jet-black hair and a set of long legs attached to an
unpadded thirty-six-inch waist. He elicits playful looks from
divorcées years younger than he. They all love what they see:
Liam Neeson goes to sea.

This morning, as usual, he wears a black T-shirt over black
jeans and white rubber boots. The dark clothes, he'll tell you,
are just the thing for anyone working on boats and docks. They
help hide stains from the muck which sometimes comes up

with lobster traps and scallop rakes, and they camouflage blotches from the grease and light oil which spit out of pulleys, winches, engines and anything else made to turn in or near salt water. The white rubber boots were the only ones he could find in size 11EEE, and since he often wears boots for twelve or more hours a day, he says, they could be rainbow-colored as long as they're comfortable.

Between pulls on a Marlboro, he talks about the past. For the longest time, he says, the only things that interested him were fish, fishing, salt water and sin. Throughout the 1970s and 1980s everything else blew right by him. He bought the newspaper for the sports section; if the boat was carrying a Nam vet, he'd tune out the guy's chatter; if a news segment came on the tube, he'd click away until the screen emptied of talking heads.

He says he didn't purposely avoid a bigger world, he just never knew he was supposed to care. Around the house when he was a kid, fish and fishing pretty much monopolized the conversation, his dad and Gramps fierce competitors who loved the sea and little else. There was no war or draft when he turned eighteen, and Washington, D.C., seemed a million miles away. All he had to do, he thought, was concentrate on partying and fishing. And party-hearty times it was, he adds, listing some of what he recalls: Dope was everywhere. Sex was easy, no big deal. People were dancing their brains out. The music rocked. Belushi lived. Things were funny and laughing a snap. There were jobs in the city and fishing had never been better. About every week there was a new record for landings of scallops, cod, halibut, you name it. And talk about good things: back then fishermen were paid in cash. No checks. No records, Just liquid cheese to squirt around town.

It wasn't until much later that he realized how incredibly small a space he was living in. His pals were all fishermen. Most of the women he knew were either fishermen or daughters of fishermen. He socialized at fishermen's hangouts and talked shop while he relaxed. His dope dealer was a former fisherman. He got his hair cut at a two-chair barbershop owned by a former deckhand. He bought his three-bedroom house from a fisherman and moved into a neighborhood that had been home to fishermen and their families for more than 250 years. The one church he'd visit—and only for weddings, funerals and memorial services—was the Seaman's Bethel on Johnny Cake Hill, where the pulpit is shaped like a ship's prow and the walls are lined with cenotaphs listing the names of boats and local fishermen lost at sea dating back to the whaling era.

That self-referential world exploded in 1987, when he and nearly a dozen other captains, plus boat owners and processors, were targeted by the IRS during Operation Big Fish. Under siege by an unfamiliar foe and wanting to know all he could about the enemy, Mako says, he turned into a news junkie. Suddenly, he couldn't get enough of CNN or Peter Jennings; he started buying Boston papers and would read the front page before glancing at the box scores.

Up to then, he had never had any dealings with the federal government other than the Coast Guard. Also up to then, he'd never known he could despise a place and its population before visiting it, but he grew to hate Washington, convinced it was headquarters to a genuinely demonic force that preyed on the workingman. Since he had never filed a tax return and had kept no records, the IRS did the math and tagged him for five years of back taxes, plus interest and penalties. To this day, he swears the IRS agent assigned his case broke his own nose by tripping over his own goddamn feet; at his trial, though, the judge found him guilty of assaulting a federal agent. He served seventy days in jail and shouldered yet another hefty fine.

Mako shakes a fist and snarls, still upset by the gross injustice done him, and continues to steam. He recalls how he was almost clear of his IRS and court bills when, son-of-a-bitch, the feds reappeared on the docks. This time, he claims, they came and threatened his existence by ordering him and everyone else in the trade to cut back on their days at sea. It was a freaking lockout, he asserts, adding, It didn't matter that fishing hadn't changed very much in centuries or that fishermen were only doing what the government had been encouraging them to do forever: supply the nation with fish product.

And that's when it started, the blame game on, Mako says. The witch hunt was under way and fishermen were losers from the get-go. He didn't hear a peep about foreign boats using drift nets or anything about factory ships flying Liberian flags or acid rain or mercury or oil spills. Instead, American fishermen were labeled rotten and trashed.

Like other skippers, Mako went to the initial round of public hearings on proposed changes to the fishing business and there-after called it quits. He had seen and heard enough to form a response to it all: fuck 'em, fuck it. He saw no reason why he should have to defend himself or seek compromises. He hadn't done anything wrong. And he can't remember one meeting when anyone actually discussed something. What he witnessed were fishermen shouting and cursing while the feds talked at, not with, their audience, and the lab coats spoke in a language no fisherman could understand beyond its tone of doom and gloom.

He homes in on marine biologists and slams them for offer-ing bad assumptions as good science, all of which fed the media and the greenies with half-baked facts and figures. How, he won-ders, can a lab coat go to sea for a week or two a year and claim to know more than an old-timer who has shipped out forty weeks a year for fifty years in a row? And since biologists never study the best way to catch fish, like fishermen do, he reasons, their sampling nets and dredges are bound to come up with only a few fish. Even the dumbest doped-up deckhand knows that when you put shit in, you get shit out for results, he says, concluding his recitation of the company line around the docks.

Personally, he adds, what fuels his skepticism of fishery science comes out of stories told by crewmen aboard the research boats based in Woods Hole. Most of them are New Bedford men, and they often return from a voyage with a whistle-blower's report. Usually, the crewmen talk about scientists too seasick to leave their bunks and experiments going bust due to gear made in a college lab instead of a dockside welding shop. In many cases, the crewmen describe biologists as liars, fudging their findings to declare success and stay in line for tenure and yet another grant to save the ocean.

Watch out, Mako warns, and vents: Faaaah-uck. In a quieter voice, he says, It's frustrating, so-way-so, when people you don't like or trust spew crap as facts which decide your future. He thinks that's unfair and un-American, and he's positive it's contrary to what he was taught and once believed this nation to be about. The best thing he can do is keep his head low, work the shadows and fight the pricks best he can.

Again, he raps his knuckles twice on the *Amy-C*'s wood and this time whispers to her, his lips nearly kissing the coaming, and assures her that they'll make it through any storm coming their way. In their relationship, fisherman and his boat, hope is dogma. Together, they'll weather the blow. Together, they'll battle the sheriff. The ocean's a horn of plenty, and as a team, they'll strip it bare. Don't worry, baby, he coos.

Mako turns away from the *Amy-C* to stare at a figure waving his arms while standing next to a car parked at the end of the pier. It's Johnny Big Boots, Mako says as much as groans. Big Boots is a minor fence and a major crack dealer and about as trustworthy as an unhitched line around a cleat, sure to slip under pressure. What's up, Big Boots?

Business, Mako, Big Boots shouts, his arms still flapping. Cheese calling.

Mako says he's so broke and in need of coin that he'll listen to any Joe Blow offering cheese. He returns to the *Amy-C* after talking with Big Boots and tells her, We're getting there, baby. He strokes her nose, then steps away from the boat to tell me in a voice just above a whisper that he's in trouble at the bank. They're going to seize the *Amy-C* if he doesn't pay off the entire note—$31,000—by the end of the month. They claim he defaulted on the boat loan; he says he's behind on payments, but not much.

He blows a kiss to the *Amy-C* and follows up with a promise to keep her beyond reach of the bank. It's the only reason, he adds, why he'd ever agree to do a job for the King of Blowback, Johnny Big Boots. While he's committed to finding the money to get the bank off his back, he says one simple, way-so, fact bugs him: the *Amy-C* is worthless to anyone except him. Certainly, no lobsterman in his right mind would invest a dime in buying her. It makes him wish she was a better boat and he was less crazy.

In fact, the *Amy-C* will cost the bank thousands just to junk her properly. But the bank's motives are more personal than financial. The chief loan officer, Janice, is Mako's old girlfriend, twice his fiancée and at least once almost the mother of his child. They met in high school, dated on and off, her brief marriage to a fellow banker never in the way, and up until last May they'd lived together, for eight or nine years. He's not sure of the exact number and remarks it's just that sort of thing that used to get Janice so mad at him. But, oh-boy, yes, he remembers the day they broke up. He calls it the day of no more china, since every plate, cup, saucer, pitcher and bowl in the house was smashed to pieces. He always thought the *Amy-C* was one of the few things she liked from their days together; they had some great times aboard her, he says, and shrugs.

Mako bought the *Amy-C* in 1990 or 1991. Again, he's not positive, but knows it was around the same time the feds started floating plans for quotas and caps on days at sea for scallopers. The thought of being denied access to the ocean and fishing

blew out his candles, he says. Frantic, he searched for a boat and
a license in a part of the fishery the feds weren't interested in,
lobstering, and found the *Amy-C*. Although his friends warned
him off, sure no one could hold two unrelated jobs in the fishing
business and be successful at both, he says he listened only to
himself because he felt his life was at stake. He points seaward
and explains, Without the sea, there's nothing. It's all he knows.
All he cares about, really.

Thanks to Janice, a junior loan officer at the time, Mako fina-
gled generous terms on a loan and, what the hell, overpaid
for the *Amy-C*, her gear and license. He didn't care: only 20 percent of the dough came out of his pocket; anyway, back then, it
was boom times for area lobstermen, McDonald's had just
introduced the McLobster Roll and he imagined Burger King
couldn't be far behind. Better yet, European and Japanese con-
sumers had taken a fancy to lobsters and had sent the price surging. Buyers for the American restaurant industry groused about
the price spike, but continued ordering more tons of product
than ever.

Within a year of when he set his first trap, the regional lobster population plummeted, the stocks whacked as clawmen
doubled or tripled their traplines to cash in on a soaring market.
The effects of human greed were soon eclipsed by a series of
oil spills, which fouled the habitat, and by the mid-1990s the
inshore lobster industry had collapsed. Locals were forced to
reset their gear offshore, in deeper, cleaner and colder water.
For Mako, it turned an easy one-hour commute to his old mark-
ing buoys into a four-hour marathon, the added fuel costs and
extra wear and tear on the boat making profits more elusive
than ever. From 1999 to 2002, the regional catch was down a
stunning 8.2 million pounds. More bad news followed: a shell-
eating disease started ravaging the offshore stocks, so disfigur-
ing the lobsters as to make them unsalable.

They'll be back, with more than ever, big and red, too, Mako says. He can see it happening at the edge of the horizon and swears it's moving his way and will soon be within reach: a million lobsters on the march and steering for his traps. Not one for science but a firm believer in traditional theories, he claims every living thing in the ocean moves in cycles, the population of each species part of a giant balancing act and either waxing or waning in a steady tempo. It's the reason he's so sure the lobster stocks, along with cod and groundfish, will rebound in record numbers. In the past, both his dad and his grandfather experienced years when they figured the ocean had been Hoovered, hardly a cod to be found, he says, and they taught him how to deal with it: tighten the belt and wait for the inevitable uptick. The one thing you don't do is push the alarm button.

Mako climbs aboard the *Amy-C* and reassures her yet again of smooth sailing ahead; he'll pay off the bank and you can bet on it. As he heads below to restring wiring to the bow light, he says he'll be brewing extra coffee on the galley stove in the morning. You're going to love it, Sailor.

The *Helen-L* was Mako's first command. She was built in Alabama and worked as a shrimper before arriving in New Bedford in 1974. She was rigged for scalloping without any modifications to her hard chine and rather flat bottom, and in three years of work, five captains came and went. They were frustrated by her southern lines, good for Gulf waters but ill-suited for duty in the North Atlantic, making her a rib buster in heavy seas and a hobbyhorse in everyday swells. They also fought with her owner, a man far too preoccupied by gambling debts to invest a dollar in the boat's upkeep or new gear. After the owner died—the Coroner's Office labeling it a suicide and most fishermen calling it a well-disguised hit—the *Helen-L* sat idle at the dock while the estate languished in probate court. In 1979, Mako's dentist ended up buying her, along with several other colleagues looking for tax loopholes, and while working on Mako's teeth, he made a deal with his twenty-three-year-old patient.

Of course, there was a catch, Mako said. In return for the captain's chair, he had to work months for free to revive the *Helen-L* and make her seaworthy again. And while he knew he was signing on to a dog hobbled by big problems, he didn't understand how sick the puppy really was until he started to work on her. He became her slave for fourteen hours a day, Sundays included, and after twelve weeks, with only three off to go fishing and reline his wallet, she was ready to work. When he finally set off for the fishing grounds, he was out to make money and prove wrong old farts on the docks.

Many skippers, his dad included, told the dentist-owner he should stick to gums and stay away from boats, that Mako was a bad choice to steer his investment, far too young to command an offshore fishing boat. They believed that only experienced, older seamen could handle the job and dismissed Mako's early days at sea (ages eight to eighteen) as a marginally instructive period when the kid was more an audience than an actor. They saw better talent available, particularly among those mates in their thirties and forties aching to be captains, and they were sure any of them had the grit Mako lacked to command a veteran crew through a crisis. When things go wrong at sea, the old-timers understood, little gets fixed without one voice, one decision maker aboard; in their experience, when the chorus sings, it's the prelude to disaster.

Mako's first two trips were blessed by fine weather, but each was only moderately successful. Scallop landings were below average for the fleet, as were Mako's marks as captain. The crew grumbled because they didn't make as much money as they expected, while dockside gossip focused on the equipment malfunctions which dogged the boat. Mako was blamed for them all, from a balky generator, which cut short one trip by two days, to a crack in the gooseneck in one of the rakes, rendering it inoperable. Even the clogged toilet on the second trip was deemed Mako's fault.

As captain, Mako had to absorb every punch. While the pay from his first trip went to a lawyer, he put his earnings from the second trip into insurance, the cash going to pay for teams of welders and mechanics to examine every bit of gear aboard the *Helen-L*. Like the old salts grading his performance, Mako felt he had two strikes against him. Three and he'd be back working as a deckhand. Only a landing of twenty-five thousand pounds or more of scallops would quiet the critics, secure his job for the rest of the season and put him on the road to owning the Corvette he so wanted in his driveway.

He and his crew of six left Pier 3 on the first Tuesday of October 1979. Weather reports predicted calm seas and winds under 20 knots for days ahead, the nearest low-pressure system almost twelve hundred miles away. After rounding Gay Head and putting Nomans Island off the starboard beam, Mako set an east-northeast course at Bell 1, bound for the northern edge of Georges Bank. For guidance, he relied on a subpar radar unit and a brand-new LORAN-C, plus a compass that had never been adjusted. If the electronics failed, he'd have to sniff his way home, going from buoy to buoy, and pray for no fog. He had traveled the route scores of times and knew the danger points; besides, only the old-timers could swing a sextant, and most boats in the fleet sailed without star charts or declination tables. Pushed by a 900-horsepower diesel and carrying twenty tons of ice and enough food and fuel to keep men and machinery going for three weeks, the *Helen-L* cruised at 8.2 knots.

Urged on by a combination of greed and daring, he steered for risky business, wanting to nose the Canuck Line and hit rarely visited scallop beds where gaffers would be his for the taking.

Most skippers, Newfies and Americans alike, prefer to stay three or four miles from the border, wanting that much room for error in their equipment, plus a bumper for drift and error in the gear aboard whatever Coast Guard boat is watching them from afar. If caught, a fishing boat crossing the line is subject to huge fines and burdened with enough paperwork to keep a lawyer on the meter for months. When questioned via radio by personnel aboard jets and cutters dispatched to investigate his venturous ways, Mako said he was merely a citizen exercising his rights in the pursuit of happiness.

In a little more than two and a half days of dragging along the border, the *Helen-L* bagged nearly seventy-five hundred pounds of product. As hoped, the scallops were mostly gaffers, with an average of fourteen to make a pound of meat. Mako wanted one more day of that sort of production before retreating from the line and easing the pressure on himself and the crew. He had the men working watches of ten on, six off, with no breaks in the tedium of setting tows and shucking scallops. Speedballs and crystal kept him going twelve on, four off, and when he wasn't at the wheel or checking the autopilot and LORAN, he was on deck working a knife. While he opened approximately four thousand scallops a day, each crewman handled closer to sixty-five hundred shells, and he sensed mutiny if he didn't reduce the workload within the next thirty-six hours.

Mako's dad had taught him that it was the skipper's job to scrutinize the sky at dawn, the horizon a giant billboard that can be read like a menu that lists everything the ocean will be serving up during the next twenty-four hours. On the morning of day three on Georges Bank, Mako saw the eastern sky go bright in reds and oranges, signaling a one-course meal of endless slop. While he didn't know the proper name of the high-flying clouds that looked like cotton candy (cirrus), he recognized them as another harbinger of rotten weather ahead. Further confirmation of deteriorating conditions came in a blink, when he checked the ship's barometer. In only a few hours, its needle had gone from under the s in FAIR / GOOD FISHING to the D in STORM / BAD FISHING, at the low end of the scale. What he couldn't understand were the marine weather forecasts predicting colder but fair weather for the next few days.

Like every captain he'd ever sailed with, Mako wasn't going to worry about the weather until compelled to do so. Most boats in the New Bedford fleet fished through gales, the gear out and the men working until Force 10 (50 knots of wind) conditions set in. If it blew over 60 knots, he knew the drill, having weathered blows pushing up thirty-five-foot seas. The one precaution he took involved flying saucers, ordering the off-duty watch to secure the galley. If they were in for a roller-coaster ride, he didn't want dishes tumbling off the shelves and costing him a buck each to replace. In a similar fashion, it was work as usual aboard the seven other New Bedford draggers within forty miles of the *Helen-L*. They exchanged information over the radio and, as one, the eight skippers cursed professional weather forecasters sitting inside windowless offices.

By ten a.m., it was pouring, and with the temperature a bone-chilling thirty-five degrees Fahrenheit, the rain carried an icy edge which stung exposed skin and caused shivers as it trickled down the insides of oilskins. The wind was out of the northwest, its speed steadily increasing, with gusts over 50 knots, while the waves were running twelve to fifteen feet and growing by the minute. Mako began to understand that every nasty remark about the *Helen-L*'s miserable ride in a gale was only half right: she was twice as bad a performer as anyone had said. Broadside to the waves, she rolled seventy degrees, becoming a catapult in tension as she dipped one rail at the top of a wave, and then it was bombs away as she slid into the trough and buried the other rail. From the wheelhouse, Mako watched a muck-out shovel scoot across the deck, hit the rail and fly end over end into the ocean. That prompted him to string safety lines fore and aft and order the men to tie on. If someone went overboard without a line to their waist, there'd be nothing to do but say a prayer for a dead fisherman.

In his fight at the wheel, Mako discovered he could keep the boat stable enough for the men to keep working as long as the punishment came straight at them, either right up the ass or smack on the nose. But once the seas topped the twenty-foot mark, he couldn't steer downwind any longer without clearing the deck; too often, waves would climb the transom and break atop the *Helen-L,* pummeling her iron and sending her out of control down the back side of the next wave. By late afternoon the rain had turned to snow, and with the storm growing worse, its energy boundless, the wind at 60 knots and gusting over the 75-knot limit on the ship's anemometer, Mako called it quits. All gear was lashed to the deck, the crew sent inside, and he stood watch at the helm. There was only one course to steer and it meant fighting with the wheel every second to keep the *Helen-L*'s nose poking into wave after wave, each a giant and every thirteenth or so a colossus. Weather forecasters now predicted short-lived blizzard conditions for his ocean quadrant and called for clearing skies before dawn. As a group, the eight New Bedford captains decided to remain on station and ride out the storm, hoping to reset their gear in the morning.

Sustained by radio conversation with his colleagues, plus pots of coffee, Drake's cakes and toots from a high-octane blend of coke and crystal, Mako wrestled with the helm through the night. Newfound energy sprang from a predawn weather forecast, the adrenaline flowing out of anger as he listened to the latest update. Meteorologists were now predicting three more days of blizzard conditions, with winds topping 60 knots the entire time. Meanwhile, the weathermen cautioned, seas would build into thirty- to thirty-five-footers, while visibility would remain lousy, always less than two miles and near zero in whiteouts.

The eight New Bedford skippers greeted this news with vows to neuter the entire staff of the National Weather Service. They also decided to leave the fishing grounds and seek shelter. Mako and four other skippers set course for the nearest safe harbor, in Nova Scotia; the remaining boats, each burdened by one or more crewmen wanted by Mounties for bad behavior during some previous visit, had to travel the extra miles to Maine. The Canadian Coast Guard granted permission to cross the line, and Mako estimated the cost of the side trip at fifteen hundred gallons of fuel, as well as lost time and a sizable bar bill while they waited in Nova Scotia for the seas to moderate.

Approximately fifty miles east-southeast of Cape Sable, at the tip of Nova Scotia, Mako suddenly felt his luck change. It came in a glance, when the snow let up for a moment and there, dead ahead and less than one mile away, he spied a gift from the gods with his name on it. He had always dreamed of claiming salvage rights to some abandoned boat, and now—thank you, Poseidon; thank you, Aeolus—he had a shot at owning an abandoned sailboat. She was a weird-looking thing and busted up in places, but she appeared tight, floating high on her lines, and just the sort of useless toy which rich-ass rotsmen insure for big bucks.

The snow swallowed the dreamboat, but things were all clear in Mako's head. First, he'd pick through the sailboat's gear and sell whatever he and his crew didn't want; then he'd hold her ransom and force the insurers to pay dearly for her release. Considering the sailboat's tiny size and the storm's enormity, he couldn't imagine anyone was still alive aboard her. He only hoped her crew had been swept overboard, saving him the bother of burial at sea. There was no way he'd arrive in port with dead men in tow. That would be asking for trouble: cops, delay and paperwork up the yin-yang.

Mako gathered the crew in the wheelhouse and they applauded his plan. It'll be greasy easy, he told them. He'd toss a harpoon with a small grappling hook attached to the tip, while Bemis, the first mate, steered as close as he could to the prize. He reckoned they had one chance and if they ended up ramming the sailboat, fuck it, let her sink, at least they would've tried. All were confident of success, relying on Mako's skill as a harpooner gained during two seasons as stickman aboard *Magic,* an old swordfish boat that ended up in a scrap yard. Both he and the boat would've stayed in the harpoon trade if it hadn't been done in by the efficiencies of long-liners and a crash in the swordfish stocks.

Mako steered the *Helen-L* in a circle, exiting the arc to aim straight for the sailboat. Bemis took the helm as Mako set up on the port rail. The crew crowded the wheelhouse portholes, ready to assist and cheer their captain.

I was aboard the sailboat. Her name was *Godiva,* after the chocolate company that ponied up the cash for me to build her and compete in an upcoming single-handed trans-Atlantic race. Designed to handle the North Atlantic from end to end, the thirty-two-foot racer was riding out the storm under bare poles, sea anchors set. I was in the cabin repairing sails when, all of a sudden, a fishing boat on a collision course filled the view through the leeward porthole. As I popped my head out of the hatch, the threat of disaster only multiplied, as I saw a Valkyrie pumping a spear aimed at my head. Preternaturally strange, the creature was half covered in snow and appeared to be perfectly balanced on the fishing boat's pitching deck, as if the weapon it was two-handing had somehow lifted it into the air. I aimed a flare gun at the spear thrower's head and pulled the trigger. The shot went high and wide.

Thought you were dead, the creature shouted, and lowered his spear. A man again, his power over a heaving deck gone, he grabbed for the rail as an odd wave, half again as big as the aver-

age twenty-five-footers, hit the fishing boat and sent her careen-
ing out of control into the trough. The gods didn't answer my
prayers and she continued steaming westward, showing a slab-
sided stern with lettering that said HELEN-L, NEW BEDFORD. Seconds later, she was gone, shrouded by spume and snow.

That night Mako and his crew sat at a table inside a Canadian
bar talking about the storm and that crazy fuck all by himself in
the sailboat. If only the guy wasn't alive, Mako kept repeating.
The crew echoed his thoughts, each man believing himself
robbed of riches and frustrated by it. Now, sadly, they all agreed,
the sailboat would be of no use to anyone, no doubt already
pounded to pieces by the storm, which was still gathering
strength. What a waste, the men said, and ordered yet another
round of drinks.

The *Helen-L* pulled into New Bedford Harbor twelve days
later, arriving late at night to an unexpected crowd gathered
to greet her. Mako was especially surprised to see his dad and
a contingent of old-timers, their arms stretched to take the
Helen-L's dock lines. They had monitored events during the tem-
pest, their ears to the radio and to stories told by storm-battered
crews, and they wanted to welcome home one of their own, the
boy-captain suddenly anointed a full-fledged skipper. They figured anyone able to handle a crew like his and a dog like the
Helen-L through a blow as dirty and mean as any seen in years
was fit to skipper their boats. He had made his bones, but best of
all, Mako recalled, the *Helen-L* landed twenty-seven thousand
pounds of scallops. It put his name on the high line for that
month's landings and it also gave him the down payment he
needed to buy a ghost-gray Corvette.

New Bedford's the place for custom marine metalwork, none
better in the East, and I visited town months later to pick up an
order. There was a clear shot of the docks through the windows
at the fabricating shop and one boat caught my eye, the *Helen-L*.

Nobody was aboard, but the harbormaster said her old skipper
had moved on and up. He pointed to a top-of-the-line ninety-six-
foot scalloper and told me to ask for Mako.

Hearing my introduction, Mako insisted there was no time to
waste. He had to buy me a drink.

Pour yourself some syrup, Mako says, and points to the *Amy-C*'s
cabin, where a coffeepot jiggles atop a one-burner gas camping
stove. The brew comes out of the pot thick and still boiling.
Meanwhile, Mako stands on the dock and leans into a bolt cutter, snapping one-half-inch galvanized chain. He's out to flatten
a two-hundred-foot spool into twenty strings and says a couple
of inches either side of ten feet don't matter none at all.

Again and again, the chain yields to Mako's pressure, demonstrating why no lock around the house is safe from a tool in
his hands. Although he fades after a twenty-yard sprint, a wheezing, unrepentant smoker, he's unbeatable in tests of upper-
body strength. His years of handling two-ton scallop rakes and
beefed-up, rule-busting nets, as well as lobster pots and anchor
rodes, harpoons and gaffs, winch handles and hand pumps,
eight-foot oars and mile-long lines of baited hooks, and hawsers
thicker than most people's thighs, all that chest and arm action
gives him an edge in bar fights, second-story burglary work,
fence climbing and when shooting pool without a bridge.

In a work mode, there's nothing glittery about Mako. No
rings. No watch, bracelet or necklace, any of which can snag on
a line and lead to disaster. Among mariners, rings are notorious
for causing more than just trouble at home. Half-Finger Matt
knows this better than most and will gladly exhibit the mess his
marriage got him into at sea. In the 1960s, he was out fishing on
Georges Bank when a burr in the boat's pullback wire sliced
open his rubber glove, hooked his wedding band and carried

him nine feet off the deck and into the pulley hanging off the
A-frame. As he flashes four and one-half digits, Matt always
thanks the donkeyman for not daydreaming or picking his nose.
If the man at the winch controls had delayed one second, Matt
suspects, he'd be known as Half-Hand Matt; two seconds late,
and it would've been Half-Arm Matt; anything over two seconds
and Matt says he would've turned into juice and been quickly
forgotten as Dead Matt.

Sometimes at night, and always when his boat docks at a distant port, Mako goes out on the town wearing two diamond
studs, one next to the other on his right ear. He favors pricey
stones in simple settings. While he admits to enjoying the flash
they emit and the attention they bring, he mostly wears them
for practical, not decorative, reasons. He considers the stones an
emergency stash, just the thing to keep the cards coming when
cash is low and the poker hand hot. Additionally, they're his tickets to freedom if he ends up in jail, using them as surety to
attract help from bail bondsmen loath to deal with out-of-town
fishermen.

Using two pieces of duct tape stuck to the dock as markers,
one ten feet from the other, Mako lays out another length of
chain. As he goes, he drags everything—chain, bolt cutter and
both feet—over the dock planking. The foot action is the same
for most mariners, the shuffle their only practiced move on a
dance floor. In Mako's case, the sea has reshaped his carriage
and an ancient adage keeps him from changing things: One
hand for the ship, one hand for the sailor and both feet on wood
or tar for love of life. When a seaman reaches for a sail, net or
drag, he looks to his legs as twin pivot points to chase the job as
it swings overhead. In rough weather, sailors employ both feet
as anchor posts, one to snub and counter roll to starboard and
the other to offset roll to port. Of course, these sea-bred habits
are hell on street shoes, and he goes through three or four pairs
a year.

Mako takes a break, reaches for a butt and curses while staring at the water, as calm today as it has been for the last three days. His eyes jet skyward, not a cloud in sight, and he repeats himself. More cursing follows.

For him and most New Bedford fishermen, cigarettes are almost as much a constant in life as swearing. Around the docks and especially aboard ship, *fuck* does it all, a multipurpose verbal tool and ever handy. It's used to clear the throat of air, saliva, food and stale thoughts. It helps pin down emotions and opinions, while the edge of its delivery neatly cuts through fat and gristle. Often, it opens a topic; thereafter, it can shave, rasp and whittle context. It can also puncture something annoying, and it's invaluable when hammering home a point or staking a position. Likewise, fishermen rely on it to fill any gap in a thought pattern, conversation, rant, soliloquy or broadside.

He starts up again: This finest-kind weather only makes him wish he was at sea, taking advantage of the flat water to fish and fish some more. He'd be out there right now and making big money if only he hadn't scheduled this week for the annual haul-out and survey of the *Sweetie-Pie,* the eighty-eight-foot scalloper he captains. She's due to come down the ways in four days—just in time, Mako thinks, for the weather to turn rotten.

How's the coffee? he asks, quickly adding, Hope it's thick enough. He likes it extra-strong in the morning, a preference shared by many sailors at the start of a watch and in need of an eye-opening jolt of caffeine. Earlier in the morning, just after dawn, he served a cup to Captain Rapoza, skipper of the *Marta and Maria,* who took one sip and threw the rest into the harbor. The poor guy, Mako says, just made dock after the worst trip of his career. One of his crewmen lost his left hand.

Mako takes the last drag from the Marlboro, flicks what's left into the drink and talks about the injured crewman: A greenhorn named Jorge Something-Or-Other. He came over from the Azores a few months ago on a tourist visa and stayed to work with his cousin aboard the *Marta and Maria*. Three days ago Rapoza had them near Georges Bank and they were pulling in the net. Jorge was on the winch and, somehow, he put his hand under the feed to the drum. It's the last place to put anything you ever want to see again.

A man who has seen worse and heard far too many similar stories to dwell on detail, Mako keeps his delivery speedy and shorn of emotion, saying: No one heard any screams. No one saw any trouble. Eyes were on the net. Ears were plugged with noise. It's always the same at pullback: the engine roars, pulleys screech, water slaps everything. So, when they do find Jorge, he's half dead. His hand is severed above the wrist and there's nothing but pulp in the coil. They deal with the guy best they can and Rapoza steams west to meet Coasties on the fly. Two hours later, the chopper picks up Jorge and takes him to Hyannis. Rapoza follows at full speed.

Mako picks up a broken link of chain and throws it as far as he can off the dock. He toys with another broken bit of chain and warns, Here's the really shitty part: by the time Rapoza gets to the hospital, Immigration has already processed Jorge. Some interview, 'cause the guy doesn't speak English and he's fresh out of the OR, puking probably, too, from the gas. The pricks tape the deportation papers to the morphine drip machine, like they're out to ruin every dream.

Again, a broken link flies out of Mako's hand and lands in the water with hardly a splash. At the moment, he says, Rapoza is seeing a lawyer about putting a stop to the fed bullshit. Mako feels that losing a hand on the job is more than enough payment for entry into any country. Besides, he says, Jorge wasn't doing anything that hasn't been done a million times before. He's just another grunt trying to put together the cheese to send for his family and set up here. Same as his cousin. Same as Rapoza. Same as half this city.

It burns his ass something wicked, Mako says, knowing some

of his tax dollars were used to screw Jorge. And it really steams him knowing that the rest of his tax dollars go to feed idiots sticking it to fishermen and blue-collar grunts everywhere in this country. Damn, in his opinion, the system is now so out of whack that it's killing the workingman and destroying the cities where he lives and that he once helped build. Believe it or not, he challenges, New Bedford used to be fat city. Alive, healthy, too, and hopping. Now downtown is a ghost town. People are out of work or not sure if they'll have work in a month or two. With the way things are going for fishermen and factory workers, he says, the future is good as gone.

He points to the small groundfish and quahog boats which haven't left the dock in months and will probably continue to rot in place, their fishing days over. He then pokes the air, gesturing at one smokestack after another lining the shore, each attached to an empty mill complex. They used to be critical pieces in the engine room and helped propel the country from the bottom of the pile to the top of the heap. Today, he labels it all broken crap, each bit a toxic leftover from the past and worse than useless: it's falling apart, leaching poisons, and somebody or other has to pay for the cleanup.

Before all the regs and rigmarole hit fishermen in the early 1990s, and before the mills closed years before that, Mako recalls it was not only okay to make your life at sea or in a factory, it was all you could do. There were no options. No plan B. Everything you were taught was about making product. Fish. Fabric. Clothing. Tools. Widgets. Whatever. But always stuff you could see and feel and actually use. However, as the electronic age blossomed, the city withered, losing tens of thousands of jobs, none of which Mako expects to reappear. That leaves fishing as the only vital industry left in town, but, he cautions, fishing could go belly-up at any time. One court order of the wrong kind, he says, and it's over. All he's sure of: fishermen are on the wrong side of tomorrow, same as mill workers used to be.

He growls and goes loud, contorting what comes out of him into the sound of a moose in pain. In the old days, he would've quieted the beast inside him with dope; next Halloween, though, he'll be eight years sober, which, he notes, is less than half the time he was a junkie, from age seventeen to thirty-eight. He gathers air, arches his back and this time launches a terrific Faaah-uck.

A ship's horn responds. It's a short blast from the *Sea Miner*, a seventy-eight-foot scalloper at the end of the dock. Pike, her captain, shows himself on the bridge. Faah-uck, he echoes Mako's sound. The noise grows as five deckhands join in and compete to be the loudest. Mako pumps his fist, his lips in a tight smile, a man glad for the company he keeps.

Pike disappears inside the wheelhouse and issues one long blast from the horn, alerting bystanders and marine traffic that the boat is leaving the dock. Upharbor, near the swing bridge, a fuel barge on the move immediately alters course to give the newcomer plenty of room to maneuver. Until water rushes under the hull and allows the rudder to do its job, fishing boats are ungainly machines. Pike coordinates the action, matching commands he telegraphs to the engine to orders he yells to crewmen at the dock lines.

Mako watches with a critical eye as he walks to the *Sea Miner*, ready, if asked, to tend a snarled line or offer advice. He has been steering fishing boats in and out of tight spaces since he was a kid aboard the family dragger. He learned the ropes from his dad, who, by all accounts, was a taskmaster and tougher on his two boys than he ever was on his other crewmen. Mako said he wanted to kill his father dozens of times while they were out fishing, and he swears he would have if the man hadn't been one of the best fishermen in the fleet and its number one brawler. Some left hook the old man had, he recalls, reflexively stroking an ear probably walloped by Dad.

The *Sea Miner* picks up speed as she enters the channel, her 1,200-horsepower diesel sending a thin, oily ribbon of smoke out the stack. Her wake hits the sides of boats tied to the dock and sends them rolling, their chines dipping in and out of water with the sound of wet kisses. Mako lights another butt and tracks the *Sea Miner* as she powers for the gate in the hurricane dike and the open water beyond. He stays at it, no doubt stuck on what he loves to death: fish, fishing and the sea.

Once, years ago, Janice booked a vacation for the two of them in the Berkshires. She thought one week away from water would do him a world of good and, at the time, he was up for a new experience. They returned in separate cars, with Mako arriving days earlier than scheduled in a rental. He said he had been bored out of his gourd. He also said he felt like the rock teachers draw on blackboards to illustrate the difference between potential and kinetic energy. He kept waiting for something to push that rock over the cliff and eventually gave up, realizing he could stare at a mountain for one hundred years without it ever blinking or his rock ever moving. It further convinced him that the only mountainscapes worth viewing were at sea. Live through a storm throwing fifty-foot waves at you again and again, he said, and the Himalayas lose any snap to their punch.

A creature of the ocean, Mako demands fluids. Liquids in flux nourish him, and only the act of fishing sustains his being. Neither man's architecture nor the enduring sweep of nature's landscapes interest him very much. He's used to jiggling, wiggling and constant motion, and only the ocean can do a proper job of winding him up. Locked in a perpetual cycle of creation and destruction, building forms and surfaces as quickly as it tears them apart, the North Atlantic is literally what makes him tick.

A seventh-generation fisherman, he believes he came out of

the womb encoded for one thing: survival at sea. Certainly, he adapted long ago to the corrosive effects of salt water and conditioned himself to be as aggressive as the elements from which he derives identity: fish and sea. Like the tide, his blood ebbs and flows in tune with the phases of the moon; he's at his loudest and rowdiest when the orb is full. And at any hour of the day, his mood can shift in a flash, his temperament as mercurial as the ocean itself.

The instant his boat leaves the dock, Mako brightens, a new man reborn in the light of an open-domed temple, and he stands taller, as if suddenly unburdened by doubt and conflict. It's not that he hates being on land, but after a few days of being high and dry, the itch for the sea returns. On land, he sees boundaries everywhere, bothersome reminders of that place he'd rather be, at sea, where he transits limitless space, all of it wildly fresh and pathless. As captain, he runs the show, a benevolent dictator of a tiny, self-propelled island populated by five or six other pirates joined in common cause: to grab as much sea booty as they can set their hooks into. Aboard ship, there's no phone to answer or avoid. No bills to worry about. No girlfriend or ex to bug him or his men. And once they reach the fishing grounds, life becomes wonderfully simple: the hunt is on and instinct and desire merge.

Mako and his kind of independent fishermen are a threatened species, their numbers steadily dwindling. Indeed, freebooters like him appear doomed just like the cod stocks, the two of them, hunter and prey, destined to join an ever-growing list of what's missing from American territorial waters.

Starting in the late 1800s, as harpoons gave way to nets, hooks and drags, almost every local boat was owned and operated by an individual, a fleet of mom-and-pop businesses, which, by and large, treated crewmen as extended family. This arrangement began to fall apart in the early 1980s, as boat maintenance and construction costs skyrocketed, and the pace of change went into high gear a decade later, with the advent of federal regulations and the collapse of fish stocks. Today, most of the nearly three hundred commercial fishing boats in New Bedford Harbor are parts of mini-fleets operated by large corporations, and the consolidation of ownership progresses at a rapid rate. The *Sweetie-Pie*, Mako's command, is among the few of the newer, larger draggers still owned by an individual. According to Mako, it's not whether his man will sell out to the big players, but when. He can only hope it's years from now and not months.

Independent fishermen are also being sent into the margins by the disassembly of another tradition, this one going back three hundred years, concerning shipboard rewards. Since whaling days, fishermen worked as shareholders, their pay based on performance, with each man earning a percentage of the landing's value. Nowadays, under corporate flags, an increasing number of captains and mates draw salaries and sign on as company men. It's a trend most observers predict will continue until the entire officer corps becomes salaried employees. Meanwhile, the push is on to duplicate things for crewmen.

Mako swears he'll never relinquish his stakeholder status. A regular check would not only penalize him for being among the best captains in the business, it would also deny him future earnings from price escalations at the dock for scallops. He feels entitled to partner status, since it's his nose for scallops and decision making that generate boat revenue. And since he runs things the old way, working on deck as hard as any crewman, in addition to his duties in the wheelhouse, he argues, he should be paid the old way. Besides, he'll be damned if he ever says *Morn'n, boss* to some guy sitting behind a desk and telling him what to do and how to do it. He'd return to the forecastle before that would ever happen, and he'd shoot himself before he'd ever sign on as a salaried deckhand.

The *Sea Miner* clears the hurricane dike and steams for

Nomans Island, where she'll turn and steer for Georges Bank. Her entry into open water breaks the spell cast over Mako, and he leads the way back to the *Amy-C*. He resumes work on the chain and warns off any help. There's a chance the chain could end up as evidence in court. For a stick ($1,000), he's making twenty anchors for Johnny Big Boots, who supplied all the parts. Mako says he knows that deals with Big Boots often backfire, but until he has a future worth considering, the *Amy-C* safe from a predatory bank, he can't let consequences get in the way of a payday.

Finished cutting links, Mako starts attaching shackles to both ends of each iron string. He calculates the holding power of a finished anchor at two thousand pounds, making them worthless trinkets to anyone on boats in the fishing fleet. In fact, such an anchor is suited only for the kinds of pleasure boats—fifteen- to seventeen-footers designed for family fun—that rarely visit this harbor, where most fuel and ice is sold by the ton and tetanus shots are advisable before touching the water. In New Bedford, Mako says, these anchors are good for only one thing: smuggling pot.

It's common practice among hay-riders to hire various middlemen, like Big Boots, to buy and assemble materials for a night run, including a large supply of black plastic contractors' bags. This arrangement helps build walls separating the importers from notice by dock busybodies, wharf rats, cops and DEA agents, but today it only entices Mako. He declares himself one of those dock busybodies and is keen to horn in on the action. Already, he's on the lookout for telltales of illegal activity, and while he's doubtful he'll discover much before sunset, he's confident the night will offer up the information he's after. Around the docks, he says, the best secrets come out in the dark. It's when pirates emerge and get down to business, unloading their boats of illicit catch; it's also when importers report for duty.

Once his research is finished, the hay-riders identified, Mako plans to approach the boat's skipper and engage him in some dock business—extortion, in this case. The skipper can deal either with him or the dozens of fishermen he'll send to the boat in search of night work. He'll settle for hush money, but he'll push—oh, Jesus, yes sir, he'll push—for a berth as a full-share crewman. He has done plenty of smuggling over the years, but he's out of practice and can only hope his back is up to the task of loading hundreds of eighty-pound bales.

Small weed shipments—one hundred bales or less—are usually unloaded at the dock, the wee quantity easy to stow and requiring only a few minutes to toss into the back of a truck. Large deliveries, though, demand cautious planning, and no product crosses the docks. Instead, it's picked up from a freighter, and as the boat steams to an unlit shore, the crew stuffs bales into contractors' bags and strings together thirty or more bags to form a raft. An anchor, just like the ones Mako is making, is attached to each raft and the whole mess is thrown overboard at the stash site—someplace close to land and hard by rocks or shallows. Even with good binoculars, beyond fifty yards it's difficult to identify the rafts as anything but garbage. Days later, or whenever the smugglers are sure it's safe, they'll assemble road transports and retrieve the weed using small boats equipped with big motors. An experienced crew can move upwards of thirty tons on a single moonless night.

Today, no boat would enter the harbor showing one bale of pot, but Mako recalls an earlier period when boats pulled into the docks with bales stacked above the rail. One night in 1982, he says, he tied up ten minutes after another boat also loaded with reefer. There were five U-Haul trucks waiting on his delivery, seven for the other boat, and nearly forty tons of cargo to sort out and load into the right vehicles. It was a Three Stooges episode, a real madhouse that night, he says, adding wistfully, Finest-kind, them days. Just the best.

The freewheeling era of pot smuggling ran for nearly fifteen

years, beginning in the early 1970s. During that time, most
importers, ground crews, cops and wholesalers rode for the
same brand, the mob. The brakes come on after the bust of the
J&M, a dragger nabbed with twenty-five thousand pounds of
weed. The feds acted on a tip, the first one ever from the docks,
and that initial and anonymous act of betrayal made everyone
wary. Mako likens that tipster to a mugger who beat up the old
order pretty bad. From then on, he says, the rat population grew
and grew. The erosion of solidarity at the water's edge continued unabated, and today, guys will flip on their mother.

It was the end of the Cold War which snuffed the go-go days
of local smuggling. From Truman to glasnost, Russian trawlers
and subs nearly monopolized the attention and budgets of the
armed forces. But as soon as the Berlin Wall turned into a souvenir racket, the area's military hardware was redirected to
shadow the only handy substitute for Red shipping, the Northeast's fishing fleet. Air force jets and navy ships and planes began
tracking draggers to hone their radar and night-surveillance
skills, while the Coast Guard redeployed its assests to fishery
patrol. Like most New Bedford fishermen over forty years old,
Mako yearns for the return of a previous world order.

Mako concedes that the feds can force the smuggling action
to pause now and then, but die? Never. There's too much
oomph behind it for it to ever stop. Part of the momentum
comes out of a 350-year tradition of smuggling in New Bedford,
plus its well-established infrastructure in service to the import
trade. Mostly, though, what impels the business and ensures its
longevity is a harbor population of nearly three thousand fishermen, most of whom would happily sign on for night work without lights. At heart, they're pirates; by profession, they're risk
takers; and the pay for smugglers is attractive, often irresistible.

Finished for now with the shackles, Mako starts making eye
splices to connect line to rode. He learned how to work rope

from a book his dad gave him on his seventh birthday. It came wrapped in a warning: Learn every knot in this book or you'll never go out on the boat. Mako says his father tied a string to everything he gave his son and yanked it on whim. He recalls his admission exam for entry aboard the family dragger as torture. He was eight and the test was an all-day affair, his father quizzing him on knots and basic navigation techniques; it ended after a swimming test involving a fifty-yard freestyle sprint, followed by bobbing in place in survival mode for an hour. Since then, he estimates, he has made a billion eye splices and says he'll have to kick himself if he doesn't finish each anchor splice in under five minutes. His first attempt takes three minutes, forty-five seconds, and he expects to gain speed as he goes. Just warming up, he says.

After the third splice, the rope flies out of his hands and, with a disgusted look on his face, he cuts loose a string of *fucks*. All he wants to do is go fishing. All he can think about is fishing, nothing else. He'd be okay if he had a reason to go lobstering. But he emptied his traps two days ago and must wait at least another day until there's enough meat in the cages to cover his fuel expenses. She's a thirsty girl, the *Amy-C,* he says, and reports that she guzzles seventy-five to ninety gallons a day, depending on the weather.

He lights a cigarette and slowly surveys the harbor. His inspection begins at the bulkhead, land's end, where the water gently sloshes against cement and riprap and leaves behind mustaches of brown foam, which, a second or two later, are licked away and replaced with new ones. Along the edge of the pier, the sea grass circling the pilings sways with the seductiveness of a hula dancer; minnows appear to be part of the act, darting in and out of the grass skirts and occasionally lingering to nibble at the hems. Toward the middle of the channel, an ebb tide, just now kicking in, carries garbage back the way it traveled

for the previous six hours. Downharbor, by the mud flats near
the South Terminal, the water appears freshly combed, the surface uniformly rippled by a 5-knot breeze. Capping it all is an
unblinkered sun.

Watch, Mako says, and points to a spot off the *Amy-C*'s stern.
With patience, it's possible to see water squirt colors into the
air. Ingots of gold appear to leap out of the drink and disappear
without making a splash. Glints of rubies are trailed by flashes
of sapphire. Emeralds, too, show themselves, sparkling greens
that explode in the air like the fizz out of a freshly opened can of
soda.

While it's merely the dance of light atop a patch of hydraulic
fluid fouling the harbor, Mako prefers to imagine it as the bling
of money, each color flagging a treasure awaiting him. He
believes millions in gems, gold coins, old tools and instruments
are on the harbor bottom, all of it dropped overboard during
the past four hundred years. He can't count the number of Vise-
Grips and screwdrivers he has lost and money, oh-man, he says,
there's a small fortune in silver which slipped through either his
fingers or his pockets. Also down there is the ring he gave Janice,
which she tossed into the harbor after they broke up last year.

When the harbor was last dredged, in the 1960s, the spoils
were dumped in a field south of the old Pairpoint Glassworks
site, and Mako says one person found a gold coin from the early
1700s in the dried muck. As a kid, he joined scores of others
searching the toxic muck for other pirate treasure, but, like all of
them, he came up empty. Maybe today he'll hit gold, he says,
bending over the *Amy-C*'s stern, a harpoon in one hand to stir up
the bottom and a net in the other to nab treasure. Urged on by
thoughts of pirates with greasy fingers and made desperate by
his need for cheese to pay off the boat loan, his arms swing into
action.

———

Pirates have been using the New Bedford waterfront for over four hundred years; indeed, the city's written history begins with crooks working the water's edge in 1602, its first page a tale of deceit by freebooters masquerading as friendly white guys as they scam the natives. This establishing spirit of connivance was endowed by the legacy of Captain Bartholomew Gosnold, along with the passengers and crew aboard the *Concord,* a privateer owned by the City Council of Dartmouth, England.

After putting the Scilly Islands astern, Captain Gosnold set course for Virginia and primed the *Concord*'s guns, a commander eager to exercise his royal license to plunder Spanish shipping. Cut from sod and not sailcloth, Gosnold proved himself an incompetent navigator, as well as a mean-spirited, often seasick ship's captain. Utterly lost and long overdue in Jamestown, the crew on half rations, Gosnold faced mutiny. He was saved by the cry *Land-ho* when a lookout sighted Cuttyhunk Island, nearly six hundred miles from his original destination.

The *Concord* soon dropped anchor in what would become New Bedford Harbor and the crew was promptly greeted by genuinely friendly Wampanoags. In quick time, Gosnold got down to business; although language was a problem, a deal was struck and understood by all: the English would trade cheap tools and trinkets for food, animal pelts and sassafras root. At the time, sassafras was thought to cure gonorrhea when ingested in its fermented form (root beer) and worth, ounce for ounce, nearly as much as silver. Once the *Concord* sat below her lines, weighed down by a fortune belowdecks, Gosnold set sail before settling accounts.

Since then, the city waterfront has been home to sin and sinners and lawbreakers. While seafaring pirates would come and go, favoring the harbor for its protection against storms out of the north and British warships patrolling the coast, smugglers took root and flourished. By 1660, the docks were doing a brisk trade in commodities banned by the Puritans running the show in Plymouth and Boston. Rum was unloaded here and sent by small boats and wagons to buyers from Maine to Rhode Island; other attractions beckoned willful sinners, especially the whorehouses at the shore, among the first in America. The harbor was condemned from the pulpit by the Puritans' chief guide on the path to salvation, Reverend Increase Mather; later, his son Cotton burnished the setting by denouncing the waterfront as Lucifer's kingdom.

During the War of Independence, local smugglers rechristened themselves and their boats, becoming privateers in service to both the Continental Navy and their own pocketbooks. Intimate with local waters and well-practiced in the art of stealth and night work, they bedeviled the Royal Navy, capturing supply ships and disrupting lines of communication. Tired of these pesky water rats, the Brits invaded New Bedford and torched the waterfront, plus every boat at anchor. From those ashes, smugglers rebuilt their operation and resumed business as privateers during the War of 1812. This time, though, they worked as switch-hitters, just as willing to prey on British shipping as they were to abet merchants in Halifax wanting to maintain trade with New England.

Once the ink dried on the Treaty of Ghent (1814), most smugglers became short-haul deliverymen in service to drug addicts throughout America. Whaling ships often returned from the hunting grounds off India, Arabia, Chile and China carrying chests of drugs—mostly opium—along with the standard cargo of oil, ambergris and whalebone. The whalers would lie offshore and rendezvous with overcanvased speedsters designed to outrace Malays, and the slow but reliable whalers carried home the precious freight for sale up and down the coast. The tonnage of drugs landed here from 1810 to 1860 made it the nation's top import center for opium, hashish, coca paste and reefer. During the Civil War, with whaling already in decline and the hunting

grounds switched to Arctic waters, the legal drug trade moved
to other ports and smugglers returned to their old ways. Throughout the Civil War, city smugglers did most of their business
with the Confederacy and effectively connected Richmond to
Halifax.

In the twentieth century Prohibition meant boom times for
area smugglers. There were sign-up sheets to prevent traffic
jams in the intricate systems of tunnels connecting the waterfront to dozens of sites in the business district. The underground pathways were built over the years by smugglers in
partnership with men in the coal delivery business, and locals
refused to share their byways with outsiders. Joe Kennedy, for
instance, was forced to locate his operation in an inconvenient
slice of the waterfront—old-timers call a small cove at the foot
of the Delano family cemetery Big Joe's Mudflats.

When the Wets won their battle in 1933, the import trade
went dormant and smugglers worked exclusively as fishermen.
The Depression and war kept them at their nets, the contraband
business on hold until the late 1960s, when the demand for pot
surged. At first, weed was the only product on the night menu,
but it wasn't long before coke and heroin were also being smuggled. By the mid-1970s, the import business was employing hundreds and on its way to becoming a major regional industry.

Mako gives up the treasure hunt and swishes the harpoon
through the water like a swizzle stick to clean its tip of muck.
Someday, he says, he's going to have enough cheese packed
away not to do anything but fish. Being on land only reminds
him why he used to take dope. And if he can't go to sea, where
his brain and heart are stowed, he's ready to walk.

A man in no rush, Mako saunters down Pier 2 at eye level to
nearly thirty heavily scarred and dented workhorses of the sea.

They come in reds, blacks, whites, greens and many shades of blue borrowed from sea and sky. All are streaked in rust and caked in salt. On display are draggers, a few long-liners, one crab boat and two derelicts stripped clean of usable parts. The smallest boat on this dock is seventy-two feet long, while her big sisters are half again as long. Belowdecks are engines varying in size, extra-large to jumbo, 850 to 1,550 horsepower. They consume anywhere from thirty-eight to seventy gallons of diesel an hour; additional fuel demands come from onboard generators powering the ship's lights, compressors and pumps, refrigeration gear and hydraulic systems. Most of the vessels are tied in rafts three boats wide and use truck tires as bumpers. For colors, the only ones in sight are Jolly Rogers and Nam MIA flags.

All the boats share common design elements which evolved over hundreds of years of head-to-head combat. In profile, their most prominent shared feature is a high nose showing lots of flair, just the thing to lift a boat as a wave approaches and to stop a monster overtaking her in a following sea from pitchpoling the works. They're also beefy, big-boned creatures, not a hint of anything sleek or dainty about them. Wide in the middle, no-nonsense throughout, these boats feature grossly oversized machinery and rigging, each bit purposely designed for all-season business, twenty-four hours a day. The winches, for instance, weigh more than many tractors and can pull up tons of both treasure and trash. Pulleys come as large as manhole covers, and portholes are made of bulletproof Lexan more than an inch thick.

The groundfish boats carry nets which balloon into strainers the size of football fields; at the dock, the nets are wound around winch drums that only the arms of a giant squid could span. The scallopers pack twin dredges strong enough to rake the bottom at 8 knots and scoop up almost everything in their path, including coral, grass and weed, muck, boulders, pieces

of shipwreck and, of course, bivalves, along with fish and lobsters. They sometimes also snag surprises, like unexploded
ordnance—torpedoes, aerial bombs and mustard gas canisters—
and, as of last week, the skull belonging to some lost mariner.
The long-liners sit low in the stern, awaiting fuel and ice up
front to level the waterline and offset all the weight at the taffrail
from a winch and barrels of meaty, stainless hooks with shark-
tooth barbs. The crabber is a retired scalloper and set apart from
the others by stacks of giant traps rising off her deck to the
height of two men, one standing atop the shoulders of the
other.

Many of the boats carry the names of wives and children the
owners don't see enough of, while they imagine they can somehow transfer their love of the boat to her namesakes. Other
name boards presume success: *Eureka, Masterful, Paydirt*. A
handful play it safe and honor the gods: *Poseidon, Aeolus, Thor*
and *Elvis*. However, a few challenge those same gods: *Sea Ruler,
Invincible, Dawn-Maker*. The remainder echo dreamscapes or
ancestral homes: *Four Aces, Utopia, Rio Sado, Pico, Limerick*.

Outward-bound, these vessels leave the dock as self-
contained machines able to stay on the hunt for weeks and go
anywhere the chase leads. Only hurricanes and gear failures can
force them to run for shelter. Each is among the largest fishing
boats in the American fleet, and together with the other 250
commercial boats in the harbor, they explain why city docks
handle nearly $300 million in landings a year. Dutch Harbor,
Alaska, lags far behind in second place, unable to challenge New
Bedford's title: Fishing Capital of North America.

As he strolls the dock, Mako tries to match a boat to the
anchors he's making. He identifies two draggers as the best in
the import trade, but doubts they'll be handling reefer or powder anytime soon. A lot depends on when pictures of the two
boats and their crews are replaced by others on the wall of the

DEA office in a downtown bank building. Mako thinks a more likely contender is the *Sea-Kitty.* He says she had a run of rotten luck lately. First, she lost a dredge. On her next trip, the winch busted. After that, the rebuilt winch busted and the generator had to be replaced. In all, Mako estimates, the owner is out $200,000 in repairs and lost income.

He reckons the bank is all over the guy for late loan payments and threatening to seize the boat, along with his firstborn if he doesn't fork over some cheese, pronto. They corrupt people, banks do, he says, claiming they're the single biggest force making a boat owner change course from straight to crooked. He saw it happen all the time in the 1970s and 1980s, when boat mortgages routinely involved balloon payments once every few years. A month or two before doomsday, owners would start prowling the docks in search of night work. The owner's age, ethnicity, whether or not he took drugs—none of that mattered. It was all about not losing the boat to some bank.

A seashell dropped by a gull crunches under a white rubber boot and Mako pauses to grind it into dust. Afterward, he puts a shoulder into a dolphin and a Marlboro to his lips and sets his gaze on the *Amy-C,* at the next dock. She sits in profile, an old lady showing every year of her age. At the sight of water gushing out of a thru-hull fitting linked to the bilge pump, he looses a soft, rhythmic series of *fuck*s, as if saying a mantra.

He has almost three weeks, plenty of time, he says, to pull together thirty sticks and save the *Amy-C.* But, Jesus, man, he adds, he has to watch his step, no hurried or sloppy moves allowed. It wasn't that long ago when his picture hung on the wall of the DEA office. As it is, Coast Guard ships on fishery patrol carry a copy of his file, while others circulate inside the old Custom House on William Street, where fishery agents keep shop. He says fishery agents usually confront him with his mug shot every time they board the *Sweetie-Pie* and then add,

We got your number, mister. He confides that this pleases him
and he wouldn't want it any other way. The same sort of thing
used to happen to his dad, and he'd hate to think the old man
was one up on him in anything to do with fishing and the sea.

Mako considers himself an expert wiggler, the fish in him the
dominant part of his being. Ever since he made captain, he estimates, one-fourth of all his fishing trips have included a shakedown by Coasties and fishery agents. But in all that time of
gunning for him, he was ticketed only once—for an expired tag
on a fire extinguisher. He knows where to hide illegal catch, having learned the ins and outs of concealment from every skipper
he ever sailed with. While he appreciates their tips, he feels he's
a natural at the game, and at this point, he has tricks to teach the
old-timers, even his dad. And when it comes to lying to fishery
agents, he doubts there's anyone better than he is. Like a bar
owner, he keeps two sets of logbooks; and like an expert thief,
he stays current with newly honed tricks of the trade: every
month he meets with a computer wizard, learning the latest
techniques in fiddling with the electronic bracelet the feds
clamped on the *Sweetie-Pie.*

On land, out of his element and shorn of his slippery powers,
he is not as elusive. He mentions ports from Florida to Maine
where his name appears on some police blotter. Often, he says,
he was just stupid, arrested after a bar fight or on trespassing
charges after collapsing drunk and doped up on somebody's
front yard or stoop. Before he was twenty-one, he knew most
of the guards at the local jail by their first name. But he made
a smart move early on: after his inaugural trip as captain, he
put every dollar from his share on the desk to the best lawyer
in town and kept him on retainer. If he hadn't done that, he
believes, he would've known the names of the wives and kids of
every guard at the hoosegow.

His view astern doesn't inspire any regrets, he muses, but,

Jesus, he sure wishes there weren't so many foggy patches. He claims the low-flying clouds as his own making, manufactured during decades of fast-lane travel as an unconstrained boozing, snorting, dope-shooting and sex-crazed fisherman with a short fuse and cash to burn. As a teen, and throughout his twenties and thirties, it was fish h·rd, play hard. While he still fishes as hard as ever, he pulled back the throttle on play in the early 1990s. He remembers the day: he awoke after a wild night out and saw his car in the driveway looking fresh out of a demo derby. Then it hit him. Had he killed anyone driving home? It's not that he couldn't remember; rather, it was scarier than that because nothing registered in the first place. The next day his brother took him to an NA meeting.

He blows a kiss to the *Amy-C* and wishes he could take out a loan and be done with worrying about her and himself. But his brother and two sisters all have kids and no spare change, and his dad is the last person on earth he'd approach for a penny. His house off Arnold Street is almost paid for, but the bank remains deaf to his pleas to remortgage it; hell, no one there will even return his phone calls. His truck is worth chump change, but his diamond earrings should net two, maybe three sticks on the street. And he has tons of junk to sell. A pack rat, Mako has littered his backyard with boat parts, and the basement is filled to the floor joists with marine odds and ends. He started posting flyers the other day advertising gear for sale and awaits his first customer.

Predictably, he looks to the ocean for relief, salt water a panacea for any malaise lodged in his pocket, body, heart or soul. As soon as the *Sweetie-Pie* comes down the ways, he's off to Georges Bank to clean it of salable product. If the scallop rakes snag a lobster or a fish, that creature be mine, he says, unconcerned by either laws or lawmen. Usually, the hardest part of poaching is finding buyers for the goods, yet he claims to know a dozen processors willing to pay top dollar, no questions asked. But most of the *Amy-C*'s rescue money will be legit, he says, coming out of his pay for landing more than thirty thousand pounds of scallops on the next trip. Others in the trade would call that number a silly dream; Mako, though, says he's out to beat the all-time record—sixty-three thousand pounds—set by the *Victor* in the 1980s, He owns the third spot on the leaderboard and swears the high line will be his before he dies. It's his destiny, and it's as simple as that, he says.

Mako returns to work on the anchors for Johnny Big Boots, who's due to pick them up later this afternoon, and I say goodbye. I'm shipping out in the morning and must pack for a two-month trip, maybe longer, depending on the winds encountered along the way. But Mako insists I return around five p.m. He has something to give me for the journey ahead. First, though, he has to fetch it from home, and he promises it holds great power: It will keep you alive, Sailor.

Anchors done and gone, Mako says, greeting me back at the *Amy-C*. Big Boots drove away happy minutes ago, and Mako curses himself for not feeling better about things. The stupid job is astern, there's a stick of liquid cheese in his pocket, and his father waved at him from the window of a passing car without stopping to chat about the good old days, back before fishermen became pansies and wooden workboats gave way to iron palaces with stereo systems and air-conditioning. That's three good things in a row, Mako notes, yet he won't feel better until there's water under his feet and he's steering for the hunting grounds. And, damn-dammit, he wishes he could remember where Janice stowed all the paperwork to loans for the house and the *Amy-C*. They're at home somewhere. He leans over the dock and blows out the carbon, one nostril at a time.

A fresh butt in his mouth, he sends a cloud carrying soothing words into the *Amy-C*'s wood. Don't worry, baby, no banker will ever touch you again. His eyes shoot skyward as he says, They can't take her from me. She's his lifeboat. If his world sinks, she's the one thing which can keep him going. He might turn on the TV tonight to news that the greenies or lab coats have convinced some judge to close the whole damn ocean to commercial fishermen. Or maybe the owner of the *Sweetie-Pie* will call him in the morning to say he's going to cash in and sell the boat to some corporate fleet operator. If he didn't have the *Amy-C*, he doubts he'd ever get a good night's sleep. His skills aren't transferable to land, and he fears he'd just jones, wither and die without a near-daily fix of salt water.

A fish jumps clear of the harbor surface. In a flash, Mako's on the *Amy-C*'s stern and staring into a bull's-eye of rippling water. Shiners, he announces, his hand wagging as it tracks the path of a juvenile bluefish. They're common visitors to the harbor twice a year, once as they migrate north and again when they head south in the fall.

Another shiner leaps above the surface and belly flops a few yards from the boat. Reflexively, Mako reaches for his harpoon—Mr. Sticker, he calls it—and sets up on the transom. As he waits for the fish to return, he carefully runs a forefinger over the harpoon's cutting edge, a curved toggle tip of high-carbon steel, razor sharp. The toggle tip rotates on a pin and lies flat to the shaft when thrown, making for a clean entry into flesh. But at the slightest tug, the tip rotates outward like butterfly wings. When it's used by a pro on a large sea animal, the metal can be extracted only by digging it out with a knife. When used by anyone on a small bluefish, it will split the swimmer in two. But Mako's not after dinner and says he'd never eat anything that came out of this harbor. He's merely responding to some internal message sent to his brain and now prickling his

skin. When Mr. Sticker calls, he says, he answers on the first
ring.

While javelins are made for throwing, harpoons are meant
for thrusting. The user's power hand cups the end of the
wooden shaft, while the other hand guides the iron tip to the
target, leaving arms and shoulders to do the work. As a weapon,
it's effective only in close combat, which partly explains why so
many New Bedford whalemen died on the job. It was normal
for the harpooner to urge the oarsmen to climb up the back of
the beast. He knew any distance beyond a few yards was useless
to his cause; he needed to plunge the stick a foot or more into
blubber. What chances the whale had to escape and/or turn its
predators into prey disappeared after the introduction of bow-
mounted harpoon guns in the late 1860s.

Closer, please, Mr. Fish, Mako whispers, and thumps the
transom several times with Mr. Sticker. In his days as the harpooner aboard a sword boat, he was known as one of the few
white guys in the top tier of a trade dominated by men of color:
red, black, brown and yellow. Traditionally, like Tashtego and
Queequeg, the best in the business hailed from islands: Martha's
Vineyard, Cabo Verde, the Azores, Fiji and Samoa.

That's it, fishy, closer, Mako says, and prepares to launch.
Hands at the grip points, the shaft goes tight to his right cheek
and he puts his left foot forward, his legs bent at the knees. With
the machine cocked, the veins in his arms start stretching their
fabric and his eyes grow large, bulging in their sockets and
showing lots of white. The target nears and when the shiner
darts leftward, Mako twists at the waist, following it. When, for
a moment, the fish dives, he straightens. The fish accelerates,
but he's already up to speed.

Mr. Sticker barely raises a splash as it cuts through the water.
Two shiners race into the area, attracted by a cloud of blood
and guts. The harpoon emerges from the drink with bits of

flesh hanging off the toggle tip. No fizz to that pop, but good exercise, Mako says, using his fingernails to remove shredded bluefish.

He likes to keep his skills with a stick honed, always hoping for the day a swordfish or a tuna crosses paths with the *Amy-C*. Since both sword and tuna are scarce in local waters, hammered by foreign fleets and drift nets, the chances are slim that he'll see one near the boat. Even so, he believes a man should always be ready to make his dreams come true. Either species, depending on weight, could be worth thousands at the dock, and no doubt, within hours of its sale, the fish would be on a jet bound for Japan or Korea. Mako says harpooned meat is the very best, firm and extra-tasty, and entirely different from hooked fish, which drown on the line and go soggy as they dangle.

He kisses the iron and uses his T-shirt to dry it. He bought Mr. Sticker in a typical dockside deal: he needed a harpoon; another fisherman with a harpoon and in need of cash sold it for everything in Mako's pockets: $64, plus nine bags of dope and a half pack of butts. Mako knew it was special the moment he handled it and felt his fingers glide into the proper grip points, each marked by a dip in the hickory shaft made by other fingers during 150 years of use. It bears the maker's mark of Lewis Temple, a former slave who opened a blacksmith shop on the docks in the 1830s and quickly established himself as the premier designer and manufacturer of marine weaponry. The toggle tip was his invention and it set the standard until harpoon guns were introduced. If he ever loses Mr. Sticker, Mako says, there's a twin on display at the Whaling Museum; if that one ever disappears, he adds, it will be a crime of passion.

Of all his different jobs at sea, Mako ranks harpooner as the best. Nothing purer, he says, just a man chasing a big fish with a stick. Aboard the sword boat, he'd move to the end of the bow pulpit, the fish in sight, and attune himself to the boat's motion, at one with her every dip and roll. With his legs acting as gimbals, balance assured and both hands free for trigger work, he'd concentrate on the target. He says he'd drill a hole into the fish's head as he studied its moves and wouldn't stop until he knew what the fish was going to do before it did. He can't remember any trick to it and doubts there is one. You just become the fish, he says. It's no big deal, guys have been doing it forever.

A glance at the *Amy-C*'s clock urges him to stow Mr. Sticker and make speed for the shipyard before the office closes. Whenever *Sweetie-Pie* is in dry dock, he meets daily with the yard owner to inspect any work charged to the boat's account. But first, he says, your gift. He darts into the cabin and then hands over a four-leaf clover encased in Scotch tape. He calls it life insurance and claims it will ward off pirates and shipwreck and bring me home intact, all pieces in the right places. He found three of the lucky charms the other day while playing center field in a softball game. The other two are already in use, one in each back pocket to his pants.

I return to New Bedford three months later in the middle of a heat wave. At dawn, the temperature is in the low eighties, the air stirless, thick and sticky like a dog's breath. It's low tide and there's a rank smell of muck, fish bits and seaweed around the docks. Swarms of seagulls identify the boats which pulled in during the night from the fishing grounds, their decks not yet cleaned of debris. One of them is the *Sweetie-Pie* and Mako is aboard hosing down her iron.

Greetings and pleasantries astern, he says they pulled in two hours ago, ending an eleven-day trip. They had near-perfect weather, a gentle sou'westerly cooling them during the day and going dead at night. Best of all, they hauled in scallops the size of butter plates and landed more than 650 bags (forty pounds to a bag) of meat.

The *Amy-C*? Still got her, he answers, though she cost him plenty and he doubts he'll ever stop second-guessing the deal. He thought he was home free when he hooked up with the hay-riders—tipped by a crew loading only deli food—and weaseled his way aboard. He and five others cruised thirty miles offshore to rendezvous with a freighter which was supposed to be chugging up the coast. They'd spent two hours on station waiting for the mother ship when a Coast Guard chopper appeared overhead, its lights turning night into day. When questioned via radio, the skipper lied, saying the boat was merely testing and debugging newly installed equipment.

That took care of waiting any longer, Mako says, and the boat sped for home. As a group, the crew preferred a shakedown at the dock to one at sea, figuring the devil they didn't know, shore patrol, had to be better than the one they regularly battled, fishery patrol. They kept the throttle wide open, unsure if the blip at the edge of the radar screen was a Coast Guard cutter, and threw Mako's anchors overboard, useful only as weights to sink dozens of boxes of contractors' bags.

A thirty-seven-foot Coast Guard boat met them at the dike and escorted the fishermen to the dock. Mako says everyone aboard was a pro and could tell a good lie. He, for example, posed as a factory tech fine-tuning some new refrigeration gear. He doesn't care if the Coasties believed him or not. The boat was clean and there's no law against wasting diesel.

Although he and his crewmates were paid well for less than eight hours of no-risk work—$3,000 per man and considerably more for the boat's owner—Mako claims the whole thing sucked. They were set up, he says, used as decoys to lure the sheriff their way while the real action went down. He explains: While the chopper was buzzing the fishing boat, a small plane was dropping packages of powder to a group of speedboats circling forty miles away. The entire operation was masterminded by Spanish speakers with no interests in the fishing business or the docks. They manned the speedboats and took care of landing chores. More than two tons of powder made it to shore.

To Mako, it's all very disturbing. First, he says, a bunch of damn Spics made fools out of fishermen. Just as bad, the scheme was flawless, the planning impressive and far more thorough than what fishermen usually concoct. It also effectively bumped the docks out of their long-held position as the number one spot for night work. Mako suspects that the Dominican and Puerto Rican gangs which control the sale of dope on the streets now represent the future for the local import trade. And that means, he adds, fishermen will be second-string players in a game they invented. He hopes none of the old-timers sniff the changes in the wind; he'd hate to listen to his dad on the subject. While he doesn't consider a new hierarchy in night work the end of the world, he feels it's certainly a step in the wrong direction.

Another disappointment: his four-leaf clovers were a flop. He was relying on them, along with prayers to every sea and sky god, to fill the *Sweetie-Pie*'s hold with treasure after she came down the ways and headed out to Georges Bank. The weather turned dirty, Mako reports. A gale blew for three days and kicked up twelve- to fifteen-foot seas; thereafter, a stiff breeze and eight-foot waves dogged them until they made dock. The *Sweetie-Pie* landed eighteen thousand pounds of scallops, about average for the fleet at the time, but far below Mako's usual number. He dubs his $7,500 paycheck from that trip a crisis maker. He had nine days to find twenty grand or it was goodbye *Amy-C*.

He hit the street, selling his diamond earrings. He hit fellow lobstermen, stealing from their traps. He hit up friends, pressuring them to buy junk from his basement. He bought dope, stepped on it three times, and resold the milk powder as top-grade product. Finally, he put on his only suit and walked into the bank with $14,000 in a paper bag, ready to tell whatever lie it took to keep the *Amy-C.*

He won't say what happened during his meeting with Janice, only that she deposited the cash and rewrote the loan at a jacked-up rate. He does say that he and Janice have gone out to dinner a few times since then, but, he adds, repair work is making him nervous. Janice is now a regular at the archery range in Acushnet and a deadeye at fifty yards, and he wonders if she'd aim for the shoulder or the aorta, wing or kill? He decides it doesn't matter as long as he has *Sweetie-Pie* and *Amy-C* to keep him at sea and away from land, where he only seems to make trouble for himself and others.

A voice shouts to Mako. It's Captain Gupp, skipper of the *Three Marias,* which is tied to the dock a boat length from the *Sweetie-Pie.* He wants to know if Mako is going to the Fishery Council meeting later this morning at the Holiday Inn?

Hell, no, Mako answers. The weather's too fine to be anywhere but at sea, and he's heading out after lunch to collect a million bucks' worth of lobsters from his traps. Besides, Guppy, he says, what's to talk about? The war's on and he didn't start it.

Three

PINK

A BIG RIG WHIZZES BY and sends a cloud of dust my way on the sidewalk. I curse the driver and a moment later, the truck nearly capsizes, bouncing wildly, the noise alarming, as nine of eighteen wheels roll through a pothole. The driver pulls over to check for damage. The iron and the rubber pass inspection and he moves to the troublemaker, where we meet and, together, stare at a large hole in the road.

Shit, ya-know, you could bury a horse in something like that, the driver notes, and heads back to the wheel.

The truck resumes course and I linger at the cavity and gaze at the droppings of coffee grounds inside the hole and all around it. There are pounds of the stuff on the ground, all of it from truckers trying to make an extra buck by detouring to the docks to pick up seafood for delivery on their route. If the truck's not refrigerated, ground coffee helps neutralize the stink from dead fish packed in melting ice.

Insurance companies own boxloads of stories involving enterprising truckers who didn't use coffee or didn't use enough of it. One misadventure is this week's talk of the docks. The action began in mid-July, when a moving van packed with home furnishings pulled up to a fish house and loaded two pallets of fresh seafood crated in shaved ice. After dawdling at Foxwoods casino, the crew drove to Philadelphia to unload some of the fish cargo. They made another stop in Ohio, but the fish was rejected due to spoilage. Come Illinois, the stink curling their noses, they abandoned the rotten fish at a highway rest area. They eventually rolled into the Flint Hills of Kansas, their final destination, and a real estate agent met them on behalf of the owners, who were en route from Boston. That evening the agent returned to lock up the house, a pleasant ranch in the middle of a leafy neighborhood on the outskirts of a college.

Two days after the moving van left, neighbors called the cops about the smell of rotting flesh coming from the house. Local police investigated and called the staties, who brought along a search warrant and specially trained dogs. Once inside, the dogs started rolling on the carpets, sofas and stuffed chairs, behavior which prompted their handlers to summon a forensics team. When the family from Boston finally arrived, they pulled into a madhouse scene. On the ground—you're under arrest, the cops shouted, guns drawn on suspected murderers. Mom and Dad were cuffed and shuttled to jail. The daughter was put in the custody of Child Services. The dog, a yellow Lab in heat, was jumped by a K-9 shepherd. Litigation is expected to continue for years.

More than two hundred trucks a day travel this stretch of macadam servicing the docks, fish houses and scores of small operations, from welding shops to lawyers' offices, dedicated to fish, fishing and fishermen. City road-repair crews often refer to this slice of the northwest waterfront as Fuck-It Place. They can't keep up with roadway decay, and after years of trying, their cause patently hopeless, they'd prefer to abet natural forces at work and blow the road to pieces. The root cause of all the potholes is unstoppable: the ground is unstable, all of it fill and all of it sinking.

The fill arrived during construction of the interstate highway linking Cape Cod to Providence, Rhode Island, in the mid-

1960s, and more fill was added as spurs to the highway were gouged out over time. Up to sixty-five dump trucks a day tipped their loads into the New Bedford Harbor, adding nearly 15 percent to the waterfront's total acreage. In the process, the fill obliterated numerous marshes, coves and shoreline jigs and jags in place for more than nineteen thousand years. That's when the Laurentide glacier, which blanketed the region during the last ice age, began retreating westward.

City fathers believed the harbor makeover would lure more fish to town at a time when the fishing industry itself was undergoing radical surgery. For centuries, the fish trade had been a fragmented, site-specific affair, the market reach of any port hamstrung by the logistical constraints of ice. From boat hold to skillet, ice alone kept fish salable; it was used at sea, at the dock, at the processors and packed in wooden boxes for distribution to a retail environment dependent on ice for storage and display. Like planets circling different suns, boats in the New York area serviced Gotham; fleets in the Chesapeake fed Philadelphia and Baltimore; New Bedford supplied Boston; and similar, localized efforts operated up and down the coastlines. After World War II, this business model began to splinter as proximity to markets became less and less important, thanks in large part to Freon, plastics and a consumer rush for plug-in appliances.

In the 1950s, advances in commercial refrigeration systems allowed ports to ship seafood ever greater distances, the mileage zooming with the advent of the Interstate Highway System, Styrofoam boxes and airplanes. By the early 1960s, after most American households had replaced the icebox with an electric refrigerator equipped with a separate freezer compartment, a vast new market opened to dockside businesses. Grocery stores began offering seafood behind glass in a cooler, as well as in the frozen food aisle. The plastics industry kept improving both the insulating and the display qualities of fish containers and created the packaging needed for expansion into single-serving fresh and frozen seafood. For fishermen and fish houses, it meant boom times, with long-term growth assured as more and more non-Catholics added fish to their diets.

Fish processors in the Northeast needed room to expand, and New Bedford offered itself as just the place to do it. The shoreline's new architecture meant plenty of land was up for grabs and almost all of it accessed deep water. The city kept land rents cheap and offered long-term leases, along with tax breaks and other incentives to attract occupants. Additionally, the city advertised itself as a place free of zoning problems and pesky neighborhood groups opposed to truck and boat traffic and smelly fish. The interstate was nearby; the railroad was at the doorstep; and an airport able to handle jets was two miles away. Better yet, New Bedford was home to a large immigrant population willing to take low-paying jobs on production lines. Already, the city was home to the largest fishing fleet in the East and an infrastructure was in place geared specifically for use by boats and fish houses. Further enticement came with New Bedford's history, its identity a national brand linked to the sea and fish.

Numerous processors from metro areas in New York, Boston and Philadelphia pulled up stakes and moved to New Bedford. They left behind headaches caused by cramped quarters, high rents and rising operating costs, and no longer had to suffer through planning board meetings. At the same time, local fish houses blew out the walls to double or triple their footprints. A host of fishermen and fishing boats reset anchor in the harbor, many of them from Maine and Newfoundland and others from New York, New Jersey and the Chesapeake. By the end of the 1960s, the local fleet included more than three hundred boats, almost all of them offshore draggers and among the biggest and most efficient machines in the industry.

Trucks keep rolling noisily down the road, every driver wearing a union-issued cap and a few decked out in satin jackets bearing the Teamsters logo. That logo is a reminder of the chemistry that transformed the local fish business into a national industry during the 1960s. An important catalyst in the mix was the mob, which promoted waterfront development and offered a range of services, from loaning money to brokering deals with supermarket chains. The mob also had the ear of city hall, and when necessary, it could whisper commands and get things done around the docks in a timely fashion and on the public's dime.

New Bedford had always been a darling of the Mafia's New England division, which was based in Providence and run by Raymond Patriarca and family. Demonstrating an insatiable appetite for sin and illegal products, the city was a cash cow to the mob and money squirted into its coffers from almost every crooked angle: dope sales, betting, jukes, vending machines, prostitution and swag. But the big money came out of the waterfront, which, up until the feds intervened in the 1980s, conducted all its business in cash. Receipts were rarely issued or requested, and fish houses offered themselves as ideal fronts for both skimming and laundering schemes. On top of that, the mob controlled the import trades.

The Patriarca family recognized the millions to be made by centralizing the production of seafood in a place they already owned, as well as the additional millions to be made by shipping the goods aboard trucks they also owned. The Providence crew called in the pros to design and construct a nationwide distribution grid for fresh seafood. Jimmy Hoffa personally oversaw the project; by 1967, the system was up and running, with trucks, transfer depots and airplanes working in concert to ensure overnight delivery of fresh fish to every major market in continental America. From 1959 to 1970, the reported income of fishermen tripled, $30 million to nearly $100 million, and it's a safe guess that unreported income more than tripled. As one old-timer confided, In them days, best to figure things went like the old comedy routine: one for me and one for Uncle Sam; two for Uncle Sam and one, two for me; three for Uncle Sam and one, two, three for me.

The road to the city piers angles inland at Wamsutta Street and the water view disappears behind the sun-bleached facades of Steel Space buildings, not a one with any flair or frills showing. Some are fish houses and others belong to businesses servicing the fish houses, including machine shops making assembly line parts and outfits supplying immigrant workers for the assembly lines. Signage on the fish houses directs truckers and deters others: NO RETAIL. NO TRESPASSING. Surrounded by cracked asphalt, not a tree or a blade of grass in view, each site is attended by one or more dumpsters, which attract squadrons of local fliers, the gulls circling, diving and crowding the top edges.

Strips of thick plastic hang across openings leading to the fish house loading docks, and forklift drivers tuck their chins as they· bust through the fly barrier to load fish boxes into trucks. On the side of each box, and written in sloppy fashion with an extra-wide Sharpie, there's a short description of contents: dabs, monk, cod, haddock, yellowtail, halibut, skate, scallops. The noise coming out of each building identifies what's going on inside: the whirl and clatter of descaling machines signal a run of whole fish being prepared for market, while the *thump-thump* of a bench cutter severing heads and tails pinpoints a fillet operation. All of them, however, produce a dull roar of streaming water, the sound of hundreds of spray nozzles cleaning fish of sand, slime, precious oil and lots of taste.

Behind one of the fish houses, a group of workers enjoys a break. They're all dressed in white rubber boots and rubber aprons, and they all wear hair nets. A few sit at a picnic table and smoke as they chat. Each one of them hails from Central America, with most of the crew Guatemalan, and they represent the latest ethnic majority among workers in fish houses. Processors have always relied on the hard up and newly arrived to fill jobs they offer in an oppressive environment, noisy and smelly, with few benefits and lousy pay. On an average shift, each worker is expected to fillet thousands of fish, a knife in hand and moving up to ten hours a day. A few years ago, Brazilians formed the majority of fish house workers. Before them, it was Mexicans. And from the early 1960s to the late 1980s, Portuguese islanders (from the Azores, Madeira, Cabo Verde and São Tomé) took care of business.

In the distance, peeking above the giant Frionor seafood plant, an icehouse at the water's edge beckons as it puts on a show. With the temperature in the high eighties and the air sticky, the dew point near at hand, the rooftop compressors crank out their own weather. Great clouds rise out of the main exhaust vents and fade into nothingness as they empty themselves of water, producing a constant drizzle above the eaves. At either end of the brick structure, more hot vapor exits vents and liquefies, filling the air with a fine mist. Eerily, the microclimate also produces sounds of birds in pain. For ten seconds every few minutes, the noise of high-pitched squawks and screams cuts through the din of heavy machinery. It seems to be coming out of the walls.

At this time of day, two p.m., and especially in this kind of heat, the icehouse should be doing a brisk trade; instead, oddly, the place looks abandoned. The company trucks are parked in a row, windows up and doors locked. There are no boats at the dock, and the ice chute and large-diameter hoses used to fill boat holds are stored flat against the brick wall, their metal and plastic bits drummed by water dripping from the eaves. And while the place sounds as if it's running full tilt, no one appears to be at the controls. The front door, which usually guides large volumes of traffic, is closed tight.

———

Howze, someone hollers. The voice comes from the icehouse dock.

I can't locate the source—until, that is, the caller waves and shouts again. Over here, Sailor. Come. Sit.

It's Pink, and there's always time in the day to sit with Pink. He's all that remains standing and lucid from an earlier generation of dock facilitators who kept waterfront businesses running smoothly until they vanished from the scene in the early 1990s. They catered to mom-and-pop boat operations and often worked hand in hand with the mob; this arrangement left the facilitators high and dry as the corporatization of the fleet progressed, along with the disassembly of the mob's base by government DAs. Pink's obituary will be one of the last entries in the log documenting the American passage from the world's largest exporter of fish to the world's largest importer of fish.

In his heyday, Pink could fix almost anything broken at the water's edge, and he still exhibits a knack for unknotting problems. These days people trust him as a levelheaded insider true to his word; in the past, people both trusted and feared him, their dread stemming from his position as the mob's point man on the city docks. The old-timers in the fishing community relied on Pink to arbitrate disputes, and they rarely second-guessed his judgment, knowing their case couldn't be appealed or his verdict disregarded. While a few of the old salts never liked Pink—Mr. Sharpie, they called him—and even more hated what he represented, they all considered Pink an integral cog in the dockside machinery.

Pink preferred to work quietly and in the shade, but when pressured or facing a deadline, he'd step into the open, flex his muscles while buttonholing targets, and issue edicts to watermen and city hall. He made sure that whatever happened on the docks stayed on the docks; conversely, he managed to keep the cops far away, the waterfront his beat, not theirs. He's one of the reasons why the waterfront operates on a mostly self-serve basis, able to thrive separate from landlubber standards and free of bothersome oversight by city officials, regulators, inspectors, licensing boards and, God forbid, the local DA's Office. Pink was the man you wanted to see when process servers, probation officers, wiseguys or lawyers were on your tail. He rarely turned away anyone in trouble with state, county or city authorities; however, if the feds were involved, he steered clear. His reasoning: Feds are blivets and always cause a big mess, he says. They all think they're Eliot Ness or J. Edgar himself and let me tell you, there's no getting through that sort of cementhead construction.

Nowadays, Pink spends half the year in Naples, Florida. When people approach him for a favor, he excuses himself from duty, saying he's an old man on the exit ramp. He'll also say that he's out of touch, owning an address book full of names of dead people and no area codes, and he no longer involves himself in the kind of spats which once earned him the title Justice of the Peace. But if a favor seeker persists, requesting help again and again, and if the person demonstrates need over desire, Pink will partner himself to their cause. He says he can still pull a few strings. Much depends on the age of the individual he has to deal with. If they're over fifty-five, his calls are usually answered and a business lunch arranged. If the person is under forty-five, he first tries to reach their father.

Pink will act on behalf of strangers and friends, two-bit crooks and big shots, junkies and Twelve Steppers, dirty cops and disbarred lawyers, street workers and johns, city-reform candidates and city-machine reruns. According to Pink, there's no secret formula for being a facilitator, because everyone has a heart, head, spleen and wallet and facilitators merely twiddle the dials. He shrugged when asked what guided him in the calibration process. Each situation was different, but he felt timing

was the most important thing he had going for him. He explained: Born in 1916, me. And you can't do better than that.
Them years, twenties through sixties, made you see it all and
feel it all. Like it or not, you learned how to deal with good and
bad, basement and penthouse. And with those years under the
belt, steering a straight course comes easy.

Stinking hot out today, Pink says as I near. He points to the
cap log at the dock's edge and cautions me to stay clear of his
fishing poles.

He tweaks the line to one of three poles he's working.
They're set in holes drilled into the dock planking by the owner
of the icehouse. Pink is built like a rather tall jockey, trim, bow-
legged, with hands fitting squarely into his wrists, and thick at
the shoulders. He's dressed in a short-sleeve madras shirt,
exposing only the flukes to an anchor tattooed on his right arm,
and blue Dickies work pants leading to spotless white socks and
shoes. At the top, a narrow-brim straw hat sits at a jaunty angle.
He once saw Cary Grant in a movie wearing this sort of hat and
he liked it so much he ordered a dozen for himself. They all
sport different hatbands and he picks his crown for the day
depending on his mood. This morning, he says, he felt like
green paisley. When he dies, he wants to be buried in the hat
with the solid black band and wants to go in the box facedown,
so people can kiss his ass.

Pink fiddles with the lines strung out from the other two fishing poles and takes a seat in a beach chair set up behind the middle pole and just inside the shadow cast by the icehouse. He
begins to speak, but the screams of dying birds interrupt him.
He points to a pair of loudspeakers hanging off the building and
secured behind wire cages, safe from rock throwers. Pink calls
the noise something new and awful, but says you get used to it.
The speakers give life to an endless loop of seagulls being sliced
and diced, and while the noise is supposed to scare off every
species of bird, from the looks of things, it doesn't work. Star-

lings, pigeons and gulls appear undisturbed by the racket, and there's a pigeon nest inside one of the wire cages.

Your tax dollars at work, Pink says, explaining that the tape was originally made for Logan Airport by a crew out of MIT. It flopped there, he adds, and it's not looking bright here.

The owner of the icehouse, though, hopes the tape will deter junkies and the homeless from sleeping and shitting on his property. Pink's not sure if it works any better on the semiconscious than on birds. The scare-'em music is on, he adds, because the ice plant is operating on night mode. There's one man inside, while the other employees and the owner are at the funeral of a worker found dead the other day on a side street in Brockton with two slugs in his head. The cops are calling it a drug deal gone bad; the dead man's coworkers describe it as a horrible mistake, a matter of a man in the wrong place at the wrong time. Pink didn't know the guy, yet he sent flowers to the funeral home, along with an envelope containing cash for the widow.

What are you fishing for? I ask. It's too early for the bluefish to return, the mackerel are someplace else and flounder prefer deep water. While scup also seek the depths, fishermen were pulling them in yesterday at the docks along the South Terminal. Though tasty, scup are small and bony, demanding more work in preparation than the reward they yield on a plate.

Pink doesn't care what hits his lines and is happy to sit at the water's edge and wait for what comes his way. Unless it's a trophy, it goes back into the water. He'll be damned if he ever guts, cleans and fillets another fish in his lifetime. Don't misunderstand, he advises: he loves fish and fishing, the sea once his home. But he won't eat seafood unless, of course, someone is willing to pay him to do it. All his food—breakfast, lunch, dinner and snacks—comes from a menu, and he always skips over the restaurant's seafood section. Growing up, he ate so much fish he thought he was growing a fish inside him.

Honest to Holy Mother-a-God, he swears, it's true. He once mistook a cyst above the crack to his ass as a sac for a baby fish. Back then, in 1930, what the hell did he know about medicine? He had never heard of a cyst. As far as he knew, he had eaten so much fish that they were coming out of him.

His father was a deckhand, so there was never any money at home for extras like doctors and dentists. All the family ate was fish, more fish, lobsters, clams, mussels and more fish. Meat, he recalls, was a Christmas treat. At age thirteen, and too embarrassed to show anyone his rear end, he watched in horror as his fish pouch grew in size and turned a sickly yellow color. When, at last, the pain became intolerable, he attacked the thing with a sail needle, a pair of pliers nearby to pull out the fish. Until his skin cleared, he awoke every morning to examine himself, a mirror in one hand and pliers in the other hand. Later in life, he says, he was the only man in his unit who liked army chow. God, it was good.

Pink opens his arms, looks left and right, one end of the harbor to the other, and calls the icehouse dock the best damn office a man ever had. He has been doing business here ever since he was nine and sold a bucket of coal he stole off a barge for two cents. It's only a short walk from here to his other office, in the basement of the Barnacle Club, which has been his headquarters since the late 1950s.

Boy, oh, boy, he loved his work. If he found Aladdin's lamp and got his wish to be young again, he'd sail the same course and try to enjoy it more. He says the search is on for that lamp, because with each passing day, he finds himself spending more and more time going over what was and what he was in all of it along the waterfront. And that, he cautions, is the trouble with getting old: you start living for yesterday. He's not complaining. And listen: he isn't afraid to say *Thanks and good-bye.*

Part of his job as a facilitator involved matching buyers to sellers. He earned 10 percent of any deal he put together, like pairing someone with a spare engine to a captain with a blown engine, or finding skippers with extra gear and introducing them to fishermen wanting gear. He says he kept more balls in the air than Ted Williams and had people on the docks from Maine to Maryland feeding him information about fire sales and overstocks. He was also a part-time merchandiser, his car trunk filled with supplies fishermen often crave after a two-week voyage. As soon as a boat pulled in, he'd park and open shop. He stocked Cubans, dope of all kinds, booze and items he describes as little somethings for the missus, like perfume and gold chains. He also offered guns and ammunition, prostitutes and party rooms, and took bets. He was always on the hustle, he says, and explains why: Up until the 1960s, the waterfront was some hard place to live a decent life. If you weren't busy, a fight would find you, some jerk would come at you with a knife or a longshoreman's hook.

The work that earned him the moniker Justice of the Peace was not something he chased after, he says, moving his arms as if pushing away a problematic drunk. All of those jobs fell out of the sky and into his lap, usually landing in pieces he'd have to glue back together. He doubts anyone would ever believe the amount of legwork and time he put into fixit chores. Convinced that there's no good substitute for face-to-face contact, he rarely used the phone for business purposes. And he can't remember the number of times he had to sneeze and cough into a handset whenever some idiot would start talking about things best never said beyond whispering distance.

When it came to getting paid for his services as Justice of the Peace, he'd accept whatever came his way. Many times he was batting for fishermen with more kids than he had fingers and troubles like nobody should ever know, he says. When those men issued a handshake in thanks with nothing but calluses coating their palms, he knew he could rely on them for a favor. To this day, he can't imagine a better alibi for someone needing such a thing than six men swearing Mr. Joe Blow Whatever was with them aboard a fishing boat atop Georges Bank. It worked every time, he adds.

When Pink was in his forties, he was fortunate to turn avocation into vocation and assumed another job title: professional gamesman. He taps a deck of playing cards in his shirt pocket and credits them as a major force of good in his life. By the early 1960s, cards were his top moneymaker, and poker remains his passion. Without his fifty-two friends, he's pretty sure, he would've been a one-act show, a fisherman from beginning to end. He also believes he would've died years ago, just like his old pals who didn't make captain and stuck with boats and fish and deckhand work, none of whom are alive today.

To a man, the fishermen he started out with had to leave boatwork at age fifty or fifty-five, their bodies no longer up to the task and suffering from the effects brought on by years of heavy lifting and bruising seas. He calls fishing pitiless, an emptying occupation which forces its toilers to give up everything in its service and leaves them with an empty cookie jar and a medical file thicker than a phone book. Cut off from the sea, Pink says, his old mates quickly soured and turned into loners forced to work as security guards and janitors. Sadly, not one of them lived long enough to cash a Social Security check.

It was Pink's skill at handling people and cards which first brought him to the attention of Mr. Patriarca. The two hit it off, becoming both friends and business associates. Throughout the 1960s and early 1970s, Pink represented the New England family in any interclan gaming competition. Pink thinks the term *card shark* is demeaning, implying predatory action and conjuring images of cheats and fast-fingered play. He didn't have to cheat; once the cards came out, the man of science in him emerged, part mathematician and part anthropologist. If his parents had been blessed with a little money, he believes, he would've been a college boy. As it was, he left school in the ninth grade. There was no choice, he says. It was the Depression and all oars had to be in the water just to keep from going backward and under. During his second year at sea, a crewmate loaned him a book on how to win at cards. In one off-watch, he memorized pages of small type listing odds.

Numbers, patterns, ratios come easy to him and always have, though he's not sure why. His gift remained wrapped up until he joined the army, days after the attack on Pearl Harbor, and some officer, recognizing Pink's talent, assigned him to an artillery unit. He earned three stripes in the field before he was made an instructor and given books filled with numbers to read and geometry to memorize. It was then, he says, when he finally realized he was good at calculating shit.

He didn't get serious about cards until the mid-1950s. Sure, he says, he could calculate odds good, but he had a lot to learn about the human form at the table. It took years of self-education before he felt himself able to track and decipher human behavior, cracking the language of tells and discerning feints from the real thing. In most card games, he says, playing the odds only gets you so far. Table manners and body language take you the rest of the way. Pink prospered at the table and went from being a Barnacle Club customer to owning the joint. High rollers and fellow pros vied for seats at his tables and made reservations years in advance to attend special events, like Noel Nights, when there were no limits at any table and the booze flowed free. Behind the curtain, the mob pulled many of the levers and enabled the Barnacle Club to expand into the area's largest betting house.

As Pink often does when we haven't seen each other in a while, he recalls the day we first met, back in the mid-1970s, when Martha's Vineyard was my home port. It's a way for him to connect with a dead friend, a man he saw for the last time a few minutes before we hooked up. He had been playing poker upisland and his pal gave him a lift to the ferry landing and turned around for home, neither of them realizing that the boat was pulling out of her slip. I was merely a chauffeur responding to a stranger walking into a coffeehouse saying he'd pay anyone $150 for a ride to the mainland. Today, Pink doesn't mention the wet ride and steers directly to his old friend, saying, You got-a miss someone like Napoleon. The connection made, Pink settles into his beach chair, comfortable with private thoughts of the dearly departed.

Napoleon Madison was the medicine man of the Gay Head Wampanoags, keeper of secrets, tradition and lore, and invested with the power to heal. He was also an expert at cards and a regular at island poker games featuring a mix of pros and wealthy seasonal visitors. Pots of more than $2,000 were common, and Pink once likened those summertime games to shearing fluffy sheep. Of all the players, Pink ranked Napoleon as the best, swearing nobody could ever read the guy, Chief Bluff. All you'd see at the table was a statue of one smart Indian taking your money.

Napoleon's reputation at cards was sealed at an early age, the story out about the young Indian who beat the pants off Leon Trotsky while the Russian was holed up at Max Eastman's place on the island. When his host went alone to Provincetown for the day, Trotsky occupied himself by playing poker with Napoleon. The game over, cash-in time, Trotsky told Napoleon to hit up Max for the money. Eastman had introduced them at a poker game earlier in the week, and Trotsky presumed his host would again cover his guest's losses. When Napoleon demanded payment, Trotsky laughed—until he was tackled and forced to hand over his pants and shoes. The items were returned only after Eastman chased down Napoleon—finding him at work painting a house in the Russian's togs—and cleared the debt, plus interest: a new set of work clothes.

Years later, Pink said, he and Napoleon took nearly $6,000 one night from a young U.S. Senator named John Kennedy and some of his cronies. During a rematch in Hyannis, the two of them won $9,000 from President Kennedy and his staff. In Pink's opinion, the son was like his dad at the table, a family pair with more tells than Bell had phones.

Pink breaks away from his thoughts of the dead to tweak the lines to each of his fishing poles. He nods at the response coming from two of them; the middle pole, though, merits further attention and he reels in the hook to check the bait, a minnow. The fish squirms as he handles it. Lazy, that's all you are, he tells the minnow, and orders it to get to work. The hook hits the water and the minnow starts wiggling.

No nibbles today, not one at fishing or cards, he says, and hopes some punter will wander by looking for a game. Always ready, he packs a folding table, chips and three more beach chairs in the trunk to his car. But the odds are good that he'll have to wait a few more hours before his wish comes true. Every night, one of his nephews drives him to Foxwoods, where he eats dinner and plays cards until he's tired, usually leaving for home before ten p.m.

In his prime, Pink says, he was always a better finisher than starter and made it a habit to be the last man to leave the table. But now he can only concentrate so long, and it's a little less every day. Even so, he's positive that the cards keep dementia at bay. He imagines himself, if he was forced to stop playing, as turning into a tomato left on a windowsill too long. Golden years, my ass. It's all pyrite, he utters to the sky.

Before Foxwoods, and before Pink couldn't drive a car at night anymore, the regional poker action was hosted by the Barnacle Club and Thad's Steakhouse. Thad's catered to the lunchtime and afternoon crowd, while Pink's joint owned the night and morning. Around the docks, one game he hosted still pops up in conversation. It took place in 1984, when fish prices were high, product plentiful and the future for fishermen looking bright. Captain Lamprey took a chair at a no-limit table and bought $20,000 worth of chips. After that stunning opening act, he went on to steal the show, betting his inheritance, a 160-acre dairy farm, on one hand. At the time, the farm was worth at least $200,000; at the table, however, it was accepted as a $100,000 bet. Captain Lamprey won, and while he lost big money later on in the evening, intoxicated by his big win and making one reckless bet after another, he still left the table up $17,000. It was enough to bankroll a party on his boat lasting as long as one-half pound of coke in the hands and noses of revelers.

Hearing my account of Lamprey's big night, Pink shrugs and says, If that's what you hear, fine. He has nothing to add. Names, faces, dates, events, they're all fuzzy to him. They have to be, he adds. He still worries about IRS agents and gumshoes. He used to think being an old man out of the loop was enough to guarantee no jail time. But then, dear God, he saw how the feds treated Mr. Patriarca. It disgusted him watching TV and seeing federal marshals escorting a dying man into the court-room, the poor fellow strapped to a gurney and hooked to IVs. And it ate out his heart when they sent him to the pen to die alone.

Why the hell should he have to worry about agents for a country he faithfully served forever? He says it's a question that has been bothering him for years. He always paid the tax man; hell, he overpaid just to keep the shits away. He donated to politicians of every stripe and at all levels, and never missed an election or a call to jury duty. What's more, he's a vet. He saw friends die, and Lord only knows how many he killed from his end of a howitzer. And don't for a second think he forgot his comrades. That's not the sort of man he is. Oh, no. He has vis-ited Arlington Cemetery more times than he can remember and he has tipped his hat to more crosses than the pope owns. Plus, he bought savings bonds while Korea was splitting in two and

again, later, when Vietnam was splitting this country in two. But
do you think the feds keep good books and balance things? No
sir, he answers, and claims they'd skewer him same as Mr. Patriarca if they could.

Pink resets the clock to 1972, when he was conscripted and reen-
tered government service, this time on loan from the mob to
work for the CIA. It was the start of an eighteen-month assignment as shore manager for a covert operation run out of New
Bedford and targeting lefties in Africa. Pink was in charge of
loading gear aboard the small freighters that regularly sailed
from New Bedford to Cabo Verde, with stops in Angola and the
Azores. Pink says the spooks were sending tons of weaponry to
Salazar's men (troops under the command of the Portuguese
dictator Antonio Salazar). They were stationed in Portugal's
African colonies and fighting home-brewed independence move-
ments in Cabo Verde, Angola, Guinea-Bissau and Mozambique.
He says the pressure from that job was unrelenting and he was
squeezed from two sides: by arrogant CIA officers who treated
him and his men like dirt and by an assortment of friends and
fellow dock citizens of Portuguese descent out to torpedo the
CIA's efforts.

There were days, Pink adds, when the docks and everyone on
them were a sneeze away from being blown to kingdom come.
He recalls shivering in fear while watching his men handle high
explosives and praying, always praying nobody would trip or
had a cold. There wasn't a man in his gang with any training in
handling such delicate cargo, and when he asked the CIA to
instruct them, they ignored his pleas. When he requested danger pay for the men, they told him it was every citizen's duty to
stop communism from spreading in Africa. When he asked for
life insurance policies, they said, Forget it, this operation doesn't
exist.

Once word started circulating among New Bedford's Portuguese community about the action at the freight dock, Pink says, things really went down the crapper. Local fishermen with roots in the Azores despised Salazar, accusing him of institutionalizing second-class citizenship for islanders and of pillaging the island economy, which had forced them to leave the islands in the first place. As one, they wanted Salazar to lose his stupid war, then die and go to hell. The Cape Verdeans staked out a more radical position, committed to ending Portugal's colonial rule. Their homeland was a battlefield and many had relatives being hunted, jailed or executed for participating in the freedom movement. Some wanted to string Pink up for helping Uncle Sam help their enemies.

What a pickle, Pink says. He loved his country. He loved his Cape Verdean friends and believed their stories. He disliked the CIA men. To keep the peace, he dipped into his own pocket and donated cash to the freedom fighters. It was big cheese, too, he says.

Around any dock anywhere in the world stuff disappears, Pink instructs. He calls it an age-old magic trick and a part of doing business at the water's edge. Over time, though, the pilfering of CIA gear got out of hand, with hundreds of items, grenades to general-purpose machine guns, going missing every month. While he could control run-of-the-mill thievery, he couldn't rein in men on a mission. He also couldn't go to the authorities. He would never rat on anybody. Never-never. Also, he feared sparking an investigation sure to lead to jail time or deportation for scores of people, including half his work gang. To keep the peace this time, he systematically shorted the contents of every container leaving port and doctored the manifests. Sloppy in their accounting procedures, the CIA never caught on. At the thought, Pink laughs: he thinks it's funny that the dirtiest crew he ever met refused to get their hands dirty once the gear was packed in grease, to prevent rust.

It got worse, a crisis in the works, when a group of Cape Verdeans came to him with an ultimatum: if the goods didn't stop flowing to Salazar within a week, they'd sink the freighter and torch the freight dock. It was no bluff, he says, and he was running out of chips. To save the docks, waterfront businesses and jobs, and to keep men out of jail, he invited the Cape Verdeans aboard as stakeholders in the operation. His proposal, he says, was simple: in return for maintaining the staus quo, they could ship gear to their cousins in the hills alongside Uncle Sam's cargo. The peace was kept, and for all his risk and trouble, Pink says, the only thing he got was an awful bad case of shingles. He only wishes he could have shared it with Salazar and the CIA men.

Once Portugal exited Africa, in 1975, ending centuries of benighted colonial rule, the CIA packed up and left without a how-de-do or good-bye. The freight dock returned to its traditional business as a terminal for shipping interests out of the Azores and Cabo Verde. The link had been established in the late 1800s; at first, the boats heading west had carried loads of wine and immigrants, while nowadays it's just wine and prepackaged island delicacies, like flan and canned mackerel. As always, the cargoes heading east to the islands include a little bit of everything, from kitchen sinks to TVs and heavy construction equipment.

A damn good little business, that freight operation, Pink declares. Locals get to send their relatives whatever they want at a cheap rate, and the wine sent this way is high quality. Pink especially likes Pico green wine. He also says the freight boats are perfect for moving big items off the lot, his cautious way of acknowledging a well-known dock scam run by the mob. Indeed, the night before a ship was scheduled to depart New Bedford, the mob would clear their shelves and macadam of hot goods. Stolen cars and construction materials, including tools and heavy machinery, would arrive at the dock for loading aboard ship in the dark, with flashlights and walkie-talkies coordinating the action. It was common to see pricey cars, like Mercedeses, strapped to the deck next to tractors and backhoes done up in Massachusetts Turnpike Authority colors.

Usual dock business was threatened once again in the late 1980s, when the CIA contacted the Patriarca family, requesting help in running another covert arms depot and logistics center in New Bedford. This time they wanted to support Charles Taylor and his thugs in Africa. While the local Portuguese-speaking community wasn't particularly interested in West African civil wars, Pink says he sure as hell was. He was too damn old to work again with the CIA, and a whole lot smarter. He told his boss to find another man or another port. Charles Taylor? The thought of helping that man makes Pink wonder, Who the hell comes up with these bad ideas?

A pickup truck drives into the icehouse parking lot, and the driver gets out to pound on a door which won't open until tomorrow. Pink, trying to be helpful, explains the situation— A funeral, for Christ's sake—to the man. No sympathy, all venom, the man shouts, Fuck. He drove all the way from fucking Freetown for fucking ice. And what does he get? Fucking nothing.

Pink offers to take down the gentleman's name and phone number and promises to have the owner call as soon as the factory reopens. He's not sure, but there's a chance the ice could be delivered free to Freetown.

The man swears he'll never return. He'd rather go to the goddamn towelheads at the gas station than see this place again. And what the fuck are you two guys doing to the birds? Sadists, you. Weirdos, freaks. That said, the man gets back in his truck and speeds away, the tires raising a cloud of dust soon rinsed from the air by the rain coming down from the eaves.

Shaking his head, Pink moves to the fishing poles and decides to rebait the hooks with fresh minnows. He dips his hand into the bait bucket and chases prey, As he zeros in on a target, he says the icehouse needs all the business it can get, even from foulmouthed idiots from Freetown. The local ice industry has been in a slump for years, and Pink thinks one or more area manufacturers will go belly-up within a year.

For more than a century, the manufacture, sale and storage of ice was a major industry in New Bedford. In the beginning, 1780 to 1900, a small army of men suffered through the winters, using handsaws to harvest ice from the lakes in aptly named Lakeville, sixteen miles from the docks. It was sent by wagon to the harbor and stored inside stone buildings with extra-thick rubble walls and few windows, with sawdust packed in every crack for insulation. Schooners transported the frozen blocks to New York and Boston, while a few of the larger freighters catered to the Caribbean and Central American markets, filling up with rum, sugar and mahogany for the ride home. Approximately one-half of the harvest was sold locally to fishing boats, butcher shops and the rich living on the hill.

At the turn of the twentieth century, as machines started to produce ice on demand, the old industry collapsed and reformed itself, the ice sawers of Lakeville never to be seen again. The surviving ice merchants focused on local sales, their profits waxing and waning with the fortunes of the fishing fleet. Again, in the early 1980s, the ice business hit a rough patch, forcing many players out of the game, and the industry continues to stumble.

Pink grabs a second minnow and goes for the hook, saying, You know, of course, it's all Washington's fault. The troubles here start there. They're killing fish and fishermen, the jerks. And they pretty much did in the ice trade, too. Damn, he adds, he squeezed a little too hard. He throws the now lifeless minnow into the drink and goes for its replacement.

Pink's accusation is the company line around the docks, his words echoing those of most fishermen, who source all their problems to the passage of the Magnuson-Stevens Act, in 1976. It was the government's first attempt to deal with ocean resources and those chasing after underwater treasure. Even though the oil and mining industries influenced much of the legislation, greasing every sticking point with favors and campaign contributions, their flacks kept the spotlight on the bill's relationship to fishermen. Initially, local watermen bought into the public relations campaign and welcomed the legislation, which pledged government support in the modernization of the American fishing fleet, along with a promise to protect it from foreign competition. As well, the bill authorized money for marine research in order to increase the catch by introducing science to fishery management. Today, fishermen feel blindsided by it all and consider Magnuson-Stevens a Pandora's box which unleashed one plague after another and is ultimately responsible for the deplorable state of their workplace. They also feel the legislation is the reason they're on the defensive and losing every battle in the courts and the media.

The Magnuson-Stevens Act had one jingoistic aspect which made it easy to sell to the public and chat about on TV: the two-hundred-mile limit. The water grab extended the borders and declared everything inside the new line, from flying fish to seabed oil, gas and mineral deposits, part of the public domain. Without a special license, foreigners were banned from farming on American property, their boats threatened with seizure and heavy fines. Washington ballyhooed its action as a salve to the ills of the American fishing industry caused by the rapacious practices of foreign fleets operating beyond the old twelve-mile limit. In a quieter way, the government urged oil and mining companies to explore the depths and prepare bids for licensing rights.

One pork-lined section of the bill, inserted at the behest of a flagging boatbuilding industry based in the South, authorized federal guarantees on loans made for the construction of new fishing boats. It was a limited-time offer and sent commercial lenders scurrying for a piece of the no-risk action. Suddenly, bankers with no experience in the marine trades were encouraging fishermen to build their dreamboats and not worry a whit about costs. Not long afterward shipyards began expanding their facilities and running double shifts to meet the rush in new orders.

By 1978, a new generation of fishing boats had started appearing in significant numbers in New Bedford. The basic layout of these vessels aped earlier designs, but most everything else about them had changed in a big way: bigger gross tonnage, bigger engines, bigger winches, nets and dredges, bigger electronic displays, and all of it at a bigger than ever price tag. Naturally, these beefed-up muscle boats caught appreciably more fish than their predecessors, and record landings became routine for cod, flatfish and scallops. At the same time, skippers and owners became increasingly alarmed by how much it cost to operate and maintain these überboats. And as more and more new boats came into service, all chasing the same prize, a gluttonous monster was hatched, with fishermen both parents and servants to it.

The increased fish landings kept supply high and prices low, forcing fishermen into a relentless pursuit of ever larger quantities of fish to stay ahead of supersized loan payments and staggering operation and repair costs. It commanded a change in tempo around the docks, the old, rather slow and steady beat giving way to a frenetic, nonstop pulse.

As it was for Pink in his fishing days, boats traditionally went out for two weeks and sat at the dock for ten days, allowing the crew a semblance of family life. But the owners of the new boats, each costing a million or more to build, couldn't afford any downtime and kept their boats in near-constant motion. They hired two crews, with one gang loading food and fuel while the other team finished unloading the catch. Bunks stayed warm; oven burners stayed on; and boats were often steaming out of the harbor hours after making dock. The fish never got a break, and in the span of ten go-go years, many stocks, like cod and scallops, were stressed to the breaking point. It was this near collapse of the fishery which prompted government intervention and site-management.

While the new generation of boats spawned a host of small, tech-savvy repair and support businesses, pieces of the old service sector disappeared. Most of the new boats came equipped with modern refrigeration systems, insulated holds and, in many cases, onboard ice-making machinery. The mom-and-pop icehouses were the first to close, and others, big and medium-sized, followed as the industry contracted into the hands of a few manufacturers. In the early 1970s the ice trade employed more than 150 people; today it supports less than sixty, and it's doubtful any of them feel secure in their job. Each new government regulation chopping a boat's quota and trimming its days at sea cuts into their business, as does every new model of shipboard ice-making equipment.

Watch yourself, Pink warns, and starts casting the rebaited hooks into the drink. As he goes through the motions, his pockets come to life, loosing the sound of chicks pecking through their shells. The fishing lines set, he extracts the noisemakers: two key rings with dozens of keys on each holder. He says he has been carrying a ton of keys in his pockets for forty years, but, maybe, he should pack them away when he's fishing. Any time a guard at a metal detector asks him about all the keys, Pink feels compelled to lie and poses as either a custodian or a motel owner. He doubts many believe him, but what else can he say? The truth is beyond reach; honestly, he can't remember what half the keys open.

Heading to safe storage for them inside his car, he fingers the keys as he walks, attaching a name to many and sometimes adding an address. But most of them only draw blanks: Dunno.

Dunno . . . Throwing out one key or ten keys won't lighten the load any; no sir, he's sure about that. As reminders of the past, they're not useless, and at his age, he says, he's holding on to just about everything he can still grip. Three keys on one ring set get special attention and he stops walking to rub them between his fingers. Rest in peace, buddy, he prays.

Each key comes out of an old and—like Pink's pal—now dead waterfront tradition governing cash loans. It was peculiar to the docks and grew out of the old divide separating watermen from landlubbers. For generations banks viewed watermen as shiftless, uneducated characters with no steady income who posed an unconscionable business risk. Even boat owners had a tough time with bankers until the 1970s, and when a captain did secure financing, it was always at a premium interest rate. Pink doubts that his father or any of his father's friends ever stepped inside a bank. Everyone was paid in cash; money orders were used on those rare occasions when a check was needed; and a sock under a mattress or a floorboard was where any savings went.

The docks took care of its own, Pink says, the community offering the only cures to waterfront maladies no outsider would deal with. So whenever a deckhand got jammed, crunched by money woes, he turned to the water's edge for help. While the whine for cash from dopers and boozers has been a constant on the docks, Pink thinks it's easy to tune out their noise—no different, in fact, from shutting out sounds from the endless loop of birds in pain. Requests for aid from honest fishermen always got a response, he says. For loans under $1,000, there was no interest charged and the borrower paid it back when he could. Nothing went down on paper, the arrangement sealed by a handshake. The terms for loans over $1,000 were the same, except for one thing: the borrower would hand over a key to something he owned as a token of extra thanks and promise. Maybe it was a car, Pink says. Maybe an apartment. Garage.

Boat. Office. Toolshed. Storage locker. Whatever the key opened, the lender got use of it, no questions asked.

Starting in the late 1950s, when Pink finally began making more money than he needed to live on, he says, he spread cheese around like crazy. Over time, his collection of openers paid unusual dividends, allowing him to store goods around town, in places from basements to office towers and pigeon coops. It allowed him to keep things simple and uncluttered at home, a three-bedroom apartment in an old Victorian mansion off Hawthorn Street, near the hospital. Whenever cops searched the place, they always left without finding what they came for. When colleagues in Providence needed to stash something or someone off the beaten track, Pink could provide the perfect hideaway.

He palms the keys in one hand and picks up the pace as he heads to his car, parked far from the wetness around the ice-house. As he goes, he points toward where he grew up and homes in, saying, North-northwest, five blocks away, just off Acushnet Avenue and above the old Cyr Fruit Market, which closed in 1937. Mom, Dad and seven kids (three boys, with him the oldest, and four girls) shared a four-room apartment heated by one coal stove. He says money around the house was like a ghost. It'd appear and then, poof, quick as that, it'd disappear without leaving any trace of it ever being around. Whenever he or his dad came home from a fishing trip, Mom would grab the cash and bolt for the door to square bills: landlord, grocer, gas and Edison, and Mr. Morris at the dry goods store. It was always in that order, too, he adds, and Mr. Morris didn't get many visits.

He left boats, fishing and home for the first time to fight in a war, and when he returned all he heard about was how good the war had been for the fishing industry. During his absence, two federal agencies, the War Production Board and the Office of Emergency Management, had set up offices in New Bedford and started calling the shots around town. To maximize the wartime catch, and to minimize fuel and transportation costs, the feds directed many small ports from Montauk to Maine to close up shop and send their boats to New Bedford, where the fleet grew from 50 to 175 boats. Jobs for local fishermen were plentiful and fish prices stayed high throughout the war. The newcomers, however, didn't linger long after VJ-Day, their departure hastened by homesickness and union organizers. Pink got back in time to see the harbor emptying, returning to the same sort of dump he'd left behind.

While unions had been a powerful force in the city's industrial sector since the 1870s, they stayed clear of docks until the late 1940s, then quickly retreated back to land. Their timing was just awful, Pink says. The men were all for a union, but the boat owners from away heard the talk and left, taking their tiny factories and jobs with them. With few boats around and lots of men looking for boat work, Pink considered himself lucky to secure a berth after only five months of searching. He remembers earning $1,400 in 1953, averaging $80 per twelve-day fishing trip. Since he was still contributing to the family pot, he says, he wasn't making anywhere near enough money to think about a missus or kids. Even so, he considered it an acceptable income because he was in line to decent pay as captain of the boat. In those days, if you weren't born into a boat, you had to pay some heavy dues to sit in the wheelhouse, he says.

He thinks his career as a captain might be the shortest on record in the history of the fleet. He made two trips, a skipper for a total of six weeks, before the hurricane of 1954 deep-sixed his dreams. The storm leveled much of the waterfront and destroyed nearly half the boats in the harbor, including his. While surveying his command, the fishing boat high and dry at the edge of Coggeshall Street, her back broken and port side stove in like a whale had rammed her, he remembers, his throat went dry and he couldn't get a word out. The boat owner was next to him, cursing a storm which had passed; he had no insurance. Pink says that's when he understood that he had to exit fishing and find another way to make a living. Although he kept working as a deckhand, he started moonlighting as a facilitator and got serious about cards, an eager student studying table manners and body language.

His car is now only a few feet away, but Pink stops and turns to the water and his fishing poles, which stand straight as asparagus spears. Just remembering something else, he says, and steers to the turning marker which pointed him away from full-time fishing and into a future as a gamesman and facilitator.

It was 1957, he begins. March. Cold. Wet. And blowing a near gale. He and seven other men he calls tough as the oak they sailed on left port aboard the *Acadia,* a seventy-two-foot dragger. Nobody had insulated gear back then, just wet wool under oilies and gum boots better at keeping the water in than out. There was no radio or radar aboard. And he says they navigated by guess and by stars, dead reckoning in the fog and keying on Polaris and Venus when it was clear. For weather reports, they relied on their own observations of clouds, daybreak colors and barometric ups and downs. The *Acadia'*s safety equipment included life jackets, whistles, war-surplus flares that rarely worked and an emergency kit—eight strings of rosary beads and one copy of the New Testament—packed inside an old saltine tin mounted on the bulkhead near the ship's bell. With neither radios nor helicopters around in those days, he says, rescue was rare, and most boats carried the same emergency kit.

The *Acadia* landed eighty-five thousand pounds of yellowtail, but the dockside storage and distribution system of the day could handle only eighteen thousand pounds of cargo from their boat. The rest was sold at a steep discount to the gurry plant at the head of the harbor, which, depending on the day of the week, made cat food, fertilizer or fish oil. The total catch, market and gurry plant sales combined, was worth less than three cents a pound ($2.80 per hundredweight). After deducting the cost of fuel, ice and grub off the top, the skipper or owner took his share (60 percent) and the seven-man crew split the rest, $72 a man. Pink says he spent twenty-some bucks that afternoon at the dentist's office to repair what a net full of yellowtail had cracked. The rest of his earnings went into poker chips; the game lasted most of the night and he walked home with nearly $400 in his pocket. Afterward, he didn't touch his seabag for months and then only in response to his sister's complaint about the dead seal sharing his apartment.

Love this machine, Pink either confides or orders as he comes alongside his car. It's a 1994 Fleetwood, black and polished like a concert grand. Seeing his reflection in the hood, he adjusts his hat, adding a slight angle to starboard. Again, he weighs the keys in one hand and this time isolates two tokens of special thanks, each for a loan over $25,000. He says he didn't make many of those wallet busters, explaining they were reserved for fishermen with staggering problems and excellent reputations. He gives an example: A man hauls out to paint the bottom and, son-of-a-bitch, discovers the keelson is going punk, the caulking is a mess, rot under the ice boards and so on, until he's looking at a yard bill from hell. That man could name his number.

Pink opens the car door and sunshine highlights creaseless black leather trimmed in light blue piping. He tosses the keys into the glove compartment and notes the time on the dashboard clock. Jesus, the pills, he says, and moves to the trunk, where he keeps his gaming equipment and a cooler holding several bottles of water, two chocolate bars, a banana and a jelly jar containing pills of various colors, shapes and sizes. It used to be three packs a day and scotch, no ice, with a splash of water, he says, fishing for pills. He won't share any information about his health—Feel great, dammit—and claims he's on a regimen of meds no different from that of many people who still think a lot about Ike.

When asked how many loans he made in his forty years as a community banker and how much he tossed into the pot, Pink swallows the last pill, burps, apologizes for burping and answers, How the hell would I know? He never kept a ledger. Greenbacks were the only paper involved. And it wasn't his job anyway; the borrower promised to keep track of things with his handshake. Sure, he always had a good idea where Mr. So-and-So stood on his debt, be it way-short or getting there. Of course, some loans went unpaid, he admits, but not many. Most of what went south happened because the guy died, and that took care of that. End of story. Jesus, sir, he's not the sort of a person who'd hit up a widow for cheese she probably didn't even know the mister had borrowed.

On the way back to the fishing poles, Pink detours to the northeast corner of the icehouse to show me something. He stands back from the drip line under the eave and points to a layer of bricks set at chin height, about eleven feet above the crest of a spring tide at flood. It's the high-water mark of the Hurricane of 1938, he says. He wants a brass plaque erected on the spot just like the one attached to the old Journal Building in Providence, where the storm made landfall after sweeping across Long Island. He considers the Hurricane of 1938 the single most significant event in the history of the docks.

Local politicians have so far brushed aside his offers to pay for the plaque. If they keep stalling, he says, he'll round up some of his old pals to attend a private unveiling ceremony. He feels it's important that something's put in place to commemorate the catastrophe of 1938. He continues: That storm clobbered the city and sent folks staggering into streets littered with debris from their own homes. It swept clean almost the entire waterfront. Mills were swamped. Boats wrecked. Worst of all, people died. And while other towns were able to rebuild and get on with life months after the mighty blow, he contends, New Bedford didn't start to heal until the run-up to World War II.

Pink shifts his gaze to Pier 1, about seventy-five yards away, and says the dock is pretty much in the same place where his dad's boat, the *Mary-L,* was tied when the storm hit. His boat, the *Theresa,* was moored further south, tied to a dock closer to open water. He left his house and went to the waterfront once the wind started blowing steady out of the southeast, hell's quadrant. Like any experienced fisherman, he understood northeasters as troublemakers and southeasters as killers, the direction of attack positioning the boat on the wrong, nonnavigable side of the eye. At sea there's always a chance of surviving any blow, but Pink can't think of a worse place for a boat in a southeaster than New Bedford, where the harbor mouth opens to the south and welcomes whatever comes down the gullet.

From commercial radio reports, fishermen knew there was a major storm moving up the coast; however, Pink doubts if anyone had a clue about what they were in for. He remembers starting the day feeling uninformed, really stupid, and he says he only got stupider, punch-drunk from being slapped silly by wind and water hour after hour. Aboard the *Theresa,* he checked the boat's barometer and cursed, sure it was broken. The needle was so low it was off the scale, and he thought the hairspring was on the fritz. When the captain told him that every barometer in the harbor had bottomed out, he says, you could've pushed him under an ant, that's how small he felt. Later, after he strung lines and extra anchors to keep the boat from smashing into the dock, the impossible happened: the dock started breaking apart and smashing the boat.

As the tidal surge began sweeping across what was left of the dock planking, Pink says, the skipper ordered everyone to shore. She's lost, he cried. She's a goner. Pink calls it an incredibly sad moment. He loved *Theresa* and, suddenly, she was about to die. It still hurts, he adds, because he never saw her again in one piece. As soon as he made it off the dock and turned seaward, he was blinded by spray and spume, the wind driving it into his face with the force of gravel out of a fire hose.

Pink went to help his dad aboard the *Mary-L* and was soon in full retreat, that dock also disintegrating. Meanwhile, the wind started shrieking and strumming the halyards, sounding a sailor's dirge. He and the others sidled landward on all fours, human crabs with their rears to the wind and their heads tucked in and held low. He says no man could stand upright and stay on his feet and only a dang fool would try because of all the missiles in the air. Cedar shakes whizzed by like giant razor blades. Two-by-fours came at him like spears. Entire trees took flight, he says, and limbs still in leaf set sail at nearly the speed of the wind. Doors and pieces of roofs flew high and low and bounced along the ground. His face was bloodied by shards of flying glass; his father was flattened by a fish box; the skipper of the *Mary-L* was whacked by a boat hatch, his collarbone broken and every rib on his left side cracked.

Pink and his dad took shelter in the lee of the brick-built icehouse. Right here, he declares, stomping his foot. And it was from this vantage point that he watched twenty-something-foot waves march down the harbor, each as steep as a wall, every one of them writhing and hissing and roaring sounds of the unconquerable. As they went, the waves carried boats and debris either into or over the bridge spanning the harbor. All around him, wind and water sawed and chewed and dismembered the waterfront, cleaving it of artifice. Only brick and stone structures could withstand the onslaught. Pink remembers watching one extra-big wave hit the lumberyard and wash the site clean of every stick and cinder block. The wind blew steady at over 125 knots, the peak velocity never measured, since the dials on the local equipment topped out at 125. Whatever it was blowing, Pink says, it was more than enough to rewrite waterfront history, the storm erasing most of the testimony to the past and altering the future in ways unimaginable days before.

As the storm surge began sending water down the tops of their seaboots, Pink and his dad moved to higher ground on North Front Street. From the lee of the old candleworks, they tracked the rising water, the icehouse wall their measuring stick. As he watched, Pink says, he saw the damnedest thing of his life: a flotilla of cars and trucks being pushed down Water Street by mountainous waves sweeping through the lowlands. Most of the iron ended up in the estuary more than one mile away, as did the *Mary-L,* which was sent high and dry alongside a textile mill. His boat, the *Theresa,* made it only as far as the gurry plant at the head of the harbor, where she ended up in pieces on the rocks.

Pink salutes the icehouse, one survivor acknowledging another, and moves to his fishing poles. He likens the Hurricane of 1938 to a KO punch ending a long and withering fight, its first round signaled by the bell at the New York Stock Exchange on October 24, 1929. The Depression pounded this place, he says, idling many factories, and with thousands of jobless citizens, the lines at soup kitchens were blocks long. Pink thinks the hurricane also emptied many people of the last thing they owned, hope. When the winds calmed and the sun finally came out, he says, folks walked around in a daze, everyone terrified by the future. Nobody knew when stores would reopen, if ever, or where they would find their next meal. There was no telling when the mills would resume production. No one knew if the waterfront would be rebuilt. And everybody expected locusts would be next. For months afterward, another kind of storm

battered people and took its toll, the talk of the town: suicide.
Pink says awful news was inescapable; he couldn't walk into a
bar or down the street without bumping into people talking
about someone who just ate a gun or jumped or sucked gas
from the oven. On his one block in a working-class neighborhood of tenements and churchgoers, twelve people committed
suicide. He estimates hundreds died the wrong damn way.

With the *Theresa* a total loss, and to jump-start at least one
income for the family, Pink helped his dad patch the *Mary-L*.
They labored inches from the Soule Mill Wetting Building at the
end of Sawyer Street. Meanwhile, factory crews mucked out
Soule Mill and the other textile plants at the water's edge, scrub-
bing the machinery and fixing the windows. Several days later,
in the afternoon, the electric company fired up the mains feeding all the mills and word went out that there'd be business as
usual the next morning. Pink remembers, while working late,
hearing a strange crackling noise coming from inside the nearby
mill building, but like everyone else working on the *Mary-L*, he
paid it no attention. He was home when the first fire siren drew
him into the street, where he saw flames licking the sky over the
estuary. Within hours, he counted six separate infernos, each
blaze a mill building as long as a football field and built with
enough wood to launch an armada. Back then, he says, no one
knew what salt water and muck did to open knob-and-socket
wiring. More than eleven hundred people saw their jobs go up
in smoke, including the crew of the *Mary-L*.

Fiddling with the line to a fishing pole, Pink repeats, Boy-
oh-boy-oh-boy-oh-boy . . . Then he adds, Two hundred years
at the shore gone in two days. Eventually, some of the old life
returned, like fishermen, their boats and the docks. But even
more of the past never resurfaced, the storm a casket maker for
the local water transport industry, which had been the largest
employer on the waterfront since the 1880s. These watermen

serviced the mills, transferring bales of cotton from four-masted freighters to barges, which they tugged or push-poled to factory docks lining the harbor and estuary. Suddenly, though, with the barges in pieces and the freight docks a mess of splintered wood, several hundred men were out of work. Pink says most of them either learned how to drive a truck or left town.

Until new fishing boats were built and old ones repaired, Pink and his dad survived the same way their grandfathers had: hand-lining for fish off the sides of a dory powered by homemade sails and oars. Weather permitting, Pink was on the job sixteen hours a day, out at one p.m. and in at five a.m. for the start of the daily fish auction. A few years afterward, just when he thought things were getting back to normal along the waterfront, the fleet numbering fifty boats and growing, he says, the Japs did the dirty at Pearl Harbor.

The way he sees it: One good thing came out of the hurricanes of 1938 and 1954, and that's the dike. He points to the structure in the distance, a massive federal project started in 1962 and made possible in large part by a president who took a personal interest in his old Senate seat. Closing the harbor mouth and protecting it from attack out of the south, the hurricane dike spans forty-five hundred feet of open water; it continues up the coastline, east and west, protecting factories and low-lying neighborhoods, with an overall length of three and a half miles. There's one gate, 150 feet wide, and it's the only way in or out of the harbor for water, fish and boats. Though not yet tested by a hurricane, the dike boasts one certain achievement: it's the largest structure of its kind in the Western Hemisphere, the world title belonging to a harbor in Japan.

Pink agrees with those people calling the dike an environmental disaster and says he's just as concerned as anyone about its harmful effects on shoreside flora and fauna. He understands how it restricts the tidal flow and stymies the natural cleansing action of an ocean constantly on the move. Any damn fool with eyes or a nose can see and smell a goddamn toilet bowl as big as the harbor, he says. And dammit, he adds, looking at his fishing poles like a man reeling in an old tire instead of an expected ocean prize, he knows the dike turned a great place to fish into a lousy one.

Even so, after his experiences in 1938 and 1954, he considers the dike a valuable addition to the waterfront. For the dock community, it means a good night's sleep no matter what the weather. For the city as a whole, it pays out dividends every year in the form of relatively low insurance premiums. Anyway, he says, this is a working waterfront, not some pretty place for high hats and yachts. He's convinced the naysayers will change their tune when the next hurricane hits and, at last, the dike proves its worth to people other than boat owners, fishermen and harborside businesses. As a man who made his living calculating the odds and playing them, he figures this place is in for a whopper of a storm sometime soon. In fact, he'll lay a stick ($1,000) on a Category 3 hurricane walloping New Bedford within three years.

Pink decides he'll have better luck catching fish if he sets the hooks away from the shadows cast by the bulkhead and the icehouse. He grabs a pole and aims for a landing spot off the bow to the seventy-two-foot dragger moored to Fish Island, on the other side of the channel and about forty yards away. The hooks travel an impressive distance, but he barely misses snagging the boat. He says an inch off is as good as a mile in this game and makes sure the line doesn't drift into the *Barnacle Bill*. Last year she sank twice at her mooring, her engine and deck gear now double-dipped and useless. Blown caulking hangs off her topsides, looking like fat, white worms trying to wiggle free of her seams, and both her stem and stern show enough punk to keep her from ever fishing again.

That's a blivet boat, more damn trouble than anything ten times her size, Pink says, and casts another hook, raising a splash yards from the hulk.

The last voyage of the *Barnacle Bill* ended in a mutiny, not an especially newsworthy event since there have been mutinies aboard New Bedford fishing boats for almost as long as there have been fishing boats in New Bedford. What set her case apart, meriting contempt and banishment from the docks, were the loudmouths involved. Both sides, captain and crew, used the radio to broadcast events, offensive and defensive, as they happened. By making it a public spectacle, they issued invitations to every badge wearer in town—local cops, staties, FBI, DEA, OSHA and the Coast Guard—to snoop around the waterfront for weeks afterward; the mutiny also produced enough paperwork to keep the boat wrapped up in the courts for years to come. Worse, and unforgivable, the hubbub caused the cancellation of two import schemes, months in the planning, and led to the arrest of shoreside service workers—prostitutes and drug dealers—unaware of all the plainclothes cops prowling the docks.

Damn her, Pink says, casting the third hook, and this time grouses about the blivet boat blocking his view of Fish Island. He likes to imagine the place in its heyday, well before the Hurricane of 1938 swept it clean, and the boat distracts him from that pleasure. It was once famous, a real big deal, he adds, and closes one eye to blank out the *Barnacle Bill.*

In the beginning, Fish Island was home to America's first industrial research park and came up with some of the most important recipes for progress derived in the nineteenth century. Starting around 1810, dozens of labs were built on the four-acre site, all of them in a race to unlock the secrets hidden inside whale oil and its competition: vegetable oils, coal and, eventually, crude. The Industrial Revolution relied on the greases developed here to keep things moving, and as the Machine Age progressed, with more and more gadgets going faster and faster, the labs created the lubricants needed to maintain the frantic pace. Come the 1830s, Fish Island was the world's leading center of fractional distillation, its wizardry capped in 1860, a year after Edwin Drake sank a well in Titusville, Pennsylvania, and a researcher discovered how to make kerosene from crude. By 1895, the labs were empty, the whaling era dead, and all the thousands of patents sold cheap to men like Rockefeller.

Pink first visited the island as a kid in 1922 and remembers the place crowded with homeless people, junkies, whores and fishermen. The poor squatted in the old lab buildings and fought with fishermen wanting to use them as gear lockers. Pink thinks it's amazing that this city's story has always been ass-backwards: high to low, riches to rags. For proof, he references the city's slide from the mountaintop—it was the richest place in the world from 1815 to 1855—to its modern-day position in the cellar, one of the most depressed places in Massachusetts. Since the 1970s, census data has put the city's per capita income at or near the bottom of the barrel, while the unemployment rate has been stuck in or near double digits from the late 1980s through the dawn of a new century.

Mind you, Pink says, he'd love to move *Barnacle Bill,* but he wouldn't blow her up or anything like that. Instead, he'd moor her closer to the main docks as a poignant reminder to fishermen never to involve cops in waterfront business. He believes the docks should always be able to fix itself and swears it could and did up until 1993, when he came out of retirement to squash a problem. That was the year fishermen shut down a human smuggling ring stupid enough to use New Bedford as a terminal. It was the goddamn slave trade, Pink says. A ring of Chinks was selling other, poor Chinks to sweatshops and kitchens. He's proud of the role the docks played in the Underground Railroad, the waterfront being a major depot for runaway slaves, so it blew his stack hearing that the goddamn opposite was going on.

The foreigners arrived around two a.m. aboard an unlit and unmarked fishing boat, which pulled up to Pier 1 and unloaded two-legged cargo into a pair of trucks parked on the dock. Within minutes, the boat was steaming out of the harbor and the trucks were rolling down the interstate. A night watchman at a fish house caught some of the action and estimated the cargo at more than one hundred people, all Chinese. He called the cops, who arrived too late to note anything suspicious.

In the morning, as word circulated on the waterfront, dock citizens banded together to start their own investigation. For information, they approached the Chinese fish buyers who drive here every morning from New York and Boston. Those men rolled like dice, Pink reports, omitting any mention of the tools used to extract leads: baseball bats, knives and harpoons. Within days, the mystery boat was out of commission; a fire somehow started in the engine room while she sat at a dock on Long Island. Because the slavers never returned, and because their boat never again ferried people off freighters, Pink credits the docks for shutting down a piece of the slave trade. If the cops or, God forbid, the feds had been handling things, he's convinced, they'd still be on the case, wasting money, not one good thing done.

While he's dead sure cops and docks don't mix, he's unsure if today's waterfront community would react as quickly and as decisively as it did in 1993. Many of the players are different and answer to corporate boards, not their peers; lawyers and paperwork, not handshakes, seal deals; and in many cases, deckhands get checks signed by people they've never met. Pink says the docks used to rely on a simpler, tighter arrangement, one in which every fisherman was an independent cuss working alongside an independent cuss who happened to own a boat. It worked damn good for more than a hundred years, he adds.

Pink thinks the physical layout of the waterfront is falling apart, just like him, yet both are recognizable from pictures taken in their prime, 1960 to 1990. For a short stretch after he retired, he says, he was a jerk, one of them harebrained fools who couldn't let go. It's used to bug the hell out of him watching his old world rearrange itself without anyone asking for his input. But once the pace of change started accelerating, in the early 1990s, urged on by lawmen, greenies and industry consolidation, he simply couldn't keep up and had to stop caring. Today, hell, he doesn't give a rat's ass what the docks salute. His time has come and gone. It just took him a while to realize it.

One thing, though, he adds: he's glad he won't be around for the day commercial fishing dies, most likely snuffed by a court order and/or unbeatably cheap imported fish raised on farms. At that point, the docks will turn into some sort of Sturbridge Village by the Sea, sanitized and saltless, with college boys pretending to be deckhands and former pencil pushers posing as captains. That, he says, would turn his stomach.

A fishing pole twitches and starts to bow to some creature on the line. No, thank you, he doesn't want any help. He'll deal with the fish and the other two poles. The day he needs help landing a fish at the icehouse dock is a day or two before he goes ass-up at the cemetery.

Pink sets the drag on the reel, gives and takes line, a practiced hand on the job. From the shape of the pole—a quivering, giant question mark—a fish much larger than a scup took the bait. Several minutes into the fight, the water bubbles off to Pink's left, about twenty yards away. A fin juts above the surface, its appearance too brief to allow identification of species or size.

Hope it's a great white, Pink says. He'd love to show everyone at Foxwoods a picture of him next to a twenty-foot-long killer. Slowly, he reels in the swimmer, but as the fish nears the bulkhead, it redoubles its efforts to break free. Pink struggles at the pole, his breath going louder with each *click-click* of the reel.

The line snaps with a twang. One end forms curlicues off the tip of the fishing pole; the other end disappears underwater. Good luck, fish, Pink says. He believes fishermen win sometimes and fish win sometimes. The odds, however, are in his favor. He still has plenty of minnows to use as bait and time to kill before heading out to the casino.

Seated in his chair, he gets to work on repairs, opening a tackle box he bought in 1961, a tin job which looks brand-new. He keeps the shine by coating it with whale oil twice a year, dipping into a supply dating back to the 1850s stored in barrels above a hardware shop near the docks. He leans over to position his pole just right on the ground and methodically assembles the different items he'll use to reset a hook: wire leader, new hook, swivels, pliers, knife and split shot to crimp on the line as sinkers. While he's in the middle of the chore, I decide to move on.

Aye-aye, Cap'n, Pink says, and starts to stand.

I tell him to stay seated, but it's too late and no use anyway. He dumps everything in his lap back into the tackle box and rises out of his chair. Good manners compels him upright. A goddamn pleasure, Sailor, he says, and extends his hand, eyes drilling into mine.

There's a clarity which comes out of Pink's grip. It speaks of an era when written contracts were mere formalities and what mattered was understood because of a shared set of expectations and goals. Handshakes built the docks, and for Pink, they remain the only currency worth a damn.

Four

MR. JINX

THE JOB ENDS AT DAYBREAK, the boat delivered to New Bedford after a fifteen-hundred-mile voyage from the factory in Florida, and I need a ride home. But it's all business on the docks before seven a.m., not an idler in sight. Stevedores high-step over boat rails to deliver cartons of fresh food and tinned goods to galley hatchways. Welders are hard at it, throwing sparks off the end of grinders and torches, hammering scale and pounding kinks out of flat stock. Riggers lay out wire rope for the *Janey-P*'s new drum and urge a nearby crane operator to stop looking at the goddamn radar dome dangling off the hoist and put it in place; they want the crane out of their way. Three hookers sip coffee as they walk shoulder to shoulder down the dock, exchanging banter with fishermen aboard boats manuevering for a clear shot at the channel, outward-bound. A dope dealer on a bike offers last-minute deals. Crewmen aboard a groundfish dragger mend a net strung from the A-frame, tying sheet bends to hold things together. A captain's voice carries through an open hatchway; he swears to Almighty fucking God that he'll kill the mechanic if the generator ever craps out again.

I steer for the yellow phone mounted on the east wall of the Old Fish Auction House, now home to volunteers running a Visitor's Center and also the office for the Mariner's Assistance

Program, which hosts AA and NA meetings. The yellow phone
offers a toll-free link to any of the six taxi companies servicing
the docks.

From the look of things, the taxi business currently offers
sky-high, mind-blowing travel in addition to basic ground transportation. The sign above the phone used to say, simply, CALL A
CAB. It now reads CALL A LAB, thanks to someone's work with a
Sharpie. Thoughtfully, another hand, this one using pencil, has
rated each taxi company according to its performance in different categories. One company, for example, merits three five-
point stars for DOPE and two smiley faces for PILLS; another
company gets one smiley face for DOPE and four stars for COKE.

A horn sounds as I reach for the handset. It's not from a boat,
lacking both the volume and the low-pitched tone mariners rely
on to cut through dense fog and carry a warning signal miles in
all directions. There are dozens of cars and pickup trucks lining
the parking lot, but none appear occupied. The search ends as a
motor sputters to life and propels a dark-colored pickup truck
out from behind a thirty-yard dumpster limned by seagulls. The
driver either has no sense of smell or sought out the privacy
offered by the dumpster's repelling odor of days-old galley slop,
fish guts and spent bivalves.

The truck heads toward the yellow phone at creeper speed.
The driver waves, but there's no telling who it is. The vehicle is
unfamiliar and the man behind the wheel has left little exposed,
concealed by a beard, wraparound sunglasses and a Red Sox
cap. The driver comes to a stop and motions for me to get in. I
hesitate. He rolls down the window, removes his sunglasses,
taps his left temple with a forefinger that's got a blood blister as
big and as round as a dime and says, At your service, dude.

Hake?

The man smiles, showing two missing front teeth. How-do,
dude?

It's Hake, no doubt about it. The teeth were knocked out of

him years ago during a bar fight at the Harborside Club. The cousin of a dead fisherman who went down with the boat blamed Hake, the sole survivor of the wreck, for causing the disaster. Calling Hake the son of the devil, a freakin' jinx, the man smacked him with the handiest weapon around, a Rolling Rock beer bottle.

It's good to be home, ya-know, Hake says, contradicting the scuttlebutt which had him dead, lost at sea somewhere off the Aleutian Islands, months ago. He was reported among the crew of a crab boat that sank with all hands during a winter storm in the Bering Sea. There was a wire story about the wreck in the local paper and the news elicited mostly shrugs, as this was the fifth instance of a boat sinking with Hake aboard, and because it was his third foundering involving dead crewmates. Nobody followed up on the story and many were relieved that they'd never see Hake again. In their opinion, Hake had two fouls and three strikes against him and, finally, he was out for good, and good riddance.

Been hearing that death stuff some plenty, Hake says, and pulls on a beard which grows dense and long under his chin and goes thin to sparse from his jaw to his ears. In a few months, he'll look like a billy goat.

He returned to New Bedford several days ago, and even though he's flying low, he says, way-like under the radar, he's getting used to people looking at him as if they're seeing a ghost. His landlord, for one, makes the sign of the cross every time their paths intersect. And yesterday, he saw his old girlfriend—Marcia, the one with red hair always in a ponytail. Unannounced, he went to Shaw's Supermarket, where she works in the meat department, and she almost freaked. A tray of pork loins in her hands fell to the floor. He hopes the next time he sees her she'll talk to him. He'd love to take her out to dinner and maybe, ya-know, fuck.

Since he was the sole survivor of a shipwreck, people in Alaska kept nagging him and quizzing him, demanding details of the disaster. How'd So-and-So die? What were their last words? Was there a message for me? Dude, he says, he doesn't carry a tape recorder. He's no encyclopedia. He doesn't even know why he's alive. In fact, he was sure he was dead. When he passed out aboard the life raft, he thought that was it, he'd never wake again. He believed himself as dead as his mates frozen stiff around him on the raft. Later, the crew on the rescue chopper thought they were flying home morgue meat, he says. Then, at the hospital, it blew the doctor's mind when he heard a pulse in the corpse. They ripped off his toe tag, which they saved and gave to him as a souvenir. Hake says he awoke in a hospital room not sure where he was. Heaven? Hell? Limbo? All he felt was an urge for chocolate. That's it, chocolate. He now believes he was dreaming about chocolate while he was dead and adrift and just had to have it to finish his dream. And today, what do-ya know, here he is back in New Bedford. The place has changed a little, but not much, he says.

Hake opens the passenger door and thumps the bench seat. Where to, dude?

Safety first. Shades on, I suggest, fearing that direct sunlight will sear his dilated pupils, which only add to the feral qualities of his pinched nose and closely set orbs. Next, stow the cookware. Atop the hump housing the truck's transmission there's enough evidence in plain sight to guarantee a day in lockup if he's stopped by a cop.

Captain material, you, dude, Hake commends, and begins to hide things. He puts the bottle cap he used as a cooker into the dashboard ashtray, which is free of debris and a reminder that not all fishermen are walking chimneys blowing cigarette smoke. The syringe disappears under the vinyl to the sun visor, slipped into a partially ripped seam and impossible to detect, flap up or flap down. He claims he's going to patent that trick someday and thinks it's amazing how many way-really-good ideas pop into his head all the time.

One thing that impresses the hell out of him, he says, is the delivery system at the powder house on Washburn Street. Until this morning, he hadn't been there in more than three years, but things work same as ever, superslick. It's still open twenty-four/seven. The money still goes into the mail slot. The dope still comes down the drainpipe in the alley. What could be better than that? he wonders. When he was shipping out of Dutch Harbor, the variables of island life used to drive him up the wall. Sometimes it was impossible to find dope; other times there was plenty of fuel around. Always, though, he says, price and quality would bounce like a Ping-Pong ball. Up-down. Up-down.

He double-checks the truck's interior, declares himself clean as Spic and Span, and wants to know what's holding up the show.

My seabag goes below my feet up front and the truck starts rolling, only to stop a few seconds later when a plastic tarp flies out of the cargo bed. Hake spent the predawn hours poaching clams and had to use the tarp because he couldn't find his old wire clammer's bucket. Before he returns to the mud flats, he'll have to find that wire bucket or steal one; he says the tarp had him feeling like an idiot waving a giant blue flag at the shellfish warden. Luckily, no one saw him in the moonlight and he man-aged to uncover $21 worth of clams, enough to buy two dime bags and a pack of gum. Juicy Fruit? he offers. He unwraps a stick for himself and begins to deal with the tarp.

While waiting, I recall the day Hake left for Alaska. Five of us were working on a boat tied to Pier 3 and everyone stopped what they were doing to answer the single blast of a horn from the *Miss Dig,* a ninety-foot scalloper announcing her departure from the dock, bound for Alaska. Hake was part of her delivery crew and the only one aboard who didn't want a plane ticket back to the East Coast. Local fishing boats have been coming from and going to Alaska ever since the late eighteenth century, when city whalers proved the lengths they'd go to in quest of prey. The whaling bark *Beaver* was the first to round Cape Horn (1791), snagging whale after whale off the coast of Chile, and returned with stories of a vast new hunting ground ripe for the picking. In her wake, New Bedford ships made their way to the Pacific and then up the coast, flying the first Stars and Stripes ever seen in South America, California, Oregon, Washington, British Columbia, Alaska and Russia. Again, a few years later (1795), city whalers introduced the American colors to China, Japan, India and East Africa. By the 1840s, the New Bedford whaling fleet of nearly four hundred boats was prowling all seven seas and pushing the limits of the hunt as far north and south as ice permitted.

Before the transcontinental railroad was completed, in 1869, much of the cargo, especially bulky items, headed to the Northwest was routed through city docks and carried onward aboard either slow-moving whalers or speedy, four-masted freighters. Mail was also dispatched aboard whalers, most of it originating within fifty miles of New Bedford: parents writing sons living in the various fishing camps; the home office corresponding with far-flung employees; anxious lovers writing men working in the whaling stations or tending animal traplines. Later, it was New Bedford merchants and the big money they represented, along with the Massachusetts congressional delegation, that greased the ways enabling Secretary of State Seward to overcome opposition to the Alaska Purchase of 1867. Up until the Yukon gold rush of the 1890s, when thousands of dreamers from around the world set up camp in the wilderness, only Eskimos and Russians outnumbered transplanted locals in the Alaska Territory. Come the turn of the twentieth century, the city whaler *Charles W. Morgan* made the last round-trip, New Bedford–Alaska–New Bedford, and closed out the era of blubber. However, the ties connecting New Bedford and Alaska never slackened, with ocean product, as always, entwining the two.

All set, Hake announces, back behind the wheel. The tarp now sits neatly folded under a milk crate filled with junked auto parts. He says he found some clams while tidying up and thinks they're good for eating. He's not sure, he says, because it was too dark out to read any of the signs posted on the beach. Them babies are yours for the asking, dude, he offers, and estimates that three servings are available.

It's an easy gift to refuse, and Hake understands. He won't eat any seafood other than what he catches far away from land. If it comes from anyplace within sight of a shoreline, he'll throw it back. While everyone may know the North Atlantic is polluted, he says, they should also know the Bering Sea is dirty, too. There were times when his boat would cut through acres of floating garbage. Such a sin, that, he says. He certainly didn't add to the mess and never has. Honest to God, he tries to do the right thing all the time, like early this morning. He didn't sell the clams to a fish market or a restaurant. Not him. No. He lost three bucks by going straight to the clam processor, where he's pretty freakin' sure all the product is strained, steamed good and cooked clean of bugs and crap before sale to the public.

Rolling slowly over the speed bumps lining the dock parking lot, Hake bends over the wheel to give it a kiss. Boy, he loves driving. In Dutch Harbor all his land travel was by foot or by thumb. This baby means freedom, he declares, and thanks his cousin Red for looking after his affairs—mail, truck and apartment—for so long. Hake paid the rent and insurance because he knew he was coming back, but he was never sure when. He'd make plans to leave and cancel them to go on one last fishing trip. There was always one more trip, he says, until it really was the last trip, with him dead-n-all.

The light at the intersection turns red and Hake refuses to make a right turn, worried about cops. He also warns that he'll be driving under the speed limit all the way. He has to, he says, because he isn't sure if his driver's license is up to date or even where it is. The last time he saw it was the day he needed a spreader while applying fairing compound to a boat he was working on in Dutch Harbor. Then, dammit, he lost his wallet and everything else he brought aboard a boat soon to sink.

One battle at a time, he says, promising to confront the Department of Motor Vehicles after he finishes fighting with the state unemployment office. Yesterday, he spent five hours there trying to square his change of address. While the paperwork took less than ten minutes to finish, he says, he had to wait around all afternoon before being told to come back another day. There was a problem which nobody could explain to him, mostly, he thinks, because his case officer is dumber than Dumbo, who could at least fly. But no matter how distasteful the bureaucratic process, he'll kiss Dumbo's ass if that's what it takes to get his checks rolling into his New Bedford mailbox. He says he can't poach clams forever and needs cheese until he lands a berth on a boat.

The light turns green and the truck gets under way, heading east. A moment later, Hake shouts, Hold on, and slams on the brakes. Two northbound cars race through the intersection. Other cars and several trucks follow, all in high gear and all, it turns out, seeing green.

Hake's cousin Red told him that the city's crime rate had zoomed and people were now stealing gum off the sidewalk. He wonders if they're also stealing colored bulbs out of traffic lights. While he agrees that such theft is improbable, he still wants to know about the Spanish speakers his cousin said had flooded the town during his absence and were causing all kinds of trouble. Hearing that the same Puerto Rican crew which founded the powder house on Washburn Street continues to run the operation, he nods, says, Them good people, and drops the subject.

Hake keeps his eyes on the steady stream of northbound traffic and chases an itch from ear to ankle, left wrist to pit. Supercharged by a hit of adrenaline, the endorphins in his system racing and tingling every receptor, he appears more alert than ever, ready for anything and, no doubt, among the safest, most defensive drivers in the city. A boat captain once explained why dopers were welcome as crewmen, saying, Junkies are every bit as good as any Johnny Straightlace and better once the count goes over forty-five hundred scallops a day per man. The only thing you have to watch out for is them falling asleep on you. At the moment, sleep is not an issue with Hake.

The traffic is unrelenting and Hake decides to avoid travel on Route 18, preferring to back up and head down the side streets connecting the docks to the North End. The back way meanders through a mostly industrial neighborhood of old textile mills and fish houses, and cops rarely patrol the district. He heads down the two-lane blacktop in second gear, the truck rolling slowly. He says he's searching for a way to begin his story about the shipwreck. He knows the ending, he lived, so it's a happy-like tale.

Red River. That's where he'll start, he says. That was her name. Fishing vessel *Red River.* There were six aboard and it was business as usual on a crab boat until a storm alert came in over the radio. Minutes later, the boat's fax machine spit out a weather map with isobars drawn so close together that Hake could barely distinguish one ridge of pressure from another, a tightly wound storm racing their way. The skipper sounded the general alarm, waking the off-watch to help secure the boat. Hatches were dogged. Pumps checked. All deck gear lashed down. With the throttle wide open, *Red River* sped for land.

Instead of knocking at the door, Hake says, the storm arrived swinging a sledge. A gust of Arctic air sent the boat on her side, burying the rail, the propellor spinning in the air. The gust registered 90 knots on the dial and it wasn't long before the wind blew steady over 100 knots. The skipper stayed at the wheel and the crew gathered in the galley, all the time wondering if the next roll would be the last. The mate opened the hatch and a blast of subzero air sent frozen spume and snow into Hake's face. He yelled, Close the goddamn door, but the wind shoved the words back down his throat and froze them in place. But he says what freaked him and everyone else was seeing all the ice forming on the decks and rails and growing an inch a blink.

Three men suited up and went aft to chip ice; Hake and Kevin took the bow. Hake carried a length of rebar and Kevin swung a baseball bat normally kept on hand to stun the unwanted creatures which sometimes come up with a trap. They used hand signals to communicate and Hake remembers Kevin gesturing like crazy for him to move away. He did as instructed, and moments later an icicle the size of a harpoon broke free of the masthead spreader and landed point-first where he had been standing. Hake says he feels kind of bad, because he never thanked Kevin.

The skipper cleared the decks, deciding it was simply too dangerous a place for crewmen, the handholds ice and the footholds ice and the boat rolling rail to rail. Besides, the men weren't gaining, the ice only building by the ton. Loaded down by all that weight, _Red River_ started to plow through the water, burying her nose and reglazing herself with every wave. They had only one plan aboard the crabber: steer for land. Maybe they could make harbor; if not, the closer they got to shore, the less distance a rescue chopper would have to travel. Hake says he remembers reading somewhere that a man in a survival suit can live up to two hours in slush; without one of the thick neoprene jumpsuits, that man would die of hypothermia in minutes.

They needed speed, but _Red River_ only went slower under the growing weight of ice and became more and more unstable. The horror peaked when a wave broke atop the deck and sent enough water down the stack to drown the engine. Powerless, she was a goner, and the crew prepared to abandon ship. Two survival suits aboard were nearly useless. The skipper took the unit with a broken zipper. Hake was issued the one with punctures and a ripped seam under an armpit.

The life raft was launched without a hitch. The escape route, though, looked hopeless: a ten-foot free fall from pitching deck to bobbing raft, along with a good chance of getting smacked by the hull. The mate jumped first, his aim and timing perfect. Kevin was up next, but he slipped at the rail and landed yards from the raft. Thrashing his arms, unable to kick or stroke inside the ungainly survival suit, he only gave sail to the wind and was out of sight in seconds. Three men jumped as one, holding hands, leaving Hake the last to leap. He says hitting the water felt like hitting glass and swallowing its shards. Immediately, a slushy mix streamed through the holes in his suit. At first, he says, the ice water stung his back and chest like a swarm of bees; then, quickly, his skin went on fire; seconds later, he was colder than he had ever been.

Of the five men in the raft, the skipper was in the worst shape, and the others huddled around him to provide warmth. With their weight concentrated in one spot, the wind got underneath the raft and flipped it over. Again, Hake went swimming and he recalls pushing away something bumping into his back. He thought it was flotsam. Instead, he saw the skipper sail by, the man's mouth wide open as slush swished in and out, his eyes vacant, his arms crossed and frozen in place. On the third attempt, the survivors righted the raft and spread out on its bottom. Too tired to bail, they let water slosh over them.

Afterward, Hake says, he drifted in and out of consciousness, never sure which door was opening or closing on him. He knew he was alive only because of the pain he felt from the cold, because of thoughts of the dead, because Mr. Jones was tearing at his guts. When numbness set in, starting at his feet and quieting the hurt all the way to his brain, he believed himself dead. It all went black, he reports. No angels. No bright lights. None of that stuff.

Hake steers the truck to the side of the road and stops in front of the old Frionor fish plant. He stares at its facade of melon-colored metal sheeting and gulps air.

I wait for him to finish his story and reveal the inner workings of a man at death's edge, adrift, and what preparations, if any, he made for a landing. Shipwreck, though, is always a touchy subject, especially if crewmen died, and survivors sometimes find any piece of the whole far too prickly to handle. Once, I saw a fisherman issue a haymaker in answer to an unsolicited question about a wreck he lived through. The punch was followed by a scathing verbal attack: It's none of your goddamn business, you asshole you!

Among survivors, shipwreck can also induce quiet or gab. Some mariners try never to revisit the disaster; sadly, when they're compelled to speak at a Coast Guard inquiry, the hearing room becomes their torture chamber, each question eliciting pain and every answer racheting up the hurt. At the other end of the spectrum, there are gasbags who love to depict themselves as hot shots and heroes in a drama spiked by varying amounts of their own bravado. The majority, however, accept their experience, warts and all, as part of life at sea. For them, it's important to learn how to duck the next time the sea tries to kill them.

Hake thumps the steering wheel with both hands. Dude, forget everything about ice and storms, *Red River* and all that stuff in Alaska, he pleads. For sure, he wants to dump it all in some garbage can with a lid which never comes off. If he could erase the whole damn episode, he'd be a happier man. After making it through so many different shipwrecks, he says he really-really-like believes he's blessed, a walking, talking lucky charm. Any-

ways, that's how he looks at it, he says. Sometimes, though, he
gets snagged, a shipwreck from his past hooking him like a cod
and reeling him to hell. That's when he sees the faces of the
dead, their features all deformed, as if twisted out of a night-
mare. Lately, he adds, the skipper of the *Red River* haunts him.

Here's the thing, he advises: he left Alaska to escape those
thoughts and those people hounding him for answers to questions he'll never solve. His goal: to start over without any
Alaskan-made baggage weighing him down. He sure wishes
there was a TV-clicker-like-thing able to zap any program which
streams through his brain about disasters at sea. Luckily, he
adds, each new day he feels he can edit out more and more of
the bad and keep the focus tuned on himself, the survivor and
one lucky man. And he can't imagine a better place to get a
fresh start on the day and on life in general than right here, in
front of the exhaust fans to the Frionor fish plant on bake day.
Whenever the factory cooks fish sticks, he says, all his problems
with the world disappear. He then adds, It wouldn't surprise
him, not none, if this is how the Garden of Eden smelled.

Hake keeps swallowing air spiced by sugared bread crumbs
baking in factory ovens. He stops long enough to applaud the
sensation coursing through him. Love it, just-just love it. The
factory owners would agree, but for entirely different reasons.
To them, the air is made sweet by the smell of pennies turning
into dollars, the alchemy occurring as bread crumbs costing a
few cents a pound go into an oven and come out worth their
weight in cooked fish costing upwards of $14 a pound. Five days
a week, the Frionor test kitchens try out recipes calling for more
bread crumbs and less fish.

The perfumed air swirls inside Hake and, apparently, does
magic, causing him to shout, Cured. Alaska is no more. Gone.
He says it's true: all he needs to squeeze shit out of his head is a
blast of air thick with the smell of fish sticks in the oven. Of
course, he adds, no one will ever catch him eating a fish stick.

He knows that the fish part is Alaskan pollock and that it's shipped here by rail in frozen blocks the size of washing machines. After processing, the fish sticks are distributed for sale mostly to institutional customers, like prison systems and school districts.

Hake blows a kiss to the Frionor plant and recalls that this particular spot on the docks has been home to good smells ever since he can remember. Before the fish house set up shop, this was the site of a Quaker Oats distribution center. And when a freighter would come in to unload thousands of tons of grain inside huge, dockside silos, he'd sit as close as he could to the action, dream and smell things for hours on end. He enjoyed his time here so much that he would risk a beating from his father for breaking a house rule: Never go near the docks. Every day he came home after playing outside, his mom would sniff his clothes for telltales of salt-water life and check his shoes and cuffs for signs of muck.

As a cloistered city kid from the West End of town, the child of mill workers who didn't own a car and spent vacations in the yard at home, Hake imagined every inch of rural America to smell exactly like oats and wheat being moved on conveyor belts out of the belly of a ship. When he watched *Gunsmoke* or *Bonanza* or other westerns on TV, he'd plug in what he smelled at the Quaker Oats dock to every scene of pine forests, grasslands and mountains. He didn't get it right until he was twelve, when he left the city limits for the first time in his life on a school field trip. The class visited a dairy farm and milk-bottling operation in nearby Dartmouth, Massachusetts. It was then, while standing in a barn and inhaling the stench of methane, that he realized that there was plenty more to learn and that much of it would most likely disappoint him. The docks, however, were accessible and didn't hide anything from him. There'd be no need to fill in any blanks with bad information if he stuck with the waterfront.

He remembers being fourteen, about to enter high school,

when he shared with his parents his life's ambition: he wanted to be a fisherman. He didn't want to be a fireman or a cop or a mill worker or a rodeo cowboy, only a fisherman. His folks went ballistic. Swearing that no child of his would ever waste his life aboard a fishing boat, his dad beat him raw. Mom tried a softer approach, lecturing her son on the evil which imprisons the docks and all who work there. It was a place of lost souls, she said, home to drink, drugs and awful language, and it would break her heart, as well as his dad's, if he went to sea. Hake dropped out of high school in the middle of his junior year to go fishing aboard the dragger *Melinda-Joan.*

Three fishing boats slip in and out of view behind the Frionor parking lot, all of them circling the upper harbor while waiting for the swing bridge to open. Two are scallopers and one's a clam boat, and Hake misnames them all. Once corrected, he chastises himself for making an error common among greenhorns. Before he went west, he swears, he could identify every boat in the fleet from miles away. It's something most veteran deckhands can do, able to put a name to a distant silhouette based on what they note at the sheer and transom, along with more obvious markers at the masthead (antennae array) and wheelhouse (porthole positions).

Momentarily embarrassed, Hake doesn't want word of his mistake to leak out for a week. After that, bugle on, dude, he instructs. By then, eight days at the most, he won't care; hell, it will be funny. His reentry into the docks will be complete, he projects, old friendships tight as freakin' ever, and he'll be able to name boats twenty miles away. He further predicts that he'll score a crewing job within a few days. It has got to happen, he asserts, and shares why: Because he's unbeatable on deck, the best fisherman anywhere, New Bedford included. In fact, he feels that he may have to turn down job offers. That means, he adds, that he must find out fast-like-soon which boats are bringing home the most cheese. With his skills, he believes, it'd be a shame for him to ride on a dog.

Back on the road, slow-motoring to the North End, Hake keeps an eye on the docks fronting a clam house and Eastern Fisheries, the largest scallop processor anywhere. He counts four boats blowing smoke, ready to cast off and join the other three boats circling the upper harbor. Digging into his past, he matches action to purpose: It must be slack tide or way-close, and about to go ebb, and skippers want those extra two or three knots a fair tide gives them outward-bound. Thank God, yes, it's all coming back to him, he says. He's starting to remember the local tricks of the trade. Alaska, that's something he has to forget. New Bedford, he only has to remember. And he thinks it's a million times easier to remember things than to forget them.

Next year will be Hake's twenty-fifth as a full-time fisherman. His job has taken him halfway around the world, from Rockland, Maine, to the Panama Canal and north to Nome, Alaska. Now, though, he feels it's time to settle down. Maybe start a family. He's forty-two years old, almost forty-three, and the wanderlust in him got up and went someplace else all by itself. Anyway, even if he wanted to keep moving, he's not sure where he'd go except broke. He says it's hard times everywhere for fish and fishermen and even worse for itinerant fishermen. As both the fishery and the national fishing fleet shrink in numbers, and as more and more boat owners demand drug tests before hiring crewmen, Hake deems the traveling fisherman a vanishing species. He figures it won't be long before they're extinct; three years, tops, he predicts, and then no more.

For almost three hundred years, 1700 to 1990, anchorless deckhands were a common feature of the American fishery and formed their own band of nomadic fishermen. Usually highly skilled, they were ringers for hire and would go port to port, boat to boat, as restless as the ocean, their possessions fitting inside a seabag. They didn't pay taxes, avoided census takers, and never worried about an address for mail, neither writing letters nor expecting them, all their business done in cash, and being solo acts, they had no partners or exes or lovers to deal with. The ocean was their home, boats merely different apartments in the same building, the entrances and exits unchanged. A few kept moving out of necessity, determined to stay a step or two ahead of a bounty hunter or a court order, but most took naturally to flying with the wind in pursuit of money and fish.

In the 1970s and 1980s, Hake says, there were dozens of New Bedford fishermen like him, all of them bouncing from boat to boat, rarely staying aboard for more than two trips with any captain. During the winter, they often dipped south to work the waters off Florida and Alabama; in the fall, they'd head to Maine to cash in on shrimp season; and no matter what time of year, they'd go to Jersey and the Chesapeake to mix business (clam fishing) with pleasure (gambling at Atlantic City). Back then, he explains, when a skipper felt the urge to go out, he'd round up his regulars and fill any empty bunk with either a fisherman passing through the port or a local free agent. However, once federal regulations kicked in, limiting catch size and time at sea, fishing trips became carefully planned productions, with skippers and owners leaving as little as possible to chance and organzing the boat around one steady crew.

When he heard the *Miss Dig* was Alaska-bound, Hake claims, he was the first to sign on for the delivery job, just as eager to leave New Bedford as he was to taste salmon and crab. And because he came with the boat, he had a secure berth on her for the first few months of her new assignment. It gave him steady work and coin and allowed him to meet locals as an equal rather than someone looking for a job. If he had arrived on a plane and walked to the docks in Dutch Harbor, he believes, he'd still be looking for a berth.

What surprised him, he says, is the god-awful-like reputation

of New Bedford among Alaskans. When he was meeting owners and captains, he always introduced himself as a fisherman
out of Cape May. The deceit never bothered him; hell, it only
helped him find work. Although dozens of New Bedford fishermen spent time in Dutch Harbor while he was there, Hake
never met any and could never understand why city men were
commonly depicted as extremely capable fishermen who were
also genuine pirates, thieves, drug addicts and mutineers.

He recalls one conversation he had with an owner of a crab
boat. He says the crabber was going crazy, blaming out-of-state
fishermen for destroying the Alaskan fishery. Of all the rogues
and misfits to do damage, the crabber said, none compared to
that scum bred in New Bedford. He believed city men were all
alike: first, they lie; next, they rob you; afterward, they screw
your daughters; last, before they leave, they hook all the kids in
town on dope. Hake thought it was so outrageous, he laughed.
But no, the crabber was serious and went on and on, swearing
he'd shoot any New Bedford man approaching his boat, kids or
house. Hake didn't say another word, but he knew the guy was
full of shit, because no New Bedford fisherman would ever give
up a single bag of dope, especially not to some kid.

Hake claims he's happy not only to be home but also to be
parked in the best port in the world for a deckhand looking for
work. It's all in the numbers, he says. He explains: With nearly
three thousand active fishermen in the city, he figures, job openings are as certain as sin in this harbor. Guys die all the time.
Others get sick or hurt. And every day there are fishermen waking up and saying, No more of this crap, so they retire, too tired,
too beat up, too something to fish anymore. Plus, he adds, there
are always fishermen getting busted for one thing or another or
both and forced to do time in jail. For all these reasons, besides
his skills and obvious worth, he's expecting job offers by the ton.

Another benefit of this harbor, and it's part of the numbers,
Hake says, is the sheer size of the waterfront industry. The

port's hundreds of boats and dozens of processors, scores of brokers and international buyers, all of that mass ensures the industry's longevity. Dude, New Bedford will be the last place working when they finally put up the big sign, saying, It's over. No more fish. Yes sir, it's going to end right the hell here.

Hake expands on his number theory, this time zeroing in on the advantages offered any port hosting jumbo-sized boats. In other harbors, an eighty-footer is king, but in New Bedford they're viewed as average citizens. And as the fish stocks keep shrinking, only the big boats will be able to give chase for hundreds of miles and endure the vagaries of offshore weather. While the city is home to the world's largest scallop fleet, there's also plenty of diversity within the rest of the pack, with large draggers holding licenses to hunt groundfish, along with net boats and long-liners with tickets to pick up middle and surface swimmers. These attributes, size and variety, allow New Bedford to absorb repeated hits from federal regulators. Hake says Washington can and does dent and damage things here, but they won't break the package until last call. Meanwhile, those same hits are creaming the industry's small fry, boats under sixty-five feet and ports that are home to fewer than twenty draggers.

Hake doubts that there will be either commercial fishing or fishermen left in Provincetown in a couple of years. The only fishing you'll see there is in the paintings they sell on the wharf, he says. He's just as glum about the future of ports like Gloucester, Point Judith and Portland, positive they'll be empty of fishing boats in five to seven years. He expects they'll go the same way as Newport, turning their waterfronts into lah-de-dah centers for tourists and yachts.

His predictions are shared by many watermen, their future controlled by a government that prefers an ocean farmed by a limited number of large boats owned and operated by a select group of corporations, just like in forestry and mining. Such a configuration would simplify management chores and make police duty easier and far more cost-efficient. It would also mean better record keeping, offering up more reliable data on harvests and reserves. As well, it would facilitate deal making, doing away with tiresome public meetings and lengthy review periods, and replace day-to-day head bashing with quiet partnership. Already, New Bedford corporate fleet owners are eyeing the next generation of fishing boats, extra-jumbo 150-footers. They believe the government will soon allow boat owners to gang up licenses and apply the quotas of three or four boats to one huge ocean machine. This, of course, would precipitate another shakeout and the small fry would be the first to go.

Son-of-a-bitch. Hake reacts to the sight of a cop directing traffic up ahead at a construction site. Reflexively, he swings the wheel and takes the first left, Wamsutta Street. As the truck loops around the block, it stays inside the shadow cast by Wamsutta Mills, the city's first textile factory. When it started operating in the 1840s, few people thought it would last more than a year or two; in the early 1900s, the complex was churning out more than 100,000 yards of cotton goods a day, and most people presumed the mill would stay open forever. Today, each doorway at the mill, and there are scores of them, carries the same signage: FOR RENT/SALE. Hake points to Building No. 3 and says that's where his dad used to work. When the mill closed in the late 1950s, its looms sent south for use by cheaper, nonunion labor, his dad found work at Morse Cutting Tools, where he stayed until it, too, was gutted. After that, his dad stayed unemployed until he died. Hake doesn't doubt the coroner's report ascribing death to a malfunctioning ticker, but he's not sure whether the old man's heart broke because of his son being a fisherman or because the guy couldn't find another job.

While the mill parking lot is empty of all but the usual urban detritus—bald tires, three-wheeled shopping carts, broken glass and litter—more and more vehicles appear, all of them parked at the curb. Damn, Hake says, realizing that the unemployment office is nearby and the truck has entered its aura of disappointment.

The old state unemployment office in New Bedford is a dreary-looking place, a low-slung building weighed down by brownish stucco and a flat roof. It sits all by itself at the edge of the old railyard, and it will remain neighborless until the city or the federal government comes up with the millions needed to detoxify the former depot. In the 1970s, just before the feds banned the sale of PCBs, local manufacturers stockpiled large amounts inside railway tanker cars parked on the tracks, where they leaked tons of the oily, colorless material. When the government later deemed PCBs probable carcinogens, a cyclone fence went up and the property joined the list of other city-owned lots off-limits to its citizenry.

The unemployment office won't open for another forty-five minutes, but there's a line outside the door. Hake guesses the number of people at twenty-something and labels everyone a go-getter. Usually, the early birds are purposeful, wanting to get in and out and finished with state business to start their cash-paying jobs on time: landscaping, house painting, cleaning assignments and nanny work, among others. Fishermen won't start appearing until eleven a.m., Hake says, adding, If they're not working on a boat, they're not working, period, and they'll sleep late.

Like most fishermen, Hake's no stranger to the dole. The vagaries of the industry—from fish migration patterns to oil spills to sudden changes in regulations and quotas—sometimes leave fishermen no other choice. For deckhands with a couple of kids, the biweekly check can mean the difference between treading water and drowning in debt. In 1990, New Bedford scallopers landed twenty-two million pounds of meat; four years later, the catch was a miserable two million pounds. And from

1993 to 1996, while the feds instituted rescue plans, unemployment around the docks hovered near 30 percent. During those down years, Hake says, nearly every deckhand spent time in a line at unemployment.

The truck passes the state building and Hake suddenly straightens behind the wheel and whistles a few bars from a rock anthem. Tomorrow, maybe, he'll deal with his change-of-address form. Certainly, he won't be visiting the office today; he has a nice buzz going and wants to keep it purring.

Near a defunct marina there's a clear view of the upper harbor and boats on the move. In the distance, the swing bridge starts to open; a buzzer sounds, lights flash and a barricade goes into place, halting road traffic moving on an east-west axis across the harbor and freeing marine traffic to power north-south. Seven outward-bound boats keep to the starboard side of the channel and head for the gate in the hurricane dike; at the same time, three scallopers returning home from a fishing trip enter the upper harbor and make way for the Eastern Fisheries dock to unload. With scallops fetching record prices, and with no end in sight to their steady climb in value, Hake says, he can identify every boat fresh from the hunting grounds: Dude, all of them are named *Treasure Ship*, full, they are, with pearly-white gold.

On average for the past few months, a crewman's share aboard a scalloper has been worth nearly $5,000. Hearing that number, Hake decides to speed his reentry into dock life and look for work in the morning. His resolve strengthens when he hits on the obvious: if he finds a berth right away, he won't have to deal with the unemployment office. That's the ticket, he says, and cheers himself on: Hake calling Hake the best knifeman who ever lived, owner of skills unparalleled in history. Yes sir, none better, never.

His hot air blows unchecked. In fact, Hake can say anything he wants about himself. Fishermen may be comfortable with lies and cozy up to fraud, but they can just as easily turn nasty when some bubble they float is burst in their face. Normally, the gas travels undisturbed, fishermen understanding that they all share a knack for the superlative and the fantastic; sometimes, though, challenges are issued and the four-flusher will often defend himself by changing the subject to war. Around the docks, false pride is as much a motivator of action as money and a bigger troublemaker than just about anything.

Finally, one block from my home in the mill, Hake opens up to something beyond himself, asking, How's the old gang doing?

Silence ensues. What old gang? He never ran with any crowd. Hake steered away from groups, a loner who appeared just as content to be by himself as others were to leave him alone. It was common to see Hake walking the docks unescorted and driving down the street with no passengers. Aboard ship, he rarely lingered at the galley table and wasn't known for small talk. Out on the town, he'd avoid upsetting waitresses at bars by taking a table alone and would instead stand near the counter, eyes on the TV; in restaurants, he'd either sit by himself or with his girlfriend or mom, but never with other fishermen.

I first encountered Hake a few months after anchoring in New Bedford. It was at a memorial service held at the Seaman's Bethel for three fishermen who'd gone down with the boat on that date a year earlier. A huge crowd had gathered and spilled out the doorway; I managed to get inside, where fishermen were standing shoulder to shoulder, and made my way to a pew occupied by only one person, Hake. A friendly hand reached out for my arm from the bench behind the near-empty pew, and a man said, Don't sit there. He elbowed his neighbor to make room for one more in their line. Throughout the service, hundreds of fishermen glared at that one man surrounded by emptiness, the sole survivor of the wreck; at the end of the service, the families of the deceased mariners led the procession out of the bethel and one mother paused when she came abeam of Hake to curse him in Portuguese. Hake's eyes stayed at his feet. He left the bethel through a side door.

Unbothered by the silence, Hake repeats his question and this time answers himself: Yeah, sure, the old gang's doing great. In Alaska, he tried to keep up with hometown news by reading the trade magazines and tracking the rebound in the scallop fishery. Oddly, he identifies Pete-the-Pea as his best pal in the old gang. He says he and Pete-the-Pea had way-radical times together on scallopers in the mid-1980s, when the harbor was one with excess. After they'd pull in from a fishing trip, he says, the two of them used to double-date and go through a mountain of coke before spending the rest of the night fucking their brains out. God, dude, it was great, them times.

Reminded that Pete-the-Pea died at sea in the late 1980s, lost in the same shipwreck which he and one other crewman somehow survived, Hake grunts, chases an itch running from his left ear to his right nipple, and doesn't speak again until he stops at the mill loading dock, the freight elevator being my front door. Sure you don't want them clams? he asks.

It's no to the clams, but thanks for the ride. As I search for my keys, packed inside a sock somewhere in my seabag, Hake steps out of the truck and takes hold of an unwanted clam. He rubs it like a pitcher taking hold of a new game ball, winds up and throws it at a gull at the end of the parking lot. Wobbly in flight, the clam veers wildly off target and partially explodes, spraying juice as it hits the riprap leading to the estuary. The seagull, sent flying by the sudden action at ground level, circles and eyes things on the wing; a free meal for the taking. The bird goes for the broken shell and Hake takes aim and fires again. And so begins the game, with Hake down one as the bird snatches the small dinner plate and scoots. Soon, though, other gulls appear, all of them squawking and sounding a dinner bell answered by nearly every shorebird within sight of the mill.

Seven clams later, the air is thick with gulls of different kinds: herring gulls, Bonaparte's, laughing gulls and a few great black-backs. Hake keeps at it without a single strike and, perhaps trying too hard, he throws out his arm. Whatever zip he had fades into a slow pitch. The lobs allow the birds to catch a meal on the fly, and dozens of them stay on the macadam, almost taunting him as they jockey for position as the next target. In the end, he could be feeding squirrels.

As I close the freight elevator door, Hake runs out of ammunition and yells to the birds, That's it. That's it. The birds return his noise and quickly desert him.

Jesus, will-ya, speak of the devil: your man, there, at two o'clock, Captain Creedon says, indicating a lone figure moving awkwardly down Union Street. The man is burdened by a gimp and two extra-large coffees from the Dunkin' Donuts at the corner. With his hands gimballing the coffee cups, he's forced to bend his neck and use a shoulder to quiet an itch behind his ear. Creedon hopes the guy trips and goes out like a light.

It's Hake. His beard is a bit longer at the chin and the limp is new, but everything else about him—clothes, hat, sunglasses and an itch demanding attention—appears the same as before. Creedon and I are positioned on the other side of the street and Hake doesn't notice us sitting on a bench by the *Catalpa* memorial, set back from the curb amid dead brown former greenery planted, the sign in the dirt says, by the New Bedford Historical Society. We watch Hake head for the docks and turn the routine into dangerous business, crossing Route 18 against the light and limping as he goes. Creedon says he can see it now: Two big old trucks are going to pancake your man, there.

Hake safely navigates the passage, prompting Creedon to

wag his head in disappointment. Hake turns toward Pier 1 and disappears behind a crane used to lift clam cages out of boat holds.

They say he's cursed, your man, there, Creedon reports.

Do you believe it?

Every word and more, he answers. Your man, there, is a jinx, a real Jonah. And they don't come worse than what's inside that parcel, return address: hell. Creedon has seen his share of Jonahs around the docks and knows what he's talking about.

Creedon started fishing when halibut sold for pennies a pound. In all those years of water work, he says, he has encountered every sort of fish and fisherman in the Atlantic. The good. The deformed. Some trash. Some valuable. The dangerous. The harmless. If it lived in the ocean, he handled it. And he knows Hake's pedigree: Lucifer's boy. Your man, there, he says, creates death and it's his fate to live while others around him die.

Good God, no, Creedon exclaims, he would never go out with that sort of equipment aboard his boat. Even with a gun to his head, he'd have to answer, Pull the trigger, mister. There's no way he'd ever jeopardize his crew and his boat by allowing a Jonah aboard. He makes the sign of the cross and expands the Trinity: In the name of the Father, Son, Holy Ghost and common sense, he'd never knowingly take on a jinx.

Around the docks, Creedon is considered an elder of the tribe, never messed with and usually obliged. In another setting, he'd be known as a professor emeritus in the art and science of fishing. Many of his former deckhands are now captains and he's the one they reference during a storm, be it man-made or natural, and they employ his methods when confronted by hurricanes or fights among crewmen. His scallop boat, the *Sea Hound,* was launched in 1964 and is now a contender for honors as the best earner in fleet history.

If the weather's decent and I'm in port, we team up on the

last Thursday of the month to shoot the stars, working sextants to calculate position the old way and relative to a greater whole. It keeps hard-earned skills from going rusty in the age of GPS; plus it's a chance for me to spend a few hours with Creedon while he plumbs the universe and reports on what he sees. As he works the sextant's vernier scale, precisely lowering some heavenly glow to his horizon, its fire barely kissing the line at the end of the sea, he opens up his insides. He says the process of shooting the stars connects him to forgotten gods, Ra to Apollo, and brings to mind old meanings and even more timeless mysteries. Citing his Irish roots, he claims it's the Druid in him talking. Today we're supposed to decide where we'll go on our next date with the stars.

He says he didn't know Hake's parents, other than that they were mill people and stayed far away from the docks for a good reason: Hake's grandfather on his mother's side left a black mark on the waterfront any daughter would want to avoid. Hake's grandfather's name was Dabs, and Creedon recalls him as a broken piece of work who never found the right glue until he went facedown in the harbor. That man, he says, didn't catch fish as much as chase them away, forever jamming a winch or fouling the net, one bad set after another. He'd make dock and go home to beat his wife black and blue. He'd kick any dog he saw. And he probably did horrible things to his daughter. He wasn't a boozer or a dopehead, Creedon says, just a twisted fuck.

Whenever he saw Dabs, Creedon would change directions, not wanting to breathe the man's air or have their shadows cross. He feels the only good thing Dabs ever did was to die young, dead before reaching forty. The body was found floating alongside Pier 3, and Creedon is convinced Dabs was a victim of his own making. His theory: Dabs was so off-balance from the malice he carried that he tripped over himself and fell from the dock, and so weighed down by sin and anger that he couldn't climb any of the ladders bolted to the pier.

Another of Creedon's theories, this one the genesis of the modern-day Jonah he'll refer to only as your man, there: Dabs's rotten seed skipped a generation and flowered inside Hake, filling him with punk and sponge where others carry a soul. For some reason, either by design or through laziness, Hake never sought to make repairs. Then, during his first shipwreck, when a fire ate the boat and forced everyone aboard to jump willy-nilly into the drink, separating Hake from the others, Hake went low, not high, while seeking assistance. In his prayer, he pleaded for his own life without thinking about his mates. And that sort of SOS, Creedon says, is something only the devil answers. During their meeting, a deal was cut and Ole Scratch gained another son.

Creedon says there's no other explanation, no possible nothing to answer why boats go down when Hake's aboard and why men always die near him. If anyone doubts his words, he has proof, and he pulls out his wallet to show a picture of two smiling and attractive women in their late twenties encircled by seven kids. In the background and blurred, two men, Creedon and his brother Martin, are running toward the women and kids. The wallet goes back into his pocket, and he says he always carries a sad story with him wherever he goes. Martin, he adds, died because of a Jonah.

That jinx's name was Cusk, Creedon begins. And that man harbored an unlit hole inside of him as big as China, same as your man, there. This Cusk washed up in May 1950. He talked big, this Cusk, saying he was the best fisherman anywhere. He claimed to have worked on boats in the Chesapeake and out of Maine and Novy ports, too. He got his chance to prove it all aboard the *Anna Maria,* the queen of the fleet back then. Martin was first mate.

The trip went well until it was time to grease the pull-back pulley. Cusk, as new man, got the job and climbed the main post. The instant he touched the pulley, the wire snapped and gear went loose and lost. Out came the grappling hooks and the men started trolling for the lost steel. At the stern, Cusk yelled, Got it. A second later, the engine quit. What Cusk got was the propellor and the line wrapped itself so damn bad, it jammed the shaft and almost blew the transmission.

The skipper and Martin volunteered to cut away the line. It was dangerous work and they knew it. A nasty swell was running and gave the boat a bad case of the rolls. Worse, she was hobbyhorsing something awful, her bow and stern going up and down like a yo-yo. They had to time their dives just right to stay clear of the stern as it came down off a wave same as a fly swatter weighing thirty tons or so. Each man stripped to his skivvies, said a prayer, and jumped in, a safety line tied to the waist. They took turns attacking the wrapped line, one diving while the other caught his breath. It wasn't long, maybe ten minutes, before Martin and the skipper were drained by the cold water and two crewmen prepared to take over. Before those men finished their prayers, Cusk jumped overboard, shoes and all, saying he was going to help. He landed inches from the men in the water and his splash sent them under the counter at the worst possible time. Fast as can be, the men on deck pulled on the safety lines and hauled in the dead. Their necks broken. A sad, sad, horrible thing.

Creedon pauses, his hands in fists, each knuckle white, and puts his eyes on the sky. He refocuses and continues: The crew threw Cusk a life jacket and dealt with the bodies, wrapping them in canvas and putting them on ice in the hold. But there was no time to grieve. They had a job to finish and men to take home. While two crewmen finished chopping away that bastard line, another deckhand stood at the rail with the boat's harpoon, ready to spear Cusk if he came near the workers or tried to touch the boat.

Once the prop was free, the engine running finest-kind, it was time to deal with Cusk. Each of those men had seen enough killing in the war to last them forever, so they threw Cusk a towline attached to a raft they hammered together out of pen boards. It was up to Cusk to hold on and ride the raft or let go anytime he wanted. Under no circumstances was he coming aboard. They wanted the jinx behind them at all times. Somehow Cusk stayed on that raft like a barnacle. As they neared dock, they cut the line and made him swim the last bit to land.

Cusk. Cusk. Cusk, Creedon repeats. No one saw him come ashore and no one saw him leave town. Dozens of men hunted for him and never picked up his scent, as if he didn't exist, ever. The next anyone heard of him came from Point Lookout or Moriches, somewhere on Long Island, when another boat went down. She snagged her net in an area fished forever without any trouble, and instead of the wire breaking it held far beyond specs, stopping the boat in her tracks and burying her rail. She sank in seconds. Three men died. Cusk lived. And he snuck out of port before anyone there could catch him.

Later, some Newfies pulled into the harbor and told their own stories about Cusk. They said he started making trouble on the Newfie west coast as sternman on a lobster boat. She sank. Her skipper died. He lived and went to the east coast, where he got aboard another boat. She lost power in a blow and smashed on the rocks. Seven died, but not Cusk. The Newfies said there was money in a bank account for Cusk's death. A group of them had put cash into a pot to get that jinx; New Bedford and Long Island also chipped in until there was $5,000. That was big money back then, but the measure of hate went higher than that.

One more jinx landed here in 1958, Creedon adds. This one called himself White. A wiry fellow, this White, with rat's eyes and missing most of his left ear. Said he was the King of Cod, the best fisherman in the East. He got a berth aboard the *Double-Bee,* which went down near the hundred-fathom line. A boat out of Point Judith, the *Mary Something-or-other,* found the debris and one survivor, White. He was floating atop five life jackets and wearing another one. The men who rescued him asked all the right questions: Where are the others? What happened? When? Not one word came out of White, not even thank you. The others thought he had gone mental, the wreck so bad it had short-circuited his brain. They also admitted that he scared the bejesus out of them. Those rat's eyes and his silence spooked them bad.

At the dock in Point Judith, they gave White some money and clothes, same as you'd give any shipwrecked sailor. He shook his head no when asked if he wanted a lift to the hospital, and they left him to sit at the pier and keep staring at the water. Phone calls were made, the life jackets identifying boat and home port, and within ninety minutes, New Bedford men were on the scene, looking at charts and salvaged gear, looking for White, too. Where'd he go? The whole port joined the hunt, but couldn't find any trace of the man. Some believed he entered a tunnel under some rock and returned to hell, his job over. Creedon, though, says he never hanked on to that theory; instead, he was sure White kept traveling, a Jonah's work never done.

His stories of jinxes over, Creedon stands. Slowly, some of the redness which had blossomed on his neck and cheeks begins to fade. Twice, he starts to speak and stops before a word is fully formed. At last he points to Pier 1 and says, Your man, there, has a much tougher job than Cusk or White. He explains: Today, the boats are stronger, better-built hulls and engines. Everyone carries a radio transmitter that broadcasts a Mayday around the world. There are rescue jets and helicopters and more Coast

Guard boats than anyone wants to hear about. And the safety gear actually works. In the 1950s, life rafts were jokes that came with foot pumps. It's just harder to kill a fisherman nowadays, that's all.

Creedon moves a few paces to inspect the plaque commemorating the 1875–76 voyage of the whaling bark *Catalpa*. She left New Bedford under charter to the Fenian Brotherhood and sailed for Fremantle, Australia, where she acted as the getaway boat for six Irish rebels who had busted out of Her Majesty's prison. Captain Anthony, master of the *Catalpa*, defied gunboats and sailed to New York City, which feted the six escaped convicts with a parade down Broadway. Creedon says he comes here to touch the plaque for good luck before he leaves on a fishing trip. Today, he rubs the marker.

His eyes fix on something at the bottom of Union Street. His neck stiffens and his thick, calloused fingers, crazed by lines of stubborn grease, curl into fists. Your man, there. Nine o'clock.

Still limping, and still carrying two extra-large coffees, Hake makes his way toward Pier 3. Two fishermen walking in the opposite direction see Hake and take evasive action. They swing wide of the hazard, as if sighting the signal flag U, a four-box pattern of red and white advising all approaching vessels that they're heading into danger.

It's either distance or havoc, Creedon remarks, convinced that confrontation would defeat the best intentions. Let fly a fist or a knife and Scratch wins, he says. And since it's impossible to punish what's already rotten, he doubts there's such a thing as justice when a jinx is part of the mix. He continues: Look, if you take a wormed-out board and smash it against something good and solid, what do you get? Lots of unwanted pieces of wormed-out board and a mess of worms in search of a new home.

Creedon decides on a time for our monthly date to shoot the stars and prepares to leave. A factory technician is due within an hour to fine-tune the *Sea Hound*'s new radar system. The sales-man at the Fish Expo guaranteed the unit would outperform Superman. Creedon, who always carries a tape recorder when quizzing salesmen, wants to see the proof. He still owes 20 per-cent of the price tag, and if the tech can't pinpoint the bird feeder in his backyard, something Superman could do in a flash, he won't be cutting a check today. In fact, he intends to hold back payment until the machine demonstrates comic-book pow-ers, as promised, or until the dealer agrees to extend the unit's warranty by two years.

Instead of walking down Union Street, Creedon takes the long way to the docks and heads for the overpass at Elm Street. Without complaint, he'll endure the extra distance and stair climbing to minimize the chances of crossing shadows with Hake. Watching him go, I find it impossible to imagine a more superstitious group of workers than fishermen—except, of course, Irish Catholic fishermen. Since no one has yet demystified the ocean, its push and pull on man, mind and planet as inexplicable today as ever, modern seafarers abjure science and, instead, accept traditions and oblige shibboleths dating back to Jason and the *Argo*. All of this is reinforced on the job, every sailor an oracle ready to discern and interpret the signs floating in the air and the sea. Not nearly as much intuited as learned from elders, shipboard prognostication is a twenty-four-hour-a-day affair, and the more potent a sailor's delphic powers, the better his chances for survival.

Around the harbor, Thursday is usually the slowest day of the week, with many fishermen following the Norse tradition never to launch a boat or depart on a long voyage on the day dedicated to Thor, god of wind and war. Like the U.S. Navy, which has never christened a ship on a Thursday, many mariners are unwilling to risk the wrath of a short-tempered god known to torpedo any major initiative not done in his name on his day.

More arcane, yet just as provocative, are the variety of omens and their meanings, with every seaman referencing his own personal library. For example, a single black-colored bird flying over the bow before the boat reaches the hurricane dike is all it takes to send Captain Whiting back to the dock. He considers the bird a messenger from his deceased father telling him, Go back, you dang fool. Check all systems. The crew never argues; once, years ago, the bird saved the boat: when the men returned to the dock, they discovered the batteries were about to melt or explode due to a faulty voltage regulator.

Old Man Olafson won't go down a dock if he sees a cat. It doesn't matter what kind of cat or what color it is, he recognizes it as a jinx and will postpone departure until one second after midnight. Captain Shad insists on talking to his brother in Texas before heading out to sea. Last year, when his sibling took the family to Africa on safari, Captain Shad didn't leave port during their month-long adventure. Unabashed, he explained why: Good God, man, you go one way for eighteen years without big trouble and only a fool would change course. Captain Gold refuses to leave the dock unless he's wearing his good luck cap, the one he wore at the hospital when he saw his oldest son for the first time. Twenty-two years later, the hat is held together with duct tape and comes out of a drawer in the navigation table for a few minutes while the dock lines slip free. Like the priests of ancient Rome who used the eating habits of sacred chickens to advise fleet commanders on battle plans, Captain Cherry relies on his wife's chickens for divine instruction. A certain hen has to lay an egg on the scheduled day of departure or he simply won't go to the fishing grounds.

Crewmen are just as superstitious as skippers, but they don't get to exercise their beliefs as much as the boss. Even so, when Mark Nursemen sees yellow socks on anyone at the pier, he heads straight for home, sure that the sock wearer can ruin his life with one look of their evil eye. His grandfather was run over and killed by a trolley operated by a driver wearing blue serge and yellow socks, and he says both his mom and his grandmom drilled the fear of yellow socks into his head as a kid. When Bobby Four Legs—so named because of his abnormally long arms—is at sea on a Friday the thirteenth, boat captains expect to run shorthanded for the day, knowing Four Legs won't touch a knife or venture beyond the galley until 12:01 a.m., Saturday.

Captain Blowzer describes himself as a practical man and claims there's not a superstitious bone in his body. Indeed, he'll swear to that fact while kneeling in front of a dozen nuns holding rosary beads blessed by the pope. He insists that it's common sense which compels him to abort a fishing trip if a crewman loses a bucket overboard, because, he says, anyone with brains in their head and sea time under their belt knows when you lose a bucket, you'll soon lose a net or a drag. That would mean the loss of ten to fifteen grand in gear, and it's his responsibility as captain not to let that happen. Likewise, if some numbskull trims his toenails while the boat is under way, it's up to him as skipper to race back to shore before a storm hits. The worst, he says, comes in green: God forbid you ever find a green suitcase aboard, because if it and its idiot owner aren't kicked off the boat, it's shipwreck for sure. He reacts to facts. Not fantasy. Not stupid superstition. He believes there are rules at sea and only fools wanting trouble steer around them.

Blowzer grew up on the docks and remembers his father and his uncles telling stories about Cusk and White, Jonahs and the power of the black holes inside them, about sea monsters, ghouls and ghost ships, about scallops weighing a ton or more and cod longer than limousines, about whirlpools and water spouts that suck boats down or up, never to be seen again. Whatever doubts he had as a teen regarding these stories are gone, he says. After thirty years of fishing, he's now used to the impossible happening right in front of his eyes. While he has yet to spot a two-thousand-pound scallop or a thirty-foot-long cod, he's convinced they exist somewhere in the deep and, someday, he expects to encounter them. Indeed, he has witnessed enough weirdness at sea to verify the entire marine catalog of cryptozoological sightings dating back centuries. If a fisherman reports seeing a mermaid, he wants to hear every detail and will steer for that spot every chance he gets. He dreams of meeting a tailed beauty and yearns to swim off with her to see all that has been hidden from him for so long. If people think that's crazy, he says, it's fine by him; he wants the mermaid for himself.

During night watches, Blowzer says, ghosts usually keep him company. Sometimes he can make out their faces; other times he can only feel their disembodied presence: a hot breath on his neck or pressure on his hands and shoulders. A ghost by the name of Peter is a regular visitor, and while he's not much of a talker, Blowzer recommends him as one hell of a good listener. He says he keeps asking Peter to introduce him to the spectral partner of New Bedford's most famous sailor, Joshua Slocum, the first man to sail single-handed around the world. Slocum left port in the mid-1890s aboard the *Spray,* an old oyster boat he rebuilt near the harbor. He credited much of his success to his companion, an apparition who introduced himself as the former navigator aboard the *Pinta,* and helped guide Slocum through hurricanes and uncharted reefs.

Monsters? They're more common than ghosts at sea, Blowzer says. They appear all the time in nets and rakes and dredges, and the scariest one he ever saw was a pogy with six dicks, two vaginas and an extra tail coming out of an eye socket. He caught it in Massachusetts Bay, near the old dumping grounds used by Boston hospitals for their toxic waste, including extracted radium implants and spent machine fuels from pre-1970 radiation procedures. The most common frankenfish he finds are those with multiple sex organs and misplaced appendages. Once he caught a nine-eyed fish, and he says he has thrown back hundreds of critters with three eyes or two tails. Year after year, he says, the ocean freak show is getting more and more twisted, with ever-creepier-looking fish in ever-greater quantities. Slowly, as rust eats away at the containers of the toxic junk dumped into the ocean before the Clean Water Act (1972), all those promises from the 1950s and 1960s of better living through chemistry are revealing themselves as nightmares.

Like Creedon, Blowzer won't refer to Hake by his given name, insisting on calling him either Mr. Jinx or Jinxy, sure that Hake's power is so dark that it swallows light. If Hake was ever to touch him, he'd seek a cure in a bottle of Clorox, and after washing his hands many times in the disinfectant, he'd go to a church to rinse everything in a font of holy water. With Mr. Jinx aboard, he predicts, a boat would only catch monster fish before some freak storm or accident sank the boat and all hands minus one, Jinxy.

Convinced that anything can happen at sea, Blowzer accepts as fact that there's a fisherman walking the docks with no insides, the man's soul and all his vital organs removed and already on broil. He, too, believes that Jinxy cut a deal with the devil to save his own, wretched life, and after hearing Creedon's theory on the genesis of a modern-day Jonah, he says it makes perfect sense to him.

Blowzer reaches inside his shirt, dipping below the neckline to extract a crucifix on a gold-colored chain. He bought ten of them the other day and got his mom to take the lot to a priest for a blessing. He gave one to each of his six crewmen and keeps the other three in his pocket for extra protection. He paid only three bucks apiece for the charms and claims the chain is so cheap, it will snap at the pull of a baby's pinkie and poses no threat as a choker if snagged by boat gear. At the same time, he reckons, each crucifix is worth millions as a protector from Mr. Jinx. The guy's the devil, you know, he says.

For the next week, Hake spends much of his time either limping
from dock to dock or sitting off to the side waiting to ambush
an unsuspecting captain walking to his boat. Each confrontation plays out pretty much the same way: Hake pitches himself
as the best fisherman in port and requests a job, and skippers,
not wanting to upset the jinx and be cursed for it, tend to keep
things polite. No one, for instance, turns their back on Hake or
tells him to fuck off, the usual response to an unwanted job
applicant. Instead, they listen to his spiel, their eyes roaming to
avoid being drawn inside Hake's black hole, and end up lying,
saying they'll call if a berth opens up. Before it's time to say
good-bye, each captain makes sure he's two-handing some tool
or piece of gear, anything that prevents him from shaking
hands.

Creedon steers the *Sea Hound* through the gate in the hurricane dike and heads for open water beyond the glare of city
lights. He doesn't want any artificial glow interfering with his
astral wandering at the end of a sextant. As he steers, he calls
Hake a piece of rotten work. Your man, there, he says, has the
entire waterfront on high alert and it's boom time for collar
wearers. Creedon knows for a fact that at least one dozen boat
owners have called in priests to bless their boats. He gave the
monsignor $100 to do the job on the *Sea Hound,* and he hears
that the going rate is now $150.

While there are usually a few captains in the fleet always glad
to buck the current and sail in zones of contrary winds, Creedon says there's not a one willing to deal with your man, there,
and he pegs Hake's chances of finding a job at zero. He doubts
the odds would be much better if Hake was unencumbered by
his past and was known as an easygoing, competent deckhand.
His gimp—caused by a tumble down the entryway stairs at

home—is reason enough not to hire the man. In today's climate chilled by lawsuits and court dates, Creedon says, boat owners and captains have to refuse anyone who's visiting a doctor or should be visiting a doctor. From experience, they're fearful of future testimony identifying them as the cause of injury and pain.

The waterfront was pretty much free of lawsuits until the 1970s, Creedon recalls, and he says chumming for lawyers back then just wasn't done. In those days, he adds, men with peg legs or one-handers were welcome aboard if they could do the job. And if a man was injured on a boat, the skipper kept him on for as long as that man wanted to stay. Starting in the mid-1970s, though, Creedon says, the dam burst and lawsuits started flooding the docks. Meanwhile, lawyers' offices took root at the water's edge and greased the ways, making it slick and easy for fishermen to launch claims. At this point, Creedon thinks, suing a boat owner is like bowling or some other sport most people try at least once. Indeed, he estimates that more than half the owners in the fleet have been sued at least once by a former crewman. While most of the cases were eventually deemed meritless and dismissed, they ate up time and money. Those lawsuits that did make it inside a courtroom usually cost the boat owner at least $5,000, the normal deductible in boat insurance policies, plus legal fees and bumps in future insurance premiums.

That's not all your man, there, is up against, Creedon adds, because he sees four or five men a day looking for a berth. Most are experienced pros from small fishing ports on death watch, and they come to New Bedford in a final effort to find a crewing job before trading in their shucking knife for a tool belt and a hammer. The vast majority will never get a gig, but a few will return home better off than they left. They'll buy large quantities of dope at cut-rate city prices and make a killing from resales to their hometown crowd.

Creedon pulls back on the throttle and lets the engine idle in neutral. He checks the radar and likes what he sees on the screen: no traffic. As if to chase away thoughts of Hake, Creedon marvels at this morning's jump in scallop prices, up 20 cents a pound. All it took was a phone call from China placing an order for ten tons. Finally, they want the good stuff for themselves, he says; he expects China to start buying more New Bedford seafood than Japan or Korea. Meanwhile, of course, cheap fish imports from China, including substandard scallops, will probably kill the net boats and the groundfish industry.

With only a red-colored bulb lighting the wheelhouse, Creedon takes hold of his sextant, a Weems & Plath model he bought in 1943, when he was a twenty-year-old junior officer in the merchant marine. Exiting the wheelhouse, he faces north and locks on Polaris to get a fix on latitude. Andromeda, which lies a bit to the east, is suitably partnered with Perseus, who killed the whale sent by Poseidon to devour the Ethiopian princess; Hercules lies to the west, and to the south is the sparkle of Vega, which, in another twelve thousand years, will replace Polaris as the polestar. Cloudless, the sea a treasury of small curves, it's a perfect night for astral observation and Creedon thinks we should watch the whole show. He'd hate to miss Venus taking the stage a few hours before dawn.

Come the weekend, Hake stops visiting the docks and doesn't reappear. It's not something people gossip about or research, fearful that the slightest breeze might bring him back. Months later Creedon calls with word that Hake landed a job aboard a Florida-based cruise ship. Your man, there, he says, is now after bigger game.

Five

WHALEBONE

THE FREIGHT ELEVATOR OPENS at the loading dock and the voice of a young Elvis Presley swells. He sings of hound dogs in full cry on the trail of love. Pearl, the city's leading lady of swag, acts as DJ and minds the truck radio, the volume on high. Pearl's companions are on another kind of high, dancing crazy-like, sweat-popping contortionists with their limbs moving whichever way Elvis inspires: up, down, all around.

Shake a leg, Sailor, one of the dancers shouts, her words barely audible over those of the crooning, canine-loving King.

There are three dancers, all female, and the one urging my participation is on the far side of Pearl's pickup truck. She keeps her back to me, preferring to shimmy while eyeing the mill's 138-foot-tall smokestack. Quite a dancer, she has long brown frizzy hair that appears elasticized as she leaps and twists and squiggles, coiling and uncoiling like so many strands of shock cord. Her ample curves at the midsection and tattoos of butterflies floating above twin strands of barbed wire inked above both ankles cinch the identification.

It's Char, as in Charlene. She's the manager of the Button Club, a lesbian bar hard by the docks in the city's North End. The bar first opened for business in 1817 and is probably the old-

est cat joint anywhere still breathing. Because of this, Char considers herself as much a trustee of the past as a modern busi-
nesswoman hitched to new ideas and ways for making coin in
the grog trade. Her latest promotion has proved a rousing success: every Friday night the Button Club hosts the Whalers' Ball,
and anyone dressed as a nineteenth-century sailor, tart or pirate
gets one free drink—if, that is, they manage to make it through
the door before the place fills to capacity.

Hop-hop, Sailor, Pearl now commands. She stands next to an
open truck door and within easy reach of the radio. Her feet are
flat to the macadam, but she's rubbery from the waist up, snapping her fingers and working her shoulders in time to the music.
Today, her hair color is red, at the border of orange, and not the
jet-black she usually favors. As always, though, day and night,
she's wearing enough makeup to fill every divot, line and scar,
and it glazes her face with a near-porcelain finish. She calls it
the baby-doll look and says she can pull it off only by using a
Japanese-made foundation formulated for geishas. She's creaseless up top, her hands the only reliable gauge; I recently guessed
her age at fifty-two, and she thanked me.

C'mon, hop-hop-hop . . .

The music swirls through me, juicing connections. Like the
others, my body starts gyrating to an energy source that came
online in the 1950s and forever changed the social dynamic of
America. Previously, the nation's power construct had been a
lopsided affair involving patricians and plebes, Protestant blue
bloods and the rest, the space between them only beginning to
project voice and volume in the 1920s. But after World War II, a
surging middle class was on its way to authority, a new power-
house, vital, oozing confidence and endowed by battlefield sac-
rifice, its message broadcast by irresistible agents of change.
Like Elvis. Like TV and its enabler, Madison Avenue. Like Wal-
ter Reuther and organized labor everywhere.

For this city of steeples, smokestacks, masts and union halls, the new power construct offered unlimited visibility ahead and a thick, welcome fog astern. For the first time in a generation, the city could uncouple itself from pessimism and trouble. The gloom had taken up residence in 1928, when thirty-five thousand workers went on strike and did battle with Pinkertons, cops, mill owners and hunger. The strike ended just in time for the onset of the worst economic downturn in history. Then the Hurricane of 1938 hit and sent the city reeling yet again. The pain continued as World War II whisked away many of its men and women to the front, while those left behind worked at cheap rates to churn out GI goods: parachutes, uniforms, hot-weather boots, webbing, truck tires, tank treads, artillery shells and rope.

NEW BEDFORD, SUNSHINE CITY read the headline to a story in the local paper about the city economy in the early 1950s. Even though the air hung like a curtain, thick with smog from smokestacks, the future looked exceptionally bright: area manufacturers were running triple shifts and advertising for more workers. Factories had retooled assembly lines, government contracts done and over with, and were feeding a consumer pipeline with all manner of goods, from bedsheets to engine transmissions to golf balls and cardboard boxes. Paychecks hit record levels, and job benefits rose with the tide. Nearly forty thousand people held union jobs, nearly half of them women in the textile and needle trades, jump-starting a new phenomenon: dual-income families at high-end hourly rates. When Elvis first appeared on the *Ed Sullivan Show*, the entire town paused to take in the action. Those at home clustered around living room TVs; night-shift workers altered their break schedules to catch the singer on screens set up for the occasion in lunchrooms; and crowds gathered outside the windows to TV and appliance stores, which dotted the cityscape.

The flow of money into workers' hands meant a surge in

building permits, and in a few years, 1954 to 1962, hundreds of acres of farmland were transformed into thousands of home lots featuring modern-day castles in the form of single-family ranches. By the mid-1960s the construction trades couldn't keep pace with demand, and one after the other, unions opened their membership lists to newcomers without a relative or friendly contact on the inside. Pearl saw an ad placed by the electrical workers' union calling for trainees and decided that was for her.

Pearl, the daughter of a waitress, her father unknown, camped outside the union hall in the middle of February and spent the night to ensure her number one spot in line. She said if it wasn't for Elvis on the radio keeping her warm by making her dance, bob and think about the morning, she would've frozen to death in air so cold it turned white men blue. Come opening time, union big shots were so impressed by her effort that the president of the local processed her application and guaranteed her a place in the union's training program.

She earned her journeyman's license while working for the Lavoise Brothers, a large outfit specializing in commercial work. Her first assignment lasted almost a full year: revamping an old textile mill for its next life as a production center for the manufacture of electrical capacitators. Five years later, her master's license in hand, she hung out her own shingle and quickly established herself as the electrician of choice among the city's gay and lesbian population.

Life veered after she rewired a downtown jewelry store and joined in on an insurance scam concocted by the soon-to-retire store owner. In exchange for instructions on disabling the silent alarm with one thrust of a crowbar, she was promised 10 percent of the loot from the staged smash-and-grab. The insurers paid out $90,000 for lost inventory worth one-third that amount; the two men doing the danger work split $10,000; and Pearl got the shaft, her partner passing off flakes, fakes and flawed stones as her take. Kindly, a local fence bought her share for $125 and loaned her a textbook from the American Gemological Institute's correspondence school.

Pearl laughs whenever she relates that story, claiming it was the best screwing of her life. It introduced her to a new and lasting love. She took the correspondence course and followed up with more schooling, apprenticing to a major dealer of swag based in Providence. She started fencing goods on her own in New Bedford and, eventually, with her expertise in burglar alarms, along with a growing reputation among shifty brokers involved in the Rhode Island jewelry industry, she gained the attention of Raymond Patriarca, who hired her as a consultant to the family business, among other titles. Although some of that work dried up after Mr. Patriarca was arrested, she remains as busy as ever. Last month she went to Antwerp before flying on to India; she returned via Dubai and spent a few days in Antwerp again before landing in New York to do more business.

Rarely these days, and only for good friends and lovers, will Pearl buckle her electrician's belt. She says she misses the trade and would gladly do more electrical work if only her knees weren't shot and her hips weren't a mess. All that early ladder work—up and down hundreds of times a day, with hours spent on a single rung either feeding or pulling No. 6 wire through tubing fastened to mill ceilings—haunts her come every cold snap and downpour. Today, though, it's warm, a cloudless day on broil, and Pearl appears both limber and painless. She once said that Elvis and Jean-Paul Belmondo were the only two men who could make her want to feel young again. However, almost any female under forty does the trick.

The song ends and, as one, the dancers cheer: Wooo-doggie. They gather near Pearl and catch their breath, leaning up against the truck or each other and readying themselves for another round of dancing. More oldies now. Go, Elvis, go, Char cheers. She wants to rock.

The radio station doesn't cooperate and airs an advert for an electronic gizmo, featuring a pitchman's voice as efficient and emotionless as the product itself. Pearl groans and spins the dial in search of music from the past. Nothing sampled appeals to her and Char takes over at the controls. Slowly, Pearl walks to the loading dock, signaling for me to stay put.

I had expected to meet her alone and on business. She had called earlier to arrange things, saying she needed some help in selling a piece of scrimshaw which came her way. Whalebone, she explained, wasn't her thing and she only knew two people who could advise her: me and Secretary Ricker—Hosea Ricker, that is, but she died last year. Of course, the piece is for sale and if I didn't want to buy it, she was offering a hefty commission for a hookup with someone who would.

Got-a can-zel, Zale-or, Pearl slurs, stopping short to fiddle with her dentures. When the upper plate slips, words tend to slide with the enamel and twist every *s* into a *z*. She hates when this happens and squares herself to the mill's brick facade while fixing things, a bit embarrassed, but mostly angry at herself for needing repair work of any kind.

Char abandons the radio to help her friend, putting a shoulder gently into Pearl's back and recommending a plan of corrective action: We got-a strangle that dentist of yours someday soon. She then turns my way and tries to finish what Pearl began, saying, We just dropped by to tell-ya, Later, ya-know, for whatever you-twos got cooking. So, Sailor, park shit on the back burner. Ain't that right, Pearl?

Pearl nods, unable to say anything with her mouth full of fingers.

Don't let it get to-ya, hon, Char consoles. In a louder voice, she adds, We're having us a pah-tee. Yes, oh, yes, we is. A pah-tee. Going to leave here and make us some fun.

Char gets a jump on things as she slips a hand inside the

waistband of one of the other dancers, neither of whom I know. She uses her free hand to pull close dancer number two.

Adjustments complete, the *s* sound reestablished, Pearl wishes death to her incompetent dentist. She steps closer and lowers her voice to a whisper, not wanting the others to hear, and apologizes for the sudden change in plans. She sets a new date to meet and promises it will be worth the trouble and wait. She says the scrimshaw is the finest piece of whalebone she has ever seen, perhaps the best of its kind anywhere in the world.

Pah-tee. Pah-tee . . . Char starts to chant and works both hands inside different waistbands. Yes, in-dee-dee, she broadcasts, we got to get it on. We got us orders from up high and there be no saying no to that power. Char goes on about the collision of luck and desire that brought them all together. It happened minutes ago, she says. They all met downtown, at the Magazine Store, and found each other in front of the triple-X racks. They had all gone there separately and Char believes a freakin' force out-a this world preordained their meeting and left them no choice but to pah-tee. They're now headed to Pearl's house on the eastern shore of the harbor to oblige destiny and re-create some of the poses featured in the magazines they bought. Wanna peek-a what's to come, Sailor?

Pearl orders the partygoers into the truck. *Vamanos, muchachas. Vamanos.*

They pile into the cab, with Char's lap doubling as a seat for the fourth rider. Pearl adjusts the rearview mirror and notes my reflection in one corner of the silvered glass. She puts two fingers to her lips and plants a kiss on my mirrored image. Later-later, Sailor.

The truck rolls across the mill parking lot, its sound system building volume until Aretha Franklin's voice booms. Char adds to the decibel level as she leads a sing-along. A man filling a tank at the Shell station next door stops working the nozzle to join

the choir and ogle. Once the truck motors up the hill and out
of sight, he returns to his task a bit happier, his head bobbing
as he continues singing: R-E-S-P-E-C-T. Find out what it means
to me . . .

I take a seat at the edge of the loading dock, eyes on the estuary five empty parking spaces away, and think about Pearl and
antecedents, about history and legacy, product and process.
Hosea Ricker pops to mind and stays there. She was the last of
her kind, her people arising out of an earlier time in New Bedford, back when the men were chasing blubber around the
world and the women ran the show at home.

The noise level at home suddenly spikes. A horn in the mill
parking lot starts honking at the exact moment the phone starts
ringing: Pearl's in her truck at the loading dock and calling on
her mobile phone to hurry things along. Shake the lead, Sailor,
she orders, and lays into the horn. She has scrimshaw to peddle
and she doesn't have all day to do it.

At the loading dock, Pearl barks, Git-nnn. Her command followed, she calms a bit and indicates why she's in such a rush,
gesturing at an unmarked cop car idling at the far end of the
mill parking lot. Most likely, the officer is cooping; however,
there's a slim chance that he's actually on surveillance duty. The
mill fronts a combined on- and off-ramp to the interstate, making its large, unlit parking lot a favorite meeting place for drug
dealers and buyers. Pearl says the last thing she wants to do is
wait around long enough to get caught up in the middle of
some stupid bust that appears on TV.

A few months before, the TV show *Cops* filmed an episode
here. In the video version of events local cops stand vigilant at
the city gates and intercept trouble before it can sow despair. We
were on the perps like sand on the beach, one cop told the cam-

era. Word on the street says something else: a deliveryman on a night run pulled into the parking lot and mistook a sleeping undercover cop for a dope buyer from Boston. He went to make the handoff, and when the interior car light went on, each man was as startled as the other. Realizing it was a cop, the mule dropped the package (two kilos of high-grade heroin) and ran for the blackness edging the shoreline. The cop didn't give chase—there was a problem with the logbook to correct—until a K-9 squad arrived. The deliveryman was never caught, and to date the case remains open.

Breakfast is my treat, Pearl announces, and heads for Dunkin' Donuts, where she orders two large coffees and one dozen jelly sticks. The leftover jelly sticks are destined for Char, who, Pearl says, goes ape over them. She drives on, wanting to show off the scrimshaw while downing breakfast at the end of Ark Lane, where there's an earthen pier built in the early 1800s. It offers a spectacular view of the harbor and, best of all, she notes, cops rarely visit the area. She grew up near the pier and has always considered it her sanctuary. No boat has tied up there for more than fifty years and it's off the beaten track, perfect, she says, as a place to be alone.

While idling at a red light, a jelly stick in one hand, she confides that she lost her virginity on Ark Pier to a boy named Chet. A real sweetie, she recalls. A Pole and from a family of ten kids. They lived on the first floor of a triple-decker a few houses from where she grew up. She says, they were both seventeen when they figured it out, fucking, that is, and did it atop a flat boulder close to the water. It wasn't anything like she had imagined or had seen in the movies; that sort of excitement came a little later, when she met Cora and, at last, felt her insides melt. That was the end of boys for her, she reports, and she became a player in a whole new ball game without any balls in the way.

Through Cora, she met a new crowd at New Bedford High.

Up to then, she'd thought almost all the kids in her senior class were Catholic prudes and hadn't gotten beyond French kissing. She got that one wrong, she says. While she can't come up with the exact number of gay classmates, she considers 15 to 20 percent a good guess. After high school, she knows for a fact that lots more came out of the closet. Tomorrow, if she were to go to a class reunion, she'd expect to find 25 to 30 percent flying rainbow colors.

Several blocks from the pier, Pearl slows the truck and points to a patch of brown grass near a trash can in a small park that hardly anyone uses. She says it's where her old house used to sit. Up until the late 1960s, the entire area was thick with triple-deckers; it had been a Polish district ever since the end of World War I, when war-weary immigrants left Eastern Europe and headed to New Bedford for jobs in the mills and toolworks. In those days, with the factory stacks belching soured, black air twenty-four hours a day, she says, this is where kielbasa and cabbage overpowered the stench of rotten eggs.

Most of the neighborhood was bulldozed to make way for the interstate and a six-lane spur meant to speed traffic from the city's South End to the federal project. In the end, the highway spur was routed blocks away from here and city officials covered up their mistake—issuing demolition orders before the engineering studies were completed—by building a small park. Had she owned a death-ray machine at the time, Pearl says, she would've vaporized city hall. Until that dream machine arrives, she hopes everyone involved in bulldozing her old neighborhood dies and comes back as a fly. Last summer she bought an electric bug zapper, and it pleases her to think that each sizzle she hears is some jerk from the past.

Carefully, Pearl steers between two giant rocks set at the end of the macadam and parks halfway down the earthen pier, the bumper pointed south and aimed straight down the harbor. It's hazy out, the sun at a low angle and yet to heat things up. The water is calm. Fuel barges, two tugs and five fishing boats are on the move. And the smell of low tide competes with that of coffee, jelly sticks and cigarettes inside the truck. Without ceremony, Pearl hands over the scrimshaw, which is rolled in a blanket of Bubble Wrap, and puts a loupe on the dashboard. Feel free, she says, motioning at the loupe, and returns to her breakfast.

Once the Bubble Wrap comes off, the prize fully exposed, initial shock is replaced by timidness. Pearl is quick with advice: Just pick it up any-old-where, for Christ's sake, Sailor. It's only a dildo. And the last she heard, they don't bite.

But this is no ordinary dildo; it's a dream reified. Indeed, the dildo is a museum-quality piece of art; both the sculpture and the drawings on the sculpture achieve greatness. It's also quite intimidating, remarkably lifelike and large enough to challenge any thought of the well-hung. However, it might be difficult to find a museum willing to buy and exhibit an eleven-inch dildo bearing scenes of piscatorial warfare and sapphic love.

Usually, scrimshaw enters the marketplace in rather pedestrian and predictable configurations. The shaved pieces are often turned into kitchen gadgets, like pie crimpers and serving forks, or made into ornaments, like buttons and handles for canes. Similarly, those adorned with drawings mostly depict static maritime scenes of a boat and/or a whale. Less common is the work of whalemen who used their free time aboard ship to pump out erotica, shaping whalebone into dildos or producing pornographic etchings on sperm teeth. These so-called naughty nauticals were either produced for immediate shipboard pleasure or stowed in a seabag and gifted to a land-based partner as something to remember Himself by while he was away on his next whaling voyage. Pearl's dildo is one of those rare naughty nauticals, but it's in a class by itself.

In hand, the dildo is uncomfortably accurate, veined in all the right places and delicately ridged. The column is easy to grasp in one hand but impossible to encircle, its circumference at least ten inches. It sprouts from a base the size and shape of a Northern Spy apple and carries a shallow curve all the way to its tip. The helmet is polished smooth as glass and, remarkably, is dimpled like a golf ball along the rim, two aspects Pearl swears every girl appreciates. At the top of the helmet, smack-dab in the middle of the crown, there's a blowhole emptying a channel which the scrimshander somehow drilled through the core. Pearl calls it the Juicer, and she suspects there was once a rubber ball connected to the base for squirting lubricants or warm water into the vagina or rectum. There are no chips or dings, the piece obviously well cared for by its previous owner(s). The color of the bone is perfect, a honeyed glaze over ivory.

The artwork is presented on the vertical, in two panels which run the full length of the column. The scene following the dildo's upper curve depicts a mother ship midway between victory and disaster. Off the bow, a harpooned whale is under tow by oarsmen, the sea calm and streaked in blood; under the dead whale, a giant squid appears to taunt the corpse of its enemy, its tentacles scratching the whale's bottom. Meanwhile, off the mother ship's stern, the leviathan is shown victorious, vengeful, too. The water roils around a giant sperm crunching one attack boat in its mouth, splintering the wood and impaling crewmen on its teeth. Its anger unabated, the whale is about to slam down its tail atop another attack boat, the crew of six drawn bug-eyed, their mouths agape and arms outstretched, helpless.

The second panel on the inside curve is all about pleasure of a certain kind. The drawings offer up three pairs of mermaids in warm embrace. Each duo is kissing, their tails entwined, and everybody has one hand cupped around her partner's left bosom, while the other hand works a dildo at an erogenous zone. The mermaids' long hair, cascades of curls that billow like spinnakers in a stiff breeze, and the fish scales drawn below the waist are especially well done, each involving thousands of difficult curves and all precisely spaced. Under the loupe, no mistakes are evident, not one awl scratch out of place or fudged. Moreover, the loupe reveals tiny details, like the emblems of the Petticoat Society (two spouting sperm whales under crossed harpoons) on each dildo and intricately etched facial features on the crewmen at the rail of the mother ship.

The look of the mother ship telltales her age: the rigging, sail plan, cut-in boards and rudder design are all typical of New Bedford and Nantucket whalers in service between 1795 and 1810. Likewise, the attack boats carry the lines of Nantucket and New Bedford craft from around the turn of the century. Unfortunately, there's no name board on the whaler, and the only colors flying are signal pennants used to communicate with the harpoon boats.

Pearl sets the price: Two sticks and we got us a deal, Sailor. The scrimshaw is worth many times the asking price, but there will be no sale today, my limit a measly $250. Hearing this, Pearl is disappointed. Holy Christ, Sailor, the door won't never open to that kind of hello.

She mounts the sculpture on the dashboard, leaning it against the glass in front of the steering wheel. She studies it while finishing a jelly stick and soon makes a decision. Sold, she says. She's going to keep it for herself. She thinks it will look fab in her living room. Recently, her business has been doing great, she reports, and what the hell, it's time to treat herself. She intends to display the dildo in the bookcase on the east wall, where she expects the light from a sunset to splash the piece with fiery colors, and once it's warmed up—who knows?— maybe she'll use it to stir up some fire of her own making. No matter what, it'll be one hell of a conversation piece. Char will flip, she says, and smiles.

Understand this, she adds: as soon as the dildo becomes part of her home, the price goes up-up-up. By the end of the week, she predicts, it will cost three sticks to take it away; after a month, she'll want four sticks, maybe five. Years ago, after the motorcycle accident which took out most of her teeth and scarred her face, she says, she added a new rule to her rule book: Never shortchange something or someone that's part of daily life. Crap and people come and go by the tons, so when one thing sticks around, you best hold on or sell high-high.

Oh, Jesus. Pearl reacts to the sight of someone approaching the pier and stows the dildo out of sight. It's a man in his fifties wearing an unbuttoned shirt over wool pants and sockless at his black oxfords. He carries a fishing pole and a five-gallon plastic bucket. Since it's dead low tide, he's either late or very early for prime-time fishing.

What's biting? Pearl asks, leaning out the window and waving.

Don't much matter, the man answers.

He steers wide of the truck and heads for the remnants of a nearby marina. It was built years ago by members of a Portuguese sports club out of materials rescued from dumpsters or found along the beach. Last winter the ice in the harbor made a mess of things, pulling out most of the tree branches used as pilings and crushing some of the floats made out of scraps of plywood laid atop strings of old Clorox bottles. With repairs yet to be made, the marina is useless for boats and, as it turns out, dangerous to visitors. The fisherman almost tumbles into the drink when he steps on a float and the whole platform squirts northward under his weight. Carefully, he walks to the far end of the float and sets up his gear. As he casts, his voice sends one word our way: Yes.

Pearl leaves the truck to sip coffee atop a slab of granite set back from the riprap. It's the size of a pool table and Pearl says this is where she goes whenever she needs an answer, which is why she named the slab Decision Rock. She calls it freaky, really, that in a city where disappointment is as common as Boston Red Sox caps, the rock has never let her down.

As a kid, Pearl and her pals would pretend to be either customers or employees of the namesake to Ark Lane. Although her mom, like every other parent, refused to talk about the original Ark, Pearl says all the kids knew the score and thought it cool that the world's most famous pleasure ship from 1818 to 1850 was anchored near their homes. In a neighborhood where nearly every room in every triple-decker was decorated with a crucifix or religious picture, she found both hope and relief in the fact that the entire city ward was once in service to sin and wicked fun.

In its heyday, the Ark was a one-stop shopping center for pleasure of all sorts, offering booze, drugs, gambling, music, circus acts and, of course, sex—women, men, girls, boys, animals, dwarfs and, famously for a few years, hermaphrodites. The Ark was the creation of Titus Peck and the source of a fortune which, by 1845, made him one of the richest men in the world not born to royalty. He made one whaling voyage and hated every minute of it, calling the sea an integral part of nausea. However, his time aboard ship served him well, spawning the idea of a land-based pleasure palace specializing in dream fulfillment for sailors. To start, he bought the remains of a wormy whaler and towed her toward the estuary. Where she went aground is where he built the earthen pier, almost one mile from the main docks, and got to work dollying her up.

By all accounts, the Ark was the star attraction among a galaxy of other hot spots catering to the thousands of sailors passing through the New Bedford docks every year. During the day, these mariners put on a wild show for the locals, who'd gawk at the weird-looking aliens on parade, like Tashtego and Queequeg, men wearing beaver hats in July and carrying shrunken heads at the belt and showing tattoos on cheeks and arms, fingers and hands. But at night, the good citizens of New Bedford steered wide of the water's edge and its hooting and hollering, fighting and partying, thugs, villains and everyday sailors. No place scared the virtuous more than the Ark and twice, in 1826 and 1828, the God-fearing answered calls issued from pulpits around town to burn down the Ark. Repeatedly, Peck thumbed his nose at the prims, rebuilding his joint in weeks and always making it bigger than before.

Titus Peck, Jesus, you got to love a guy like that, Pearl commands, impressed by any self-made individual who bucked the establishment and made gads of money in the process. She recalls Peck's name carving out a big space in her brain when she was twelve and happened on three men digging holes in the earthen pier in search of Peck's fortune, which he supposedly buried on Ark property. Other treasure hunters followed, including Pearl and all her chums, and her search hasn't ended. Someday, she says, she's going to get hold of a land radar unit like the one she saw on TV being used by archaeologists in Egypt.

Rising from her seat atop Decision Rock, Pearl reaches for a pebble and tosses it into the water, making a wish in concert with the splash. Try it, Sailor, she urges. It once worked for her.

She remembers the magic: She was just starting out in the swag trade and a friend from Providence called with a favor. He had a client spending the day in New Bedford who'd just remembered it was his anniversary and had no time to shop. The client would meet her where she wanted at four p.m., and Pearl suggested Ark Pier for the hookup. With the clock at five twenty-five, her patience shot waiting for some jerk who'd forgotten it was his anniversary, she picked up a pebble and launched it, along with a wish for the person to show up inside five minutes or to drop dead and never bother her again. Two minutes later, Pearl says, up drives a big black Caddy and out steps Mr. Patriarca, all sorry for the delay. The don bought a diamond necklace from her, and once business was done, she mentioned her skills with alarms systems and related a few tales about Titus Peck and the Ark. The next day Mr. Patriarca summoned her; she left that meeting with a new job in what she deems an A-one organization.

One last wish. Pearl goes for a rock the size of a deflated soccer ball and, using both hands, lobs it into the water and broadcasts her wish: Let Peck's treasure be mine.

The loud splash makes the fisherman on the float turn to investigate. Pearl waves and again asks, What's biting?

Nothing good, he answers, and returns to the business in hand.

Back inside the truck, Pearl repacks the scrimshaw, taps the box of remaining jelly sticks, and says, Dollars to doughnuts, bet you, Secretary Ricker once owned this dildo. She believes it's just the sort of high-end item Secretary Ricker would've inherited, used and sold for peanuts before she died. The dildo goes into Pearl's bag and, along with the sound of a zipper closing, she says she never liked Secretary Ricker. Not one bit. Pearl claims the lady was so condescending it was hard to believe and even harder to stomach. And if there's one thing she hates, it has got to be some hoity-toity snotnose thinking and acting like they're better than her for no good reason. The lady was broke, Pearl adds, and in more ways than one: penniless and nutso and absolutely horrible to work for.

According to Pearl, by the time I first met Secretary Ricker—a few years before she died of a heart attack at the kitchen table—anything of value inside her big house on the hill actually belonged to an antiques dealer from Boston. Likewise, the house and property had been sold in the mid-1980s to one of the city's biggest powder dealers wanting to launder cash. Pearl says the buyers got great buys, but there was a catch: nothing could be moved or changed until Secretary Ricker died. Thinking there'd be a few items worth buying at the estate sale, Pearl and Char went; but she reports that all they found was a crying shame: two card tables topped with knickknacks, jelly glasses and tattered designer clothing from the 1940s and 1950s.

More than twenty-five freaking years, that's how long Pearl says she knew Secretary Ricker. While uncertain when the Ricker money went dry, she guesses it was before they first met. She had been called to the big house to do some electrical work and instead of writing a check, Secretary Ricker paid the bill with items out of a hallway closet. The barter netted Pearl two golf club bags, each made from the penis of a sperm whale. She still owns and prizes them and figures they were worth ten times her bill twenty-some years ago; today, she wouldn't sell one for less than ten grand. In the old days, Pearl adds, that house of hers was crammed with the greatest stuff, and most of it was sold for quick cash and way-way-cheap.

Pearl went on to buy numerous pieces of jewelry and art-work from Secretary Ricker, including a seven-carat diamond ring and drawings done by a Dutch master. She insists she paid the lady good money for everything, but admits it wasn't close to market value. Again and again, Pearl says, she told Secretary Ricker to work through an auction house, not a fence. But no, not her. The lady wouldn't hear of such a thing. Every sale had to be hush-hush, and Pearl estimates the cost of stupid pride in the hundreds of thousands of dollars.

While Secretary Ricker was pleasant to guests, store clerks and people she passed on the street, Pearl swears she was as nasty as can be to the hired help. Ask anyone who ever worked for her, Pearl challenges, and they'll tell you that every day with Secretary Ricker was a Pepto kind of day. All she ever heard from Secretary Ricker were commands and corrections: change your hair; do something about your awful clothes; stand straight;

your fingernails need attention; don't speak until spoken to; and on and on like that. Pearl says it used to drive her crazy-mad, because, Christ Almighty, this is New Bedford, not Atlanta before it burned.

During her entire life in New Bedford, Pearl says, the only richies she ever met were drug dealers, shady lawyers and a couple of people who hit the Lotto. They all treated her as a fellow citizen and it didn't matter if she was selling them gems or working on the wiring in their basements. By the time she was on her own, the era of blue bloods in town had ended. With few exceptions, Secretary Ricker among them, the old aristocracy had decamped by the late 1960s, unnerved by local race riots and put off by the rising power of the middle class in city affairs. They moved to the burbs or out of state, and today the only palpable evidence of swells ever having lived in New Bedford is their old mansions. Some were converted for use as apartments or offices for lawyers and doctors and dentists; a few, like Secretary Ricker's house, were bought by drug dealers; and others were abandoned and left to rot, becoming kindling for arsonists.

As best she can figure out, Pearl says, Secretary Ricker was either born too damn late or lived too damn long. At the Button Club, she confides, people used to call Secretary Ricker Dino Dyke, the last from the old herd on the hill. Certainly, Pearl adds, she heard Secretary Ricker talk about that group of hers, the Petticoat Society. Everybody did. And maybe the stories were true. All she knows is that it involved dead people from a world she's glad went to pieces on the blue bloods. While Pearl was at every march and rally for gay rights, she never once saw Secretary Ricker in the crowd, and this makes her conclude one thing: the lady was never there when it counted, so to hell with all her gab as Missy Important to the movement.

Pearl fires up the truck and honks the horn to exchange waves with the fisherman. Good luck, she yells, and heads for the loading dock at the mill. As she drives, she talks nonstop about the most beautiful dildo in the world.

Without knowing why, most folks around town addressed Hosea Ricker as Secretary Ricker. It was never ma'am or Miss or Hosea; instead, without fail, it was Morn'n, Secretary; Hell-o, there, Miss Secretary; Evening to-ya, Secretary Ricker. And because people who didn't work for her liked her the same way they liked anyone they considered filthy rich who drove a car like theirs, ate in the same restaurants as they did, and wore rather smart, finely tailored outfits a bit frayed at the edges, they never challenged her title. She always imagined it had a certain workaday ring to it that no one would ever question and she appreciated the way it distracted people from her family's association with power, money and eccentric behavior. Yes, dear, do call me Secretary Ricker, she said when we first met. It's who I am.

Her title came out of her position as secretary of the Petticoat Society, its top officer, and an organization that might have rung a bell or two up until the 1950s, she said. So it was fine by her if others simply followed their parents' example and saluted the old lady living alone in her big house as Secretary Ricker. Any acknowledgment of her office and work pleased her.

Hosea Ricker came in with a new century, born May 2, 1900, the only child of Abigail Coffin Ricker and Captain Pelham Smith Ricker. Her father was a missing item in her life; he left for China a few months before she was born and never returned. There was a problem with the family's Far East holdings which demanded his immediate attention: one warehouse had been set afire during rioting; the office manager had disappeared and was presumed dead; and no employees were reporting to work at Ricker House, an import-export company. The secretary said there had been a Ricker in China since the 1830s, and with her father's death during the Boxer Rebellion, there'd always be a Ricker in China.

His body was never found, only his jacket splattered with blood and crumpled on the floor to his office, which overlooked the Canton docks. The jacket, however, was considered enough evidence for an English army prosecutor to convince a French army judge in Shanghai to send ten employees of Ricker House to the gallows.

When asked for more details, Secretary Ricker shook her head, saying, Well, no, nothing comes to mind. But she remembered there was a newspaper clipping mentioning something about her father's disappearance and reluctantly agreed to search for it. These things in China happened so, so very long ago, she said, leading the way to the butler's pantry, where cheap glassware and dishes occupied one-tenth the space once dedicated to extra-fine porcelain and cut crystal. On a high shelf, behind old jelly jars carrying pictures of the Flintstone family, she pulled out an intricately carved sandalwood box. She couldn't remember when she'd last handled it.

Opening the box, she discovered more than she'd expected. Oh, my, well-well, she said, putting aside the newspaper clipping to inspect a bundle of letters addressed to her from various female correspondents. There was also a clutch of strike-anywhere matches held together by dried-out rubber bands. She had forgotten about the letters and the matches, which she called unfinished business. Maybe it was time to deal with things. Maybe not. She said she'd decide over dinner, because thinking while she ate helped her digestion.

The newspaper clipping, yellowed and scissored from an English-language daily published in Canton, was one column wide, three inches long, and only told part of the story. At the bottom, it said, *Cont. p. 5,* but the run-on hadn't been saved.

What was inked dwelt on the time and place of execution—International Forces HQ, Sector 2—and hailed the court's swift action as an effective determent to would-be rebels. Oddly, there was only passing mention of her father, a subordinate clause at the end of one sentence listing the names of court officers, saying, *their work puts to rest the late Captain Pelham Smith Ricker of Ricker House.*

That's it, the secretary said, and shrugged. She returned the clipping, letters and matches to their old place inside the sandalwood box and put the works back behind the jelly glasses. As she retraced her steps to the living room, she thought it was amazing, truly quite remarkable, dear, that there was anything about her father left in the house. Because she never met the man, there was nothing for her to cherish about him, and her mother, certainly, never visibly ached for the man she'd lost. And come to think of it, the secretary added, Grandmother Smith Ricker rarely mentioned her son or, for that matter, any man. If there was a family motto, Secretary Ricker believed, it had to be a two-word slogan: Soldier On. It was a phrase she often heard around the house growing up and felt it suited the family quite-quite well. Yes, dear, we women soldiered on, we most definitely did. It's what survivors must do, she said, and took a seat in a wing chair.

While the family was rich (whale oil money wisely invested), the fortune came at a price, since most male heirs died young. Both her grandmothers were widowed early on. One lost a mate to Arctic ice before her twenty-sixth birthday; the other was twenty-four when her husband's body was dumped overboard near the Solomon Islands during an attempted mutiny. Neither grandmother knew their fathers very well, the men constantly away on business, tending shipboard matters as whaling captains and overseeing land-based operations in the Far East, and both men were buried at sea. Although there was no way to be absolutely certain, Secretary Ricker said she was ninety-nine point nine percent sure that in her line, the men had predeceased their wives ever since the three families (Ricker, Smith and Coffin) came to America in the early 1600s.

The secretary once explained that she became aware of her strength, as well as that of all Ricker, Coffin and Smith women, a few days before she turned five. It happened when she was playing with the dog and disturbed some yellow jackets in the garden. Stung here and here and here, she said, pointing to her upper lip and left eyebrow. She recalled her tears flowing like Niagara and how no amount of coddling by her mother or nanny could stem the flow. The nanny wanted to apply a compress of baking soda on the bites, but her mother had another idea. She ordered the nanny and her charge to stand by the window inside the house; meanwhile, she gathered bottles of naphtha and kerosene from the carriage house, mixed the two in a pail and doused the nest. As the wasps attacked her, she calmly torched the colony and remained motionless, head high, never wincing. The naphtha burned blue at the edges of the fireball, while the core glowed red from the kerosene, until, suddenly, the whole mess exploded like a firecracker and sprayed dead yellow jackets everywhere. Secretary Ricker said her eyes dried as she watched the drama unfold; thereafter, she never cried again.

To Mother, the secretary saluted, raising a teacup and nodding at a framed photo on a table. It showed an extremely attractive woman in her early thirties (Grace Kelly came to mind). She was dressed in tennis whites, an oxford shirt tucked into tailored pants, and about to serve the ball. She was fully extended, on her tiptoes, racquet high and an inch from contacting the ball, her form study-book perfect, a goddess at play.

Other than the driver and the gardener—a Scotsman who talked to trees and little else—Secretary Ricker grew up surrounded by women, the house filled day and night with female sounds. There were two maids, a cook, a nanny, two grannies, and Mom. The coal furnace that made the pipes rattle and the radiators hiss was named Florence. The dogs were always females (Birdie, Goldie and Girly). And the ghosts making all the noise in the attic were thought to be the spirits of Great-great-grandmother Elizabeth Coffin and her daughter Leander, both of whom perished while trying to save the mares during a stable fire in the 1840s. The two of them were quite bold while they were alive and everyone assumed they'd remain loud after death, the secretary explained. Other than the postmen, plumbers and deliverymen, she said, male visitors to the house were like rare birds, often talked about but hardly ever seen. Her mother loved to entertain and constantly filled the house with guests for ice cream socials, lunch parties, birthday parties, dinner parties, cocktail parties, holiday bashes, solstice galas and fund-raisers of all kinds, but they were always women's events.

Among the wealthy of New Bedford at the time, it was not unusual for husbands and wives to maintain separate social calendars, each tending to orbit around a club established for the exclusive use of one sex or the other. At home, they slept in different bedrooms, neither quizzing the other about extramarital affairs. Many dads among the gentry were mostly absent members of the family, detached from wife and kids, so Secretary Ricker considered her home life quite normal. Nannies were in charge of day-to-day child-rearing duties and in-home tutors prepared their students for boarding school. The girls usually went to high school at Sacred Heart Academy and spent weekends at home; the boys went wherever Dad prepped and returned home for Christmas, Easter and summer break. No matter how things were orchestrated in a family, Secretary Ricker said, there was one thing she shared with the young girls in her circle: no one really knew their father. They were like icebergs on the horizon, dear, something you approached at your own risk.

Secretary Ricker then paused, sounded a *tsk-tsk,* and said, Of course, some friends had reason seven times seven to be scared of their father. Such worry and pain those young women carried. Such unspeakable behavior they endured. Just terrible what some of those men did. More tea, dear? she asked, unwilling to say more on the subject of predatory dads.

Every day up until she died inside the federal-style, eighteen-room mansion off County Street, the secretary paused to check in with the family matriarchy whenever she came or went by the front door. She'd linger in the hallway, left hand on the doorknob, while her right hand went for the wall, fingertips to the worn spots at the base of two picture frames hung side by side. One was a photo portrait of Secretary Ricker as a baby atop the knees of her mother and flanked by Grandmother Coffin and Grandmother Smith Ricker. Baby and mother wore white smocks edged in lace and aimed smiles at each other; the two grannies stood straight as poles, their lips pursed, and wore black from chin to boot tips, their hands wrapped around large and slightly tapered candles, the lit tips at breast level.

Nearby, the sister frame displayed a postcard-sized ink-and-charcoal drawing of the Petticoat Society emblem: spouting sperms in silhouette under crossed harpoons. Secretary Ricker said her mother drew it when she was seven years old and claimed it had special powers. In fact, every time she touched the frame she felt her mother's hand atop her right shoulder, exactly as she had each time her mother either greeted her at the front door or sent her out the door.

The Petticoat Society emblem was a common sight around the house, embroidered into pillows gracing couches and chairs, sewn into the tops of ottomans, displayed in the marquetry of cabinets and tabletops, and seen in the flags at the mastheads of whale ships depicted in oil paintings hanging in the living room. The secretary inherited it all, but if she had the resources, she said, she'd commission the greatest artists in the world to paint, sculpt and cast the Petticoat colors. To her eye, there was nothing more beautiful than the Petticoat emblem.

It was my quest for facts about the Petticoat Society that had initially led me to Secretary Ricker. While the historical record contains numerous oblique references to a secret society of women involved in the early American fishery, only a few entries mentioned the Petticoat Society by name. At first, Secretary Ricker was disturbed by the crumbs of evidence I had gathered and wished out loud: Dear God turn him away or turn him into a woman. Over time, though, she softened and promised, as she put it, to serve up a nice-sized piece of cake someday. She delivered on her promise not long before her death. It happened on a Sunday afternoon, the two of us seated in the kitchen of the big house. There was snow on the ground and she wore an overcoat to insulate her from the cold seeping through the clapboards. A kettle was on the stove to refresh teacups and the oven was on full blast, baking an empty pan.

Point me toward Nantucket, she instructed.

Once she was properly oriented, her eyes tracking east-southeast through the kitchen window, she put a forefinger into motion and outlined a boomerang-like shape on the tabletop. Nantucket, she said. Using her thumb this time, she located the main settlement. Town, she declared, adding, It was our birthing room, so to speak. The Petticoat Society was born there during a mighty storm in the middle of the 1600s. She then closed her eyes for several seconds, reopening them to launch a story she entitled Genesis.

GENESIS

In the beginning, every woman in America lived in the darkness of a man's shadow, a second-class citizen stripped of voice and in service to a male master. That all began to change the day

Mary Coffin Starbuck left her bed and stepped outside the house at the harbor settlement on Nantucket Island. The air felt especially clammy to her, and even though it was early fall, the current flooding, it carried the rank smell of low tide in late July. There was no wind, yet two layers of log-shaped clouds shredded at the tips scudded along in opposite directions. Another strange thing: there were no birds in view. Usually, at that time around dawn, gulls by the dozens crowded the sky above the shoreline, while garden fliers—robins, jays and sparrows—would carpet the garden, looking for slugs and worms and seeds.

Mary went back inside to heat water for tea and to enter her weather observations in a journal she was keeping. Earlier in the year, she had been inspired to maintain accurate records by a visiting ship captain who'd shown her the boat's logbook. He'd claimed it was more valuable than gold; indeed, it was the most precious item carried aboard ship. Without it, he'd be clueless, a blind man trying to read the weather, and perpetually lost, unable to navigate by dead reckoning, never sure where he had been or where he was going.

Finished recording her observations, Mary checked earlier entries and discovered a number of disturbing matches, all of which preceded foul weather. She shared her findings with her husband, Nathaniel, when he appeared for breakfast. Her chatter meant nothing to him, except that it was delaying service. He wanted tea and biscuits and an egg if one was available. Mary stood by the stove and demanded his attention. She wanted to tell him something important. He answered by thumping the table. Breakfast, now.

There's a storm coming, she repeated, and predicted it would be an especially violent blow, not a day to go fishing.

Of course he would be going fishing. He hates it, but he does it anyway. Besides, the conditions outside looked perfect for boat work. There was no wind. The sea was flat. And the tide was rising, making it easier to launch the boat. My breakfast now, woman, he thundered.

Mary called him a stubborn fool. She was as sure as yesterday that a storm would arrive today. The one thing he should do: pull the family boat up the beach and beyond the reach of storm rollers.

My breakfast, now.

Mary didn't wince. He'd get his breakfast after promising to move the boat. Without it, how would they eat? How would they buy anything? And they needed everything.

Nathaniel grabbed his heart as if it threatened to stop working and shouted, No more insolence or feel my heavy hand. How dare she challenge his authority. He made the decisions in the house, no one else. She was to cook and obey and give him children. With the law of the land invoked, he then turned heavenward, to his Puritan God, and uttered a short prayer: Forgive her, Lord, and protect me, your servant.

Unfazed by her husband's drama, Mary said she'd move the boat herself or rally other women in the community to help her. The boat was too important to their lives to chance it being damaged or destroyed. The first snow was not far off, she reminded him, and little had been put away for winter.

Nathaniel raged, his voice boiling, hot and hurtful: No woman can speak to her husband and master that way and not expect punishment. He had no more patience. She had to apologize immediately or vacate the house. His house.

Mary didn't blink. She'd read the signs and they'd told her a storm was coming.

A witch? he shouted. Had he married a gypsy? First she insults him and now she abuses her faith. How could she imagine anticipating His actions, God on high? No man, and certainly no woman, could claim knowledge of His divine plans for the day ahead. Her words were blasphemous and needed instant repair. Loudly, for all the village to hear, he petitioned his Creator to forgive his wife, a weak and very disturbed woman. Still loudly, he ordered Mary to pray for forgiveness, first to God and then to him.

Pull the boat up the beach, she said. There is no need for forgiveness. She had already forgiven him for committing his sin of obstinacy.

His temperature and blood pressure spiking, cheeks puffed and as red as ripe bog berries, Nathaniel shook his fist. His God was vengeful and would crush her. Begone, he ordered, and made it clear that she was to leave the house before he returned from fishing to attend noontime prayers. She could sleep in the woodshed until he consulted with the other men in the community on a long-term course of action.

Pour your own tea, Mary told him, and turned her back. She'd had enough of his blather and, suddenly, she couldn't stand the sight of the man. She had loved and respected her father, the man who'd taught her to read and write and had engaged her in debate. How could he have let her marry Nathaniel Starbuck, someone as square as his shoe tips?

Nathaniel slammed the door on his way out, hard enough to make the kitchen table jump with all four legs.

Mary poured herself tea, and as she sat down, she remembered a crucial detail she'd somehow forgotten to include among that morning's entries in her journal. At dawn, the eastern sky had looked afire, a mess of crimsons and oranges which gave way to gray, thick clouds in the distance.

Nathaniel joined the other island men gathered at their boats. They had heard the shouting at the Starbuck house and now listened to Nathaniel's report on Mary's lawless behavior. They, too, called her actions blasphemy and her words devilish. Perhaps an incubus had visited her during the night? Surely she was a troubled soul.

Like Nathaniel, the men looked around and saw ideal conditions for fishing. No wind, flat seas and no birds were blessings that would keep their nets from constantly snarling and their catch safe from the beaks of gulls, Yes, they agreed, Nathaniel had done the right thing chasing her out of his house, and they promised she'd find no succor at their doors. They also agreed not to waste another minute of a beautiful day when they could be benefiting from the extra-fine weather God had sent their way.

As a group, the island men were reluctant fishermen, not very good at it and harboring little desire to improve. They dreamed of heifers and green pastures, bumper crops and streams and lakes. The ocean was their nemesis and usually churned their stomachs. Cod and halibut were viewed as clever foes, slippery and distasteful. They'd rather have corn and meat than fish and hateful lobster. For most of the men, their first experience at sea had come aboard the sluggish ships that had delivered them to the New World, a six-week voyage which had made them sick from the Eddystone Rocks to Plymouth Bay. They were all the seed of landlubbing families rooted in English sod and Roundhead tradition. Their Puritan faith bound them together as one, each a zealot, all defenders to death of their God and an English way of life. Hopefully, Reverend Mather in Plymouth could exorcise the demon inside Mary and return island life to an even keel.

Most of the men, including Nathaniel, had arrived in America as teenagers and joined the main colony at Plymouth. Later, married and starting families of their own, they'd shared a common desire to establish their own farms and viewed Nantucket as just the place for them. The island was only a day's sail from Plymouth, five hours to Hyannis, close enough to make trade and transport easy. Better yet, they considered the island's treeless topography a boon, saving them countless hours in tedious land-clearing chores. It took one year and much of their money before they understood farming as folly on their windswept, salt-sprayed home of rock and sand. Lacking options, they took to the sea, their incompetence partially masked by the sheer abundance of fish in the island's waters. Other Puritan families joined them and also took to the sea. On a good day, the men caught a full barrel of fish. Some was saved for their own use; the rest was used in barter for tea, flour, cloth, tools and just about everything else, including loam shipped from Hyannis to sustain the small garden plots.

Because of the flat sea conditions, the men found rowing easy and set their nets a mile beyond their usual fishing spot at the mouth of the harbor. They manned a fleet of leaky, poorly designed and shoddily made skiffs, each about fifteen feet long and encumbered by a wide beam amidships and stubbed bows. They were planked in green wood, which often popped fastenings as it dried and shrank; overall, the boats were suited for fishing in ponds and slow-moving streams, but not the ocean. Within an hour of when they set nets, a breeze kicked in and grew steadily in strength. Naturally, the boats started drifting with the wind, heading farther from shore. The plowmen, however, took no notice. As well, other cautionary signals went unanswered, like a shift in wind direction and a sky going from light gray to the color of oiled slate. Worry emerged when a northeast gust sent hats flying and forced leeward rails underwater. Another gust followed, and in minutes their circumstances went from bad to miserable. A full gale was on tap. Their boats leaked like sieves. And the sea was churning up a white-capped mountainscape.

The men put their backs into the birch limbs they called oars and pulled for their lives. Between strokes, they prayed to their God and sometimes urged on their partner or another duo in a nearby boat. But as soon as the clouds opened, the rain falling in sheets bent at an angle by the wind, they lost sight of land and neighbors. The wind steadily increased, and gusts throttled their words to heaven, silenced by water shooting up their nostrils and through open lips and down their throats. At the same time, the waves grew large and started rolling over the rail. To rest at the oars meant death, the skiff sure to go broadside to the sea and either capsize or swamp; to stop bailing also meant death, so one man stayed at the sticks while the other scooped water overboard using his shoes or hands. Eight boats and sixteen men were never seen again.

The northeaster slashed the New England coast above Rhode Island, but no place suffered like Nantucket, its shoreline torn up and its people tortured by heartbreak. In that one storm, the island lost approximately 10 percent of its entire population, and the property damage was extreme. Every storeroom was ruined by rain, and each house looked a wreck: windows blown out, siding stripped from the frame and roofs in pieces. The gardens were washed away, reduced to lifeless sand and rock, the harvest of tubers lost. The fishing boats that made it to shore were filled with sand and needed extensive repairs, not a bit of gear left inside them or to be found. New nets would have to be made, and while there was a stockpile of twine and pitch tar, none of the men knew how to string a net or tie a proper knot at the end of a hook.

As soon as the rain let up, the wind dying to a whisper, the men convened a town meeting to pray and devise a communal plan for healing. The prayer session went well—there was plenty to ask for—but any sense of community quickly went out what little was left of the meetinghouse windows. Each man was still punch-drunk from his bout with the storm at sea and considered his burden a hundred times that of anyone else's. As soon as one man would stand to air stories of his valiant fight for survival and go on to list his problems on land, another man would stand and speak louder than his neighbor, claiming a monopoly on pain and suffering and heroism. The morning session took a break for tea and prayers and the town meeting resumed that afternoon.

Individuals kept the focus on themselves. They were all scared, absolutely terrified of the future, and proving themselves utterly incapable of sharing. Moreover, they knew that any discussion of community would force them to deal with an issue they assiduously sought to avoid: how to provide for the twelve widows of the missing men and their fifty-two children? In the past, a widow and the needs of her brood were adopted by the entire community; there had always been enough padding to shoulder the burden of two, even three fatherless families at a time. But twelve families? Sixty-four mouths to feed when there wasn't an ort to spare?

While the men jabbered and prayed, the women of Nantucket were hard at work. They formed teams and ran an army of children and found it natural to work together in common cause. If the men felt they had other duties, involving palaver and prayer, so be it; they could help the women once their meeting ended, decisions made on the course ahead. However, the town meeting went on and on, adjourned and reconvened over and over. At the start of deliberations on day three, Mary stopped hammering roof boards back into place to see for herself what was delaying the men. It was time for them, everyone, to effect repairs and gather food.

With hammer in hand, she declared her intent to her fellow workers and soon found herself leading a column of women to the meetinghouse, where, as one, they stopped outside the doorway. That was as far as tradition and law allowed. As women, they were entitled to an earful of men-talk deciding their future, but not much more. Within the Puritan construct, women had neither vote nor say in community or family matters outside of child rearing.

Mary steamed as she listened to the blather of men caught up in self-pity, overwhelmed by circumstance and, as far as she could tell, not doing a darn thing to remedy a horrible situation. The hot air of the gasbags got to her, so she hummed and swayed, hoping a lullaby would calm the rage sweeping through her. Finally, unable to cap her anger, she exploded.

Get on with it, she yelled. We need a plan and all hands to rebuild our community.

That got everyone's attention and, at last, the men spoke as one, roaring in the name of God and common law that she be silent. Nobody was louder than Nathaniel, sure that Mary's blasphemy had provoked God into issuing the storm. Quiet, woman, he shouted. Not one more word, sinner.

Instead, Mary silenced the others, stunning the women and all the men by stepping inside the meetinghouse. She took two giant steps, paused for a moment, and resumed course, her elbows out, the hammer still in one hand, and made way to the front of the room. When the expected bolt of lightning didn't incinerate the taboo-breaking, impudent woman, she spoke to the crowd. She said they had two choices: they could work as one or die one after the other. The women of the community, she added, had already made their choice.

Gusts of affirmation came from outside the doorway and broken windows. Inside the meetinghouse, the men seethed. They were horrified by this mutiny against God and law and rushed to snuff it out. While many heaped verbal abuse on Mary, Nathaniel and three other men took hold of Mary and began to drag her away. She resisted, swinging the hammer and demanding to be heard, which prompted more men to rush her. She was as surprised as any when she was suddenly freed, her jailers reacting to a greater, more menacing force confronting them. One by one, every female over the age of fourteen filed inside the meetinghouse, their heads high and all shouting, Free Mary . . . free Mary. They struck a pose of defiance while lining the back wall, scowling at husbands and fathers, one hand in a fist and the other wrapped around some household item or construction tool—brooms, ladles, hammers, saws, axes. Several of the men yelled at their wives, ordering them to leave, and went to eject them by force. They stopped in their tracks as the women tightened formation, promising that an attack on one would be considered an attack on all, and brandished the tools in their hands as if they were weapons.

Let Mary talk, one wise man suggested, and his words were chanted by the women. Let Mary talk . . . let Mary talk.

Unsure what else to do, the male assembly turned the floor over to Mary. There was no need for her to collect her thoughts: she had gone over things dozens of times while hammering roof boards and surveying the destruction from up high. Securing food and shelter, the obvious priorities, topped her list. Next, she said, the men had to fix the boats right away, working day and night. Meanwhile, the best knitters would also go flat out producing nets. Children would help the remaining women at the cook fires and in the home-rebuilding effort.

And now the hard part, she warned: community attitudes had to change. Indeed, to survive, they needed to effect immediate structural repairs to the community's framework. The men had to commit themselves to the sea and accept fishing as their calling. The sea was their only resource and their sole exit out of this crisis. In its short history, the most money the community had ever made had come from selling the spermaceti from the head of a beached sperm whale. Cod and halibut would be their main food source, but whaling, she suggested, would be their way to prosperity. While the men hunted the sea full-time—no more half days, Sunday breaks, or pauses for prayer sessions every few hours—the women would deal with everything else, soup to nails, in charge of community redevelopment and the marketing and sale of fish products.

One more thing, she announced, and cautioned the men to listen carefully. From this moment onward, women must be treated as full-share crew members, equal rights to all over fourteen. Everyone will have a job, each as important as another, and each voice will be weighted the same at all town meetings. Hearing this, the widows in the crowd cheered the loudest.

At first, the men shouted the negative: no, never, impossible. Such a thing had no precedent in Puritan law or tradition. Indeed, the Scriptures prohibited such a realignment of power; women, the Good Book instructed, were subjects of men. But under the circumstances, what else could be done? Slowly, the naysayers replaced invective with grumbling and the men talked among themselves, eventually deciding there was no viable alternative, at least not at the moment. Mary's plan would provide for the widows and their children and smooth relations at home. At a later time, surely, the men agreed, they could return to the old system—once the women gave up trying to be men, willing, at last, to admit their feebleness and ask for forgiveness.

The men took a vote and all but Nathaniel agreed to allow the women to join the workforce. In the next show of hands, the women were granted the rights of full citizenship. Again, Nathaniel cast a dissenting vote. With females suddenly in the majority, a new officer corps was installed, and Mary was elected town moderator. She steered things straight, yielding the floor to men and women on an equal basis, and she cut short any whimpering or boasting. In quick time, she enabled individuals to form teams and arrange lines of communication. By the end of the conclave, every citizen had a job and knew exactly what was expected of them and all their neighbors. People walked out of the meetinghouse with spirits rejuvenated and got right to work. That night they prayed for strength rather than miracles.

Over the course of the next few months, the women never

flagged, evincing neither weakness of any sort nor any desire to turn back the clock. In fact, they proved themselves equally adept at business and at home repairs: come the first ice in the harbor, every house was tight and bills for supplies were paid. At the same time, the men redoubled their efforts at fishing. Record catches reinforced their willingness to learn new techniques and hone old ones. Slowly, they shook themselves free of sod and sand and began to dream of cod bigger than the boat. They reached out to the Wampanoags, aspiring students to masters, and learned native tricks of the fishing trade. Soon they were building a system of traps and weirs and practicing with harpoons. Pride in their work hit a new high when the men landed their first whale. Before work was finished on the tryworks set up on the beach to render blubber into oil, the men landed another whale. Proceeds from the kills filled the community coffers and established the preferred course into the future: men and women cojoined in the hunt for blubber and the sale of oil.

Mary was appointed chairman of the Harbor Council, in command of all dockside business, including seafood processing and sales, fleet maintenance and expansion, warehousing and port development. Four other women served with her on the council, which met twice a week. They'd gather at Mary's house after cleaning and salting the catch of the day, leaving their work clothes—aprons, shoes and outerwear splattered with fish guts—in the mudroom, and conduct business in the kitchen dressed in their petticoats. It wasn't long before the Harbor Council had a new name: the Petticoat Society.

And that, dear, is the story of a bud which would blossom into a brilliant flower. Exquisite, actually, that island flower, and like none other since the Greeks, Secretary Ricker said, concluding her tale of Genesis.

———

Of all the entries in the logbook of commercial fishing in America, none appears more important or deserving of high-line honors than the founding of the Petticoat Society. Certainly, the day Mary Coffin Starbuck took the helm is the same day fishing in America was turned on its head, never to be the same again. While necessity may have catalyzed the action at the town meeting, islanders provided the important stuff of any breakthrough achievement: a willingness to buck the prevailing wind and trash old maps for new ones of their own making. Out went the conventional dualism of God and man. In came a revolutionary trinity: God, woman and man.

By enfranchising females, islanders successfully wedded the expectations of both sexes to the pursuit of fish, and the bigger the ocean prize, the better. Out of it all, and beginning that day of the Nantucket town meeting, islanders crafted a template which would shape the future of commercial fishing in America for the next 140 years, 1660 to 1800. In the process, Nantucketers launched a uniquely American way of catching fish and selling ocean products. Their triumph led to a near monopoly in the world oil trade and the creation of a money machine that would generate nearly half of the nation's export revenues in the 1790s.

In the Nantucket construct, with fishing boxing the compass, communal desires merged and gave rise to a culture which celebrated the whale. Success on the island became a measure of a man's ability to bring home the blubber and a woman's ability to turn blubber into coin and manage the store while himself was away whaling. As the specialization of skills progressed, the island adapted, forever tweaking the system and narrowing the focus until whales filled all horizons. Soon, men had to prove themselves worthy of reproduction, all marriage proposals wishful thinking until himself had harpooned a whale and driven home the death blow with a lance. Likewise, the founding mothers rejiggered the island recipe for female attractiveness, promoting brains over beauty, business skills over social graces, the practical over the prissy, and offered generous salaries to women working for the Petticoat Society with a mind on a career, not children. For the men, the ante kept rising until it became two whales killed, then three notches in his harpoon before he could propose marriage, a race of piscatorial warriors and quartermasters in the making.

Mary died in 1717, a few months after the Petticoat Society opened its first foreign office, in London, part of its effort to cut out the middleman and take control of the oil pipeline. She lived long enough to see Nantucket whalers develop into the best in the business, unmatched as navigators and hunters, and recognized as an ascending tribe of Yankee seafarers about to corner the global oil market. By 1760, the island was outproducing the entire whaling fleets of England and Spain combined, its boats rigged as factory ships able to hunt, kill, process and package the catch without ever stopping, the crow's nest on a Nantucket whaler on perpetual lookout for the next prize. In the early 1790s, islanders were rounding Cape Horn, circumnavigations routine, and probing the furthest extent of open water to the north and to the south.

As a rule, island boys shipped out as men on the year of their twelfth birthday. In 1800, the easy pickings in the fishery gone, they were in for a long ride, the average whaling voyage lasting almost two years. Nantucketers accepted the overtime work without complaint. They had been bred for sea duty, schooled as navigators and tempered for the hunt. They'd set a course for home only when the hold was filled to the deck beams with barrels of oil and casks of ambergris. At sea, their images of home life became blurred by the fog of absence, and they increasingly fantasized about what they'd left behind. When their ship returned to the harbor, they stood at the rail, their hearts pounding, and debarked happy to be on land, glad to see Ma, Sis and maybe the wife and kids, and near delirious at the thought of a family meal, fresh meat and vegetables a dream come true.

However, within days of their arrival, the itch for the sea returned and quickly turned into an imperative. On land they were a dysfunctional lot, out of sync and clueless about the fashions of the day, and squirmed as if needing a fix of salt and blubber. Around the house, they were constantly underfoot in a place organized to run smoothly without them. Before long, sadly, most found themselves strangers to their own children and wives and mothers. Those who didn't seek out booze or drugs to shield them from the harsh light of a landsman day spent much of their shore leave at the waterfront watching their boat being recoppered, rerigged and provisioned for the next voyage—a five-week process, on average. Once the sailor and his ship were under way, the harbor astern, he could yet again relax and resume the comfortable routine he shared with twenty-six others aboard a 105-foot boat crammed with enough gear and supplies to sustain a multiyear voyage.

On any given day from 1740 to 1805 on Nantucket, females outnumbered males eleven to one, and to prosper on this man-less island women had to adapt to an environment unlike any since Lesbos was known as the Queen of the Mediterranean. The Petticoat Society facilitated climate control, stoking the flames of sisterly love and greasing the machinery of commerce and daily life. As the island grew wealthy from the oil trade, the Petticoat Society hired professionals to manage the business end of things; by 1770, it had reconstituted itself as a purely sor-oral organization, the first in America. While membership was open to all island-born females, the society's curtains remained tightly cinched, with men and all off-islanders barred from its inner workings. The old business offices were redesigned and transformed into a community hub for social activities. Once a year, in August, the island shut down for two days while the Pet-ticoaters threw their annual party, a rip-roaring bash modeled on the saturnalia of Rome. Every day of the week, though, Pet-ticoat headquarters hosted smaller, more intimate affairs. The doors would open for morning tea, served either straight or spiked with opium—so-called blackened tea and the beverage of the majority—and the doors would close after the musicians played their last number at night, the dancing over. Quarterly membership meetings were enhanced in the mid-1770s by the introduction of rites and rituals, all of them ceremonies designed to tighten the female bond, and most involving the liberal use of sperm oil, dildos and lewd dancing.

Secretary Ricker called the Petticoat Society building on Nantucket (demolished after a fire in 1811) a corral for the feminine spirit and an energy center nourishing a woman's soul, heart and mind. In less florid language, she conveyed a clear picture, saying, Don't tell me, mister, that you don't know what the men were doing aboard those boats besides fishing. My-my-my, twenty-something men together for years aboard a floating prison. Of course they were dipping the stick. And, dear, wasn't there always someone aboard nicknamed Hebone or Tripod? She continued: The island, too, was a ship, detached from land and crewed by members of the same sex. The gals only did what came naturally, like the men, but better, one presumes.

Considering the prim era—Colonial and post-Colonial America—Secretary Ricker recommended Nantucket as the most remarkable society ever constructed throughout history. She believed three things kept the women on top and at the controls: location (a twenty-two-mile-wide moat protecting the island from invasive mainland forces); buckets of money (whaling turned Nantucket into the wealthiest place anywhere, an export community able to buy whatever it wanted and ban the rest); and secrecy (a rule-breaking society sharing and obliging the oath of outlaws).

When Hector de Crèvecoeur published his book *Letters from an American Farmer*, which included a chapter about his lengthy visit to Nantucket in the late eighteenth century, he wrote about a prosperous port community populated mostly by women with a taste for opium, Parisian fashions, Greek classics and privacy. While he made mention of a secret society of women running the island show, in charge of its works top to bottom, he couldn't offer any details. Secretary Ricker cited this as proof that women can keep secrets better than men. In her opinion, it was a good test of strength: That Frenchman, dear, ate with the gals, slept in their houses, maybe—who knows?—in their beds as well, drank their blackened tea, danced with them all, and yet he remained as blind and dumb to the biggest force on the island as when he first arrived.

Secretary Ricker went on to credit Mary Coffin Starbuck for locking the gate and fortifying island defenses from disruptive mainland influences. Indeed, more than anyone, Mary allowed the indigenous island species to set roots and develop in its own peculiar way, which would've been impossible in the presence of mainland strains. Mary, Secretary Ricker said, was especially wary of her Puritan cousins and feared they'd swarm the island once they smelled money in the community purse. Through her initiative, islanders established and operated a ferry service linking Nantucket to Hyannis, along with a main terminal in New Bedford. Ferryboat captains were instructed to deny passage to unwanted types, especially emissaries from Plymouth and Boston out to collect taxes and tithes. Anyone turned away at the boat could apply for a ticket at the Petticoat office located on the New Bedford docks, where they'd be interviewed and vetted.

The shakedown at the ferry was only one line of defense and useless when it came to the dozens of ships which pulled into Nantucket every month, delivering goods and transporting whale oil to market. When one boat dropped off three preachers in addition to a load of lumber, Mary was sure there'd be no stopping proselytizers in search of sinecures if something radical wasn't done in a hurry. Her solution: Quakerism. She converted and urged others to follow her inside the fold or keep close to the Friends' shadow and thereby project a united front to outsiders. It was enough to dissuade even the most adventurous preacher from trying to establish a beachhead on the island of the damned, home to heretics, the lost and the hell-bound.

For a disillusioned former Puritan like Mary, Quakerism was a comparatively easy fit. It was the only organized religion at the time to offer pretty much the same deal to men and women in church matters; plus, it came with a big bonus: the Friends endorsed bundling and gave women a say over their beds. While the Quaker embrace of self-denial and hard work appealed to Mary's sensibilities, successive generations tended to pick and choose, cafeteria-style, what looked good to them. But no matter how islanders put things together, Bible-thumpers or lushes, there was never a call for a preacher of any sort. Nantucketers spoke directly to their God and for some, Secretary Ricker was quick to note, that meant addressing Her, not Him.

A good part of Mary was also caught up in naturalism, and she relied on the interplay of the elements to explain the phenomena which turned a gust into a raging gale, rain into snow, and sent tides from ebb into flood. Her enthusiasm for careful observation of the weather became contagious, and with a near-religious fervor, many islanders became apostles of sky and water gods and recorded detailed accounts of their doings to instruct others. None were more faithful and diligent at the job than Nantucket captains and first mates. Every time they returned from a voyage, the ship's logbook would go to Petticoat librarians, who copied each entry and codified them according to time and place. By 1725, long before Maury and Humboldt would map the seas, the Petticoat Society had published a set of pilot charts for the North Atlantic, showing currents and prevailing winds in various ocean quadrants for every month of the year. As the accumulated knowledge grew, the charts became ever more precise and were eventually released as an oversized book offering captains invaluable information on what they would find ahead, including advice on weather, whale migration patterns and islands offering food and water. The book became known as the Nantucketer's Bible, its word more valuable to the sailor than the Old Testament. Usually, this bible was stored in a leather case lined with lead, and Nantucket captains were duty-bound to ensure that it never got into the hands of an off-islander.

The good times on Nantucket ended as the clock struck 1806 and eviction notices were posted by both Mother Nature and Uncle Sam. That winter a series of especially violent storms ripped up the bottom of Nantucket Sound and forced millions of tons of sand and muck down the harbor mouth. Later, survey crews working lead lines and charting the recontoured seabed issued bad news: the harbor shoaling appeared irreversible and would most likely get worse year after year. Many islanders understood this as the beginning of the end for Nantucket as a useful port for oceangoing, deep-draft whale ships. More problematic: 1806 marked the start of saber rattling by America and England, each accusing the other of interfering with the free flow of commerce on the high seas. On the island, the tocsin clanged and shook free unpleasant memories of the last war, when the Brits had ravaged the whaling fleet and cost islanders millions. London made the first move, ordering the Royal Navy to blockade certain U.S. ports; Washington retaliated months later with the passage of the Embargo Act, which, along with other protectionist measures, banned exports to England.

The politics of the times made Nantucketers seethe, and many wanted to leave the Union to fly the ensign of an independent island-nation. Secession efforts fizzled, and as free-market trade crumpled, no group was hurt more in the purse than the American whaling industry. Not only had islanders lost their biggest customer, they also felt their survival was at stake. Better than anyone, they could read the signs of a gathering storm, and what they saw coming was the world's first war over oil, its production, transport and marketing. With the Machine Age in high gear, and with oil a necessary ingredient to keep things moving, Britain appeared intent on floating its own pipeline and destroying the near monopoly on the oil trade by upstart Yankees. Ships of the line became a constant presence off island waters, and with an outgunned U.S. Navy a day's sail away in Newport, Nantucketers viewed themselves as both an easy target and the prize the Brits most wanted.

Separately, either the shoaling of the harbor or the saber rattling would have sent the smart money out of Nantucket; together, these two developments hurried an exodus of islanders and their assets to New Bedford, a place they already pretty much owned. For years beforehand, islanders invested in city real estate and industry, representing the single biggest force in city commerce. They used the place as a service center for their boats and a headquarters for their mainland operations, prompting many to buy and maintain a second home in the city. It was Nantucket money which launched the New Bedford whaling fleet in the late 1760s, and islanders financed its growth even after New Bedford dethroned Nantucket as King of Oil in the mid-1790s. Additionally, Nantucketers were instrumental in building the city's dockside industries, its shipyards, ropeworks, copperworks, candle factories, ship chandlers and sail lofts. By the time the Treaty of Ghent was finally inked in 1814, most of the old Nantucket fleet not seized by the Brits during the war was sailing out of New Bedford. On the island, meanwhile, a skeleton crew of die-hard residents stayed active in the oil trade, but at a price: someone had to pay for harbor-dredging schemes and all the camels, giant contraptions designed to lift whale ships and float them over the mudflats to the dock.

For the American whaling industry as a whole, the timing was perfect to bust free of an island cocoon and morph into the next stage of exponential growth. Around the world, more and more machines were appearing, and budding industrialists everywhere were hooked like junkies on whale oil and its chief byproduct, grease. Without lubricants, their newfangled machinery would quickly heat up and rattle itself to death or simply melt and seize. Vegetable oils were no substitute for the extra-fine, heat-resistant grease made from whale oil; additionally, with a lock on refinery techniques, New Bedford labs constantly tweaked formulas to match customers' needs.

Britain and France tried mightily to protect their national interests in the oil trade, spending wads of cash to subsidize private contractors; when that effort failed, they spent even more to nationalize their whaling fleets. But neither country could crack the American monopoly, and both cashed out of the business at a tremendous loss. In each case, they were hobbled by insurmountable problems: an inept officer corps unschooled in whaling techniques—any posting on a whaler considered a demotion and career ender—and crews prone to mutiny after a year or two at sea. The Brits, for instance, had to write off dozens of whalers in the years 1817 to 1830; a few boats were lost to storms and poor navigation, while more ended up as firewood on some remote island after a mutiny.

At the same time, Americans were launching a new whale ship every few weeks, with most of the newcomers headed to New Bedford. By 1825, the city was host to an armada of nearly three hundred whaling barks and, most remarkably, the port handled nearly one-half of the total world oil production. With a virtual stranglehold on the business, New Bedford became the de facto home to the first modern oil cartel, and, like their twentieth-century avatar, local ship owners conspired to manipulate prices and subvert the ambitions of would-be competitors. Concurrently, they kept investing in fractionalization labs and refineries and gouged grease customers every chance they got. Extra cash dribbled in from the cartel's ownership of the distribution grid for its products, while more income came in over the transom from the cartel's cut as both mule and distributor of drugs, supplying the nation's intake of opium and servicing the Brits in their devious use of the narcotic in China. The drugs were loaded aboard whalers stationed miles offshore by souped-up coastal schooners, the original prototypes of today's high-speed drug-delivery boats.

Goodness gracious, me, there was so-so very much money pouring through New Bedford in those days that, honestly, dear, it would make a Chinaman blush, Secretary Ricker said. She was talking about rich people in the city—many of them transplanted Nantucketers—becoming ridiculously rich people during the whaling era. Families like hers operated like modern-day Borgias, occupying that thin slice of the upper crust and able to buy whatever they wanted. For old island families, the move to New Bedford was much the same as a coming-out party, Secretary Ricker added. At last they were able to mix, wine and dine and compete with their cousins in New York and Boston society. Like other Nantucket clans, the Coffins, Rickers and Smiths set such deep roots in their new hometown that no one in the families ever returned to Nantucket. Obviously, they liked their new life on the mainland, she said. And, no, dear, she has never visited the island. She's a New Bedford gal and, frankly, when the Petticoat Society left Nantucket, they kept the history but abandoned the place.

Upon arrival, the Nantucketers immediately assumed the high ground in New Bedford, building their mansions on the ridge overlooking the harbor and upwind from the noise and stench of industry and underclass. Just as it was before, the men took to the sea and left the women in charge of the money and the home front. Within a few years, after overseeing construction of nests with fifteen or more rooms, the women were hard at work shaping a town into a city dedicated to the sea and fishing, all eyes on the whale. This time, though, with mainland laws and mores to deal with, the women abandoned the limelight to both direct and stage-manage the action from the shadows. They hired a phalanx of front men to do their bidding and, thanks to their bottomless purse, the beards quickly put the city machinery and all the control levers within easy reach of their employers. The matriarchy was firmly in place by 1818, the wives and widows of whaling captains calling the shots at town meetings and council sessions. In fact, the women had their way in any community matter in which, by state and federal law, only half the community was allowed voice and vote. A local newspaper of the day verified the matriarchy's power in an editorial; it was entitled "The Good Women on the Hill." The writer thanked the city's society women for their interest in town affairs and for their ability to motivate citizens to participate. Many of the poor would go hungry and shoeless, the writer noted, if the good women didn't pay them to attend civic meetings and vote.

The Petticoat Society moved into a mansion near County Street in 1809. The new digs were gifted to the society by a member at her death, and the Petticoaters redecorated the space without concern for cost. Secretary Ricker called it a genuine wonder of the world, and claimed it was a treasury of the best of the best from any place bordering an ocean with a whale in it. Her source for this report was Grandmother Coffin, who, she said, never lied about Petticoat affairs; to her, the Petticoat Society was a church and a life rolled into one, and while she'd lie for it to keep secrets, she'd never lie about it. Unfortunately, any evidence of the clubhouse and its contents was consumed by a fire set by an untended candle during the blizzard of 1854. The storm was so powerful that no fire brigade could leave its barracks for almost two days.

As always, privacy was ensured at the clubhouse and its replacements: no men, all proceedings secret. Added security came from the tall iron fence with railings shaped like harpoons that ringed all Petticoat property, as well as the dogs which patrolled the grounds and answered only to their female handlers. The staff, including painters and carpenters, was an all-female crew. While Secretary Ricker would often smile, wink or nod when asked to confirm accounts lifted from diaries and ships' logbooks of wild, sapphic parties and sexually charged ceremonies hosted by the society, she refused to speak on the subject. Eventually, after hearing one too many graphic descriptions lifted off pages from the past, she bolted the door to that part of history: My dear, my dear, she said, just know everything from Nantucket went to New Bedford and Petticoaters recreated island life here. Nothing changed, really. The Petticoat Society never wavered. As always, dear, it was women helping women in every possible way.

According to Secretary Ricker, the organization steered a steady course—no scandal, no crisis, only growth and assurance—until the late 1880s, when its membership rolls included more women with gray hair than any other color. By that time, its core constituency—the wives and widows of whaling captains and refinery executives—had become an endangered species, the whale oil industry on the wane since the end of the Civil War. Of course, she said, women outlived the men, and the Petticoaters soldiered on the best they could without whales and men away on ships.

The whaling industry peaked in 1848 and went kaput in the 1880s, the death knell sounding when twenty-nine New Bedford ships were lost in one season to Arctic ice. Afterward, there'd be no comeback, no second wind for whale ships or those Americans who sailed aboard them. World oil production had shifted away from the sea to land-based operations, the future belonging to the black stuff and its distillates. The few whale ships afloat in 1890 were the last of their kind, and while a handful, like the *Charles Morgan*, kept working the Arctic hunting grounds and managed to sail into the twentieth century, the rest were stripped of gear and left to rot at the dock or high and dry on a beach. The big moneymakers in the sea—sperm, right, blue, humpback, baleen and gray whales—had been hunted to the brink of extinction, and whaling voyages were lasting upwards of five years, with mutinies becoming more and more common and profits ever scarcer.

The local moneymen closed out their maritime accounts and started pouring millions into textile manufacturing; lesser amounts went into building toolworks and glassworks. Mill buildings replaced shipyards on the waterfront, and marine-related businesses either adapted to the new industrial climate or disappeared. Dozens of sail lofts, for instance, went belly-up, but many ropeworks applied their braiding and spinning techniques to supply the cordage used in tires. By 1891, the docks were handling hundreds of bales of cotton for every barrel of whale oil, and the water's edge refitted itself to service the new paymaster in town: manufacturers.

Hosea Ricker was named secretary of the Petticoat Society just in time to stand death watch, the lone officer of an old ship on its way down. When she was elected to the post, there were only thirty-five dues-paying members, and she was the youngest by twenty-five years. She said the job fell into her lap not long after she cut short a European holiday to nurse her mother, who had been in a car accident and badly bruised. She soon learned that being attentive to Mom also meant being an audience to her mother's cronies, a gang of nearly twenty, each a Petticoater and all of them cards, she said. Growing up, she knew these ladies as special friends of the family and regular visitors to the house; they doted on her and she referred to each as Auntie.

The women surprised her one afternoon by announcing her election to the secretary's post, and they urged her to take control of what little was left of the organization. Its main assets were intangibles—tradition, history and, of course, the members themselves—and administrative tasks were minimal. Their last clubhouse had been a rental, and once the lease had expired, in 1906, they convened meetings at private residences. Clubhouse furnishings and artwork had been sold in 1898 to bail out members suddenly swamped by debt, and all ceremonial items had been dispersed among the group's elders. Monthly dues in 1923, her first year on the job, covered the cost for the blackened tea served at get-togethers and provided a small stipend for the society's secretary. As a society girl, expensively schooled and poorly educated (the Sacred Heart Academy, Swiss finishing school, a year at Smith and graduate study in luxury liners, hotels and gay living), she thought a job might be exciting. Up to then, she had never considered a career or imagined herself ever going to work.

They, those gals and Mother, you know, came as one, the entire group bound together by the stickiest stuff man will ever see, she reported. They had melded during battle, their cause freedom and equality for American women, a campaign the secretary invariably referred to as the Second War of Independence. A few of the older vets had put in more than sixty years of service, joining up as teens alongside Grandmother Coffin and Grandmother Smith Ricker, and called to arms by Lucretia Mott, their Nantucket-born leader and fellow Petticoater. Later, as part of a larger contingent of New Bedford women, they all served under the command of Carrie Chapman Catt and, as usual, pulled double duty as bankers to the cause.

After enfranchisement in 1920 with the passage of the Nine-teenth Amendment, the New Bedford brigade and their general had a falling-out. The locals felt a battle had been won, but not the war, and they accused Catt of selling out, more interested in basking in the limelight and collecting coin from speeches on coast-to-coast tours. Hosea Ricker's first assignment as Petticoat secretary involved peacemaking. But her efforts failed and she explained what she was up against: Each side believed they were right, a feeling of betrayal everywhere, and, honestly, dear, there wasn't room enough for give-and-take to split a hair.

When her mother recovered from the car accident and was back on the tennis court, her serve almost as good as ever, Secre-tary Ricker made her big decision: she was setting anchor in New Bedford. She loved her job at the Petticoat Society and, likewise, after years of being away, she'd rediscovered her home-town and found it, as she said, delicious. She had rekindled an old love affair from her high school days and reintegrated her-self in local society, hosting charity events and socials. Not inter-ested in men, marriage or children, she said, she followed family tradition and assumed the title of Queen Bee of New Bedford.

She often visited friends in London and Paris and while she adored Europe, she said, there was something about the Conti-nent that always got her goat, At night, it was smooth sailing, never a problem, but once the sun came up, so, too, did an ugly bit of the culture which admonished her for being a lesbian and forced many of her chums to deny their true identity until after sunset. As an all-or-nothing kind of gal, she found New Bedford, with its large population of gays and historical tolerance of, she said, queers, an excellent match for her type: hard-core and proud of it.

Although New Bedford never rolled out the red carpet for homosexuals or bisexuals, Secretary Ricker said there was never a reason for a welcoming party, simply because queers were always part of the woodwork. My dear, my dear, she repeated, no one can throw stones in this city without hitting themselves where it hurts. She added: Honestly, now, every family in these parts has its share of fruits, from the tippy top to the taproots. Queers, my dear, have always run things in town and probably always will.

She drove home her point by tapping the front page of the morning paper, her finger on a story above the fold about the local representative in Congress, Barney Frank. Ever since he took the seat held for years by Gerry Studds, Frank has won reelection by landslide margins. She moved her finger across the page to a picture depicting city fathers at a ribbon-cutting cere-mony, and she poked faces in the photo as she spoke: Yes, yes and certainly. She then motioned toward a copy of *Moby-Dick* on a nearby shelf and wondered aloud, saying, Now, dear, what exactly do you think Melville saw through the window of the Crossed Harpoon Inn that made him keep going? Too jolly for his taste, he wrote. Do tell, dear, jolly?

Secretary Ricker insisted there were two reasons explaining why neither time nor the best efforts of area Baptists could ever dull the city's gay edge. Number one, the Petticoat Society. Number two, men aboard ships gone fishing.

Six

PERFECT
WRECK

MONK IS OUT TO SINK HIS BOAT and says it's tricky business, the perfect wreck, much harder than he first imagined. Even so, he feels confident things will soon tilt his way. In another week he'll be three years on the case and three is one of his lucky numbers.

After several botched attempts at destroying what he once loved, along with what he calls more research than you can shake a stick at, there are only a few more details to work out. He considers them itty-bitty line items, a snap to finish. At last, he'll be free of that damn boat, and he says he gets a rush just thinking about it.

The future may scare other people, but not him. No sirree. He sees a tomorrow with him sitting pretty while his boat sits on the bottom and insurance cheese lines his pockets, all of them. But don't expect to see him smiling. He'll be the sad-looking guy, Mr. Bummed Out. Everyone on the docks will spot him and say, Oh, man, would-ya, there's poor boatless Monk. A miracle, it is, that he escaped that shipwreck. Awful, really, that he lost his baby out there.

See, the perfect wreck is big, way-far beyond the deed itself, he instructs. And once other fishermen stop talking about the day he almost drowned, he'll write a manual. Already he has a title, *Tune-up for the Perfect Wreck,* and he believes the rest will flow like honey out of a wide-mouth jar. He intends to keep it simple, fisherman friendly—no big words and under twenty pages in length—and offer it to men either wanting or needing to cash out of the fishing business. He feels there are a million reasons, maybe more—he hasn't done a full count yet—why a fisherman would one day decide, No more, that fishing is harmful to his health and wallet. His manual will offer step-by-step instructions on how to do it and make money at the same time. He hasn't fixed on a price to charge for his manual. Fifty bucks, he says, sounds cheap. One hundred seems a bit pricey.

When he was starting out, oh-Jesus, he would've paid whatever somebody wanted for spelling out the perfect wreck. Honest: he would have robbed Fort Knox if it meant losing his burden, that good-for-nothing boat of his, *Shell Shock,* a thirty-seven-footer rigged for clamming, groundfishing and pot smuggling. By the end of his first season working with her, he says, his romancing days were over and he started to hate her. He'll never know why it took him so damn long to realize what she really is: a death boat. Either she dies or he dies. He wins or she wins. Right now she's killing him, bleeding him dry and numbing his brain.

Christ, what are them do-nothings doing now? Monk exits the garage to check on the *screep-screep-screep* of a dump truck moving in reverse.

The sign above the garage says PETE'S REPAIR SHOP, but Monk has been running the engine-repair business in the North End since he was a teenager. The garage belongs to Uncle Pete, but no one is sure when he'll return to New Bedford. The parole board rejected his latest appeal for early release, and the widow of the man he killed vowed she'd push for lethal injection at his next parole hearing, in two years.

Monk returns with an update on the flood at the end of the block, where Belleville Avenue is one foot deep in raw sewage. A city crew is on the scene and Monk says they're only moving crap around, this way and that, and not fixing the problem. The sewer line under Belleville is more than a hundred years old, its piping calcified and the nearest pumping station inadequate, and sewage bubbles up during and after every downpour, like this morning's soaker. Monk is thirty-nine and has lived with this situation his entire life. At this point, he deems the city's inaction criminal. He dips out the door to shout at the city workers: Fix it, will-ya. Fix the freakin' . . .

He lives next door to the garage, on the top floor of a triple-decker. He grew up directly across the street from the garage, also on the top floor of a triple-decker, living with his parents, two brothers, two sisters and one grandfather. Most mornings since he can remember, he has woken up to the same view outside his bedroom window, looking northeast at the mill buildings lining Belleville Avenue and the estuary behind them. Invariably, the estuary got his attention, the water a quick-change artist, rarely looking the same blink to blink. Growing up, he'd see colors he couldn't match to any stick in his 120-count box of Crayolas. The sun, of course, had much to do with the water's sparkle and palette, as did that day's run of fabric through the color presses at one mill. If a chop was running, the wave action would stir up the bottom and enliven the show with bursts of chroma from the thousands of tons of industrial waste—heavy metals, PCBs, arsenic and mercury—dumped into the estuary over the past 125 years.

Monk reenters the garage and goes for a bottle of cheap vodka, which he keeps airborne for two pulls at the neck. The bottle slides into a workbench drawer with the clink of glass bumping glass. Smooth, he announces, and returns to *Shell Shock*. When they first met, he was sure she was an agent of change which would carry him out of the neighborhood and into prime space on the docks. Don't laugh, he warns, and proceeds: There was a time when he thought owning a fishing boat would make him a millionaire.

There was reason to his madness, he says. Grampy-J—his grandfather, Jorge Lopes—once took a chance on a boat and considered it the luckiest and best damn thing he ever did. So when Monk saw the FOR SALE sign hanging off *Shell Shock,* he was sure lightning was about to strike the Lopes family for the second time.

Hear me out, Monk says, and begins: Grampy-J was some good man and he got the jump on the man part. When he was thirteen, Grampy-J took a huge leap and did something most people never do if they live to be a million years old. He'd never brag about his big balls; that wasn't his way. He'd only tell you he gambled everything on the unknown because what he knew sucked.

He, Grampy-J, was one of nine kids and came in the middle of the pack. Back then, the 1920s-like, the Lopes family, same as all them others in their village on Cabo Verde, worked a small plot of tired land. About all they owned was their sweat and spit, a few clothes, a pig, some chickens and goats, and they shared a cow with a neighbor. Home was a one-room shack where the eleven of them ate, slept and lived. Twice a year, at pruning and harvest season, the whole gang took jobs at a vineyard near their place.

Like always on Wednesdays, Grampy-J left the farm carrying a pail of goat's milk to the dealer in town. But that Wednesday, he only made it as far as the docks in Praia, the capital, stopping to watch a tramp get ready to leave port. He had never been on a boat and didn't know a bow from a stern. All he saw was his ticket off Cabo Verde and all he heard was a voice inside him saying, Get out of here.

While the crew was busy with the dock lines, Grampy-J snuck aboard, a stowaway with a pail of goat's milk and wearing a T-shirt and short pants, no shoes or underwear, and not an escudo on him. He curled up inside a lifeboat, scared as a mouse staring at a cat, and he stayed there until the crew heard him puking the next day. The captain wasn't about to waste diesel and turn around, so the crew gave Grampy-J a scraper and a paintbrush and told him to get to work. When the tramp finally made port in New Bedford, the captain smuggled his illegal cargo ashore. Dressed in the mate's old pants and shoes, a skinny kid in big man's clothing, Grampy-J started life in America and got a job as a house painter on a Portuguese-speaking crew.

Monk guesses he heard Grampy-J tell that story in a thousand different ways, but no matter how it was delivered, he always reserved a moment for Monk. He'd save it for the end and look his grandson in the eye, telling him, Your chance is coming, boy, and when you see that boat, be sure you're on it.

Naturally, when Monk saw *Shell Shock* in North Carolina, he flashed on Grampy-J. It was his first trip to Tar Heel country and he was there on a rescue mission, hired to resuscitate the motors aboard a seventy-two-foot dragger that sank in shallow water at a marina. The boat was an old New Bedford scalloper that had found new life as a long-distance hay-hauler. She had left Jamaica and was bound for Boston when a storm hit and opened a plank, forcing the crew to make landfall. The marina operator was paid well for his cooperation, and come sunset, the crew transferred most of the cargo—twenty-four of twenty-seven tons of reefer—into U-Hauls and motored northward. After ten days with no sign of cops or Coasties, the owner arrived on the scene and put in a call to Monk. Get down here and bring your tools, he was told.

The boat was on a railway by the time Monk arrived, bottom

repairs in progress. Because the boat sank at the dock, the water in the engine room didn't reach a killer level, and Monk says he did more flushing and cleaning than repairing and replacing. After a few days of work, the job was done, all motors at factory specs or better. To kill free time before his plane left, Monk borrowed his employer's rental car to take in the sights. At a red light, he got an inexplicable urge to turn right, and fifty yards down the road, he saw *Shell Shock*.

The owner was nearby cleaning his paintbrush in kerosene after lettering FOR SALE on a piece of plywood. The man had decided to sell that same morning, explaining he was retiring after fifty-five years of fishing and clamming. He called *Shell Shock* the best boat her size on the East Coast and kept lying: When clams see her bottom, they jump into the rake . . . She slices through twenty-foot waves like a knife through butter . . . She's as solid as the day she was built . . .

Monk says he only believed one word out of the man's mouth and that was his first name, Bud. It was sewn onto his shirt above the pocket and appeared on unopened mail left on the galley table. Bud's asking price: $16,000 in cash or $20,000 by check. It was half what Monk considered a lowball number for a fully rigged thirty-seven-foot boat. He searched for reasons why she was going so cheap, and while he knew nothing about structure, he was a pro when it came to marine systems. So he overlooked the rot to home in on the engineering department. He says everything—engine, generator, pumps, controls and winches—worked but needed an overhaul. If he had been surveying for someone else, he would've steered them away from a purchase, estimating a huge repair bill, plus parts. For him, though, his time came free and he knew where to get cheap used parts.

He and Bud went on a test drive, down the river and around some buoys in open water at full throttle. As they sped, Monk convinced himself that he couldn't lose in the deal—unless, of course, he dallied and forfeited out to a more decisive man turning right at the light. He says he was in love as they pulled into the dock, his body tingling, because of the way *Shell Shock* looked under power and because she made him feel like Captain Hot Shot at the wheel.

Later, when he sat down with the hay-hauler's owner, a major player in an all-cash business, Monk says, fate once again smacked him in the head. He wanted the boat. The dragger owner wanted the remaining reefer in New England and wanted to send his boat south for another big load, so he offered Monk $16,000 to deliver three tons of weed to New Bedford. That night *Shell Shock* was moored alongside the hay-hauler and Monk started introducing himself as Captain Lopes.

While preparations for the journey ahead were straightforward, a knuckle-scraping slog from one end of the engine room to the other, Monk says the paperwork was a loopy trail through hell. Usually, maritime lawyers take care of the details in registering a fishing boat and prove themselves worth their fee. But Monk refused to hire one, identifying all lawyers as kin to the one who represented his wife during their divorce. Unable to make things happen over the phone, he drove a rental to Washington to battle a many-headed water monster: IRS, Department of Commerce (Coast Guard ticket), U.S. Navy (*Shell Shock* was a documented vessel), FCC (radio license transfer), and various agencies operating under the aegis of NOAA (the National Oceanic and Atmospheric Administration). Having bought and sold cars and small boats since he was fifteen, Monk considered himself an expert in handling extra-large machinery, like the Massachusetts Registry of Motor Vehicles. However, nothing had prepared him for dealing with entrenched federal bureaucrats. To this day, he swears he's not sure how he made it out of Washington without strangling someone.

Monk left North Carolina at daybreak in the middle of May 1989 and chugged up the coast, one eye on the compass and one eye on the future, daydreaming. He says he saw himself a man on the move, the Cape Verdean mechanic who made it big in the fishing business. With plenty of fish product to peddle, he'd get his chance to wheel and deal in catch and gear, just like the top players in the game, and he'd buy low and sell high until he ran the largest fleet in the harbor. Meanwhile, he imagined himself keeping the garage as a warehouse for his new building at the South Terminal. He planned on calling his operation Monk's Marine and Motors, Triple-M for short.

The passage northward went smoothly, and each new day of a melody cruise only heightened the anxiety of a skipper expecting the worst. He was sure a storm would hit as he came abeam of Cape Fear and he was positive he'd run aground on the Intercoastal Waterway and get busted by Coasties towing him off a sandbar. For almost two hundred miles, Monk says, he couldn't change the picture in his head. It placed him inside a federal prison and sharing a cell with Uncle Pete, the two of them arguing over who gets the bottom bunk. At the time, Monk vowed he'd never run pot again; he now considers that a promise made under duress, no different from a forced confession, and he can't be held to the bargain.

When the (19)80s were about to turn 90, Monk says, New Bedford harbor was hopping, a rock-out place where fish and cheese were pouring out of boats and pockets. With landings at historic highs, shortsighted fishermen felt they had every reason to celebrate and couldn't imagine why it would ever end. For Monk, this made it comparatively easy and cheap to snag licenses, renting them from boat owners carrying three or four tickets and only interested in the big moneymaker, scalloping. Two weeks after leaving North Carolina, Monk was on the hunt for groundfish.

While most other boats were making dock laden with product, Monk says, he got used to disappointment. He had to learn the trade while on the job, and just when he got the hang of setting and towing a drag, the feds closed the only nearby groundfish area suitable for a small boat like his. He reconfigured the deck layout to start clamming, the gear in place when a red tide moved in and shut down the shellfish grounds. Months later, after the algae bloom faded and the toxins disappeared, he went after sea clams and promptly found himself competing with 110-foot clammers equipped with venturi pumps and rakes bigger than *Shell Shock*. Those boats set the market price for clams and doomed him to slim margins; on an average fourteen-hour day, he cleared less than $150. When he decided not to hire a crewman, the solo act tortured his body; he soon found himself spending more on painkillers and chiropractors than the day rate for a deckhand. He says his troubles with clams turned love into despair and got him thinking up ways to kill *Shell Shock* and collect on her insurance. Nowadays, before he goes to bed, he says one prayer: Dear God, kill her, please.

To prepare for his first attempt at a perfect wreck, he practiced knifework until he could sever an intake hose and make it look like an accident caused by defective rubber. When he put his skill to the test, issuing a Mayday as the boat slowly took on water off Nomans Island, the Coast Guard was only twelve miles away rehearsing nighttime search-and-rescue maneuvers. Two helicopters were on top of him and lowering pumps seconds after he inflated the life raft; a patrol boat soon arrived and towed *Shell Shock* into Menemsha Harbor, a dry port, not a bottle of booze to be had; he says he felt like crying. It cost $600 to have the life raft repacked, and the Coasties levied $3,750 in fines for safety and fishery violations, all of them pegged to missing gear he'd purposely left behind.

His next attempt at shipwreck was aborted near Cuttyhunk

Island, when he sighted a deer swimming the channel and decided to herd it toward shore and safety. Shepherding duty took six hours and cost him the fuel and the hours of darkness he needed to stage a near drowning. Lucky number three was also a flop, ending when he checked the horizon before going below to do the dirty work and a flare lit up the sky. In that flash of burning phosphorus, the wannabe victim transformed himself into a wannabe hero and sped to rescue mariners in distress. Along with the Coasties, *Shell Shock* scoured the area until the search was called off, the flare shooters identified as teens joyriding aboard a stolen motorboat. His fourth attempt went awry after he fell asleep at the wheel, waking as the boat crunched her way up a beach on Nashawena Island. He missed rocks by a few feet—rotten luck, that, he says—and the tow off the sand cost $700, while repairs to the bottom set him back nearly $4,000. With a $5,000 deductible in his insurance policy, Monk says, he couldn't afford any more mistakes. It was time for research and a meticulous plan for the perfect wreck.

He can't futz around anymore, he says. A few days ago his insurance company sent him a letter saying they intend to drop all policies for wooden boat owners, the age of wood about to be declared dead. The letter didn't specify a date for cancellation, but he feels he has less than a month to do the job. It would make him nervous if he wasn't so ready.

Look at this. He grabs a manila envelope on his desk and hands over the summer schedule for Coast Guard ship postings and maneuvers. It's marked SECRET, but Monk insists that every importer on the docks has a copy. His lesson learned, he won't be rescued before he's damn well ready to be rescued. The only missing piece to his plan is something he calls the bubble-down rate, which he explains as the *tick-tick* on a clock for an old woodie to sink.

This is where you come in, Sailor, he warns. He knows that

I'm headed out aboard the tug hired to sink the *Conquest,* a decommissioned wooden scalloper, once the Coast Guard certifies her oil-free and eligible for legal dumping. He also knows that the inspection is scheduled to happen in a few days. All he wants, he says, is the exact time it takes for *Conquest* to disappear, from the moment the plugs are pulled to the triumph of water. He needs to compare that bubble-down number to the one he assigned *Shell Shock.* He repeats several times why he considers this information so important: *Jackie-B, Jackie-B . . .*

The *Jackie-B* was a forty-seven-footer that went down twelve miles off Nantucket last fall, and the inquest to her sinking just ended last week. Her owner and crew was a fisherman from the Cape by the name of Starr. He bought the boat at auction after she was seized by the feds for carrying five tons of reefer. Starr was the highest bidder, at $1,001, though he was prepared to pay ten times that. He didn't care that she had sat at the dock for more than two years while her former owner appealed his conviction and had gone rotten at the gunwale, horn timber and most knees. To his eye, the *Jackie-B* looked like an investment worth a million bucks.

He became infatuated with the boat while he was doing a short stretch at the county prison (three months for aggravated assault, yet again) and buddied up with the crew of the *Jackie-B* before their transfer to a federal lockup. The hay-riders cursed the rat on the Hyannis waterfront who tipped the feds, but they promised they'd enjoy the last laugh. The boat wasn't carrying five tons of weed; they'd loaded twice that in Alabama, secreting half the cargo under floorboards and interior planking. After their release, they intended to track down their old boat, reclaim the stash and live like kings in Belize.

Starr brought the *Jackie-B* to New Bedford and started tearing her apart. After stripping off most of the interior, all he netted for his efforts was a few pounds of mildewed shake, which he couldn't give away. He was about to rip up the cabin sole when he got word that DEA agents had already sold the treasure to a local dealer, which explained why the wood he had pulled out had been tacked on, not screwed down. This information left Starr with a decision to make: sink thirty grand into the boat to make her seaworthy again or collect ten grand on the insurance policy the feds had demanded he contract before removing the boat from the auction site.

Stealing what he needed—raft, flares, radio, survival suit, emergency beacon and fuel—off a yacht, Starr set course for Lisbon. Once the diesel ran out, he issued a Mayday and opened the sea cocks. He boarded the life raft a confident man, sure he had planned for any possible screwup. The weather was perfect, dead calm. He had plenty of food. There were fresh batteries in his Walkman. And he carried a full box of .22-caliber bullets for the rifle he packed. A veteran of the court system, he valued the absence of evidence and relied on the rifle to vent any air which might get trapped inside the hull and keep an old woodie afloat long enough for Coasties to attach a towline.

Within ninety minutes of the Mayday, a Coast Guard helicopter was approaching his position. Starr, though, didn't realize the chopper was equipped with a high-tech night-vision video camera. It taped him pumping round after round into the *Jackie-B*'s nose, which protruded several feet out of the water. The bullets were no match for her oak planking, denting but never piercing the wood. In the end, the *Jackie-B* drifted into the shipping lanes, still afloat two days later; she was sunk by a Coast Guard frigate, which rammed the hazard to navigation. At the inquest, when asked if he had anything to add to the record, Starr rose from his chair and said, It was the wrong damn gun for the job, Your Honor, Captain-Commander. Whatever You Are.

Monk says when he goes to kill *Shell Shock,* he's bringing

along a freaking cannon. Actually, it's a 10-gauge sawed-off shot-gun that came with the shop and was once a favorite tool belonging to Uncle Pete. With the right mix of powder and lead, Monk claims, it will drop a hippo in a second. He also says if you aim that mother at somebody owing you cheese, you better stand back because the guy will start shitting like crazy. Since the gun has an unsavory history best kept secret, Monks says, killing *Shell Shock* will be its final act. Afterward, into the drink it goes. No fuss. No mess. No evidence.

However, he only has two shells and says it won't be easy to find more since all the noise on the neighborhood streets these days comes from automatics firing NATO rounds. He'd have to special-order ammo for his beast, but his old armorer is dead, killed during a break-in which put more than one hundred guns on the market. The one place he knows where they'll fill his order is in Freetown, and it's operated by white-power freaks who sell jacked deer meat to subsidize their trips to neo-Nazi conventions around the country. So, first, he'd have to find a real, really-like white man to broker the deal. With his dark complexion, he figures, they'd skin him and mix his meat with the venison.

You know what, though? he asks, and quickly answers, Screw it. He'll take his chances with the freaks if that's what it takes to kill *Shell Shock*. He'll tell them he's just back from Florida or that he fell asleep in a tanning booth. But he won't do anything on that front until he hears about the sinking of *Conquest*. If she buries her bow or stern right off the bat and sinks in less than one hour, he says he won't have to buy any more shells. If she sinks slow on her waterline and air gets trapped inside all her compartments, then he'll have to go shopping.

The now empty vodka bottle slides into the darkness of a drawer without a sound. Monk, though, goes loud, hollering as if trying to reach someone beyond sight: Not guilty. No sir, not guilty. Back at normal level, he explains that he's only practicing. Besides, he ain't guilty of nothing now or ever. By killing *Shell Shock,* he will be acting in self-defense, and there's no crime in that, he notes. If he doesn't do her, he'll be the perfect wreck. She'll keep nibbling away at him until there's only enough left to fill a saltshaker.

Of course, he knows that he's not alone in the hurt department. He's not blind. It's awful luck being a fisherman these days and it's worse-awful-bad luck being a fisherman anchored to a small boat. Like him, his colleagues in the trade realize there's no place for small boats in the business anymore. Unlike him, most have left the fishing game, abandoning their boats to bang nails or drive trucks or go on the dole. Every time he visits Pier 3, it reminds him of the lost and found department at the old bus station downtown: just a bunch of junk nobody wants to remember they ever owned and nothing a junkie would even steal.

Near the bulkhead to Pier 3, there's a fifty-yard stretch of floating heaps. It's the holding pen for abandoned boats and over the years, one boat length a season, *Shell Shock* has been issued berthing space ever closer to the bulkhead. Monk tugs at a forefinger as he lists some of the unwanted baggage parked near *Shell Shock: Bullwinkle, Missy of the Sea, Barb and Dolly, Baby-D.* Them and more, he says, are all the same: each a woodie with punk and sponge everywhere, each under forty-five feet in length, and every one coated in lead paint inside and out. He feels the government should pay for the disposal of the derelicts, since all their regs, rules and quotas were nothing more than toe tags for small fishing boats.

He'd go on, but for the first time all morning the sun breaks through the clouds, and Monk salutes the sudden warm-up. Shine on me, baby, he says, stepping outside to bask in the rays, his eyes on the city crew draining the Belleville flood.

Inside the shop, the ambient light barely increases a notch. The garage doors face north, and each window is covered in iron plate carrying rebar welded in a tic-tac-toe pattern. Monk once said he got drunk one night and counted all the drawers in the garage and came up with 406,000. Three hundred is a better guess, but it's possible they contain 406,000 different parts and fastenings. Like Uncle Pete, Monk rarely throws out anything, believing its usefulness will appear sometime in the future. Although none of the drawers are labeled, he knows precisely where to look when searching for some arcane part—say, a throttle pin to a 1956 Evinrude outboard. Scattered around the shop is a history lesson in marine propulsion systems from the 1920s (a one-cylinder Lister) through the 1970s (an Olds 350 Rocket equipped with a marine pack) and up to today (an outboard still in its shipping crate).

The garage was originally built as a no-frills neighborhood repair and pump shop, its cinder-block walls laid in the 1940s atop the ashes of a triple-decker. Uncle Pete bought the place in 1965 and remodeled some of it, adding a paint booth and iron to the windows. He also ripped out the pumps and replaced them with two German shepherds on long chains. The new layout helped him and his crew process the heist of the day. At first, his gang specialized in stealing box trucks; older models were either shipped to the Azores or chopped up and sold piecemeal to local body shops, while late-model vehicles were usually sprayed a new color, issued bogus identification numbers and sold out of state. In 1971, Uncle Pete left the hot-truck business to concentrate on stealing high-end transports, like Cadillacs, Lincolns and Jaguars. Around the same time, he launched a new career as a drug wholesaler in the powder trade.

Monk started his apprenticeship at age eight, sweeping floors and rolling unwanted evidence—useless tires and rims—into the estuary and delivering packages on his bicycle to body shops around town. Along the way, and at a speedy pace, he learned the basics of engine repair. In the sixth grade, he was given run of the place and no longer had to knock before opening a door. The next Christmas Uncle Pete set him up in the fix-it trade, allowing Monk to start his own shop in the old gas station office, a separate room and visible to street traffic. Monk went to work repairing dirt bikes for friends and lawn mowers for the extended Lopes family.

At the end of junior high, Monk said, he really got into it, realizing that his popularity at school was soaring among peers and older teens, his status A-one to those needing work on their motorcycles and cars. Soon afterward, and thanks to Uncle Pete's tutoring, his relationship with motors hit a new, more sat-isfying level as he began to understand their language and could diagnose ailments from their sounds. Monk was and is a sucker for new gadgets and a compulsive catalog reader, determined to have the latest and best gear in the trade, and he put all the money he earned into tools and more tools. His reputation was made after word leaked out that he was fixing the outboards belonging to instructors teaching automotive arts at the high school.

Once, years ago, Monk made me inspect his palm, specifi-cally his life line where it's slashed by a short, thick crease. He said the crease marked the day Uncle Pete was arrested. One minute before the crease, he described himself as an average, not too-too fucked-up kid rounding the corner toward his six-teenth birthday. The next minute, he was freaking out, feeling like an ant about to be squished under a gumshoe. Five cruisers, lights blazing, and seven cops, guns drawn, converged on him as he left the supermarket with his mom and younger brother. Get on your knees. Hands up, the cops shouted. He lost his grip on a gallon of milk; the container hit the ground, broke and drenched his socks and sneakers; a moment later, he was kneel-ing in milk as his mom screamed and brother cried. He was kept overnight at the police station, where he was grilled for hours by local cops and FBI agents. He refused to believe a word they were saying about Uncle Pete. A murderer? No way, not Uncle Pete. He's a good guy, really nice. A mobbed-up dope dealer? Not Uncle Pete. He doesn't use drugs.

Monk arrived home in time to watch lawmen finish empty-ing the garage, seizing all its contents as either evidence or stolen property. In addition to Monk's tools, the cops trucked away the machines he was working on: two motorcycles, four dirt bikes, one go-kart and numerous lawn mowers. Some of the owners of these items were enraged and a few wanted to kill him. Suddenly, Monk had to watch his step, careful not to wander near homes or hangouts of unhappy customers. But he couldn't avoid traps, and after being beaten to a pulp in a school bathroom, he kissed off New Bedford High, too scared to return. When his body healed, he took a job in the repair department of a car dealership.

Like the rest of his family, he maintained silence, never men-tioning Uncle Pete's name and refusing to confront the abuse heaped on the clan by fellow Portuguese islanders, many of whom identified one bad fruit as the product of a rotten family tree. The phone at home went silent; his parents started eating lunch alone, shunned by fellow workers and old friends at the mill. Monk said his family was blackballed by the only commu-nity they knew, leading them to adopt the traditional Portu-guese islander's defense: denial at every turn. Whenever a letter arrived from Uncle Pete, Monk's dad or Grampy-J would burn it at the stove without peeking inside. They met sneers with smiles on the street and, while standing in line at a store, pre-tended not to hear their name dragged through the dirt.

In the 1970s, the vast majority living in the neighborhood were Portuguese speakers; their enclave was one of several in the city where residents considered all Lopeses to be murderers. Each of these districts was further defined and set off from the

rest of town by island roots set deep in the Azores or Madeira or
São Tomé or Cabo Verde. As a group, they were darker-skinned
than Iberians and spoke an island dialect which mainlanders
tended to mock, considering it gutter talk full of harsh sounds
and African influences. Throughout the area, islanders formed a
tight community, nearly thirty thousand strong, and since they
preferred insulation over integration, community leaders cut a
tacit deal with the local political machine: leave us alone and
we'll leave city affairs to you. Come election time every Novem-
ber, Monk's neighborhood usually posted the worst results in
terms of ballots cast versus eligible voters of any city ward.

Comfortably surrounded by the familiar from the old
country—Portuguese banks with Portuguese-speaking tellers,
Portuguese-speaking insurance agencies, lawyers, cafes, shops,
bakeries, foremen at work—people felt no pressing need to
adapt to a new climate and place. Instead, they happily obliged
old-world rules, totems and taboos, rituals and hierarchies, all of
it derived from the melding of Iberian and West African traditions and all of it steeped in Catholicism and stuck in some
ancient rut. While denial helped him get through the day, Monk
said, the family never lost hope and prayed together every night
for someone else to screw up. It was nothing you said out loud,
he explained, but that was what we were telling God, you know;
Jesus, please, send us a mass murderer from the Azores or Cabo
Verde. What we, us, the Lopeses needed, he added, was people
treating some other family as the worst thing since sliced bread
and canned olives.

Approximately five months after Uncle Pete's arrest, the heat
went off the Lopes clan, the family prayers answered when a
man up the street came unhinged while holding a revolver. First
he shot the dog, then he shot his girlfriend twice and did in two
parakeets before using the last bullet on himself. It was big news
and monopolized the community airwaves for weeks afterward.
How anyone could kill all those animals, poor souls, became a

debate topic which shuttled Uncle Pete out of the conversation. At last, the phone started ringing at Monk's house; lunch breaks for his folks became chances to catch up with old friends; and he no longer went to the bakery expecting to hear whispered remarks about his family.

While his former high school classmates were visiting Sullivan Brothers to rent tuxes for the senior prom, Monk quit his job at the car dealership and reopened his business at Uncle Pete's garage. Sure that the cops had him under surveillance as heir to Uncle Pete's empire of crime, Monk said, he was scared to fart in public and kept everything at the shop squeaky-clean. Seeking respectability, he joined the chamber of commerce, and he once attended its annual soiree at the Hawthorne Country Club, in the burbs. He remembered being the only brown-eyed, dark-skinned person in the room not carrying a tray and the only guest under thirty not snorting coke off a butter dish.

After two years as Mr. Clean, Monk got back in step with his natural rhythm. Once again, he dabbled in crime, and described his efforts as barely worth a felony, like dealing weed and reselling car stereos nicked by the Holly Street gang, headquartered a few blocks from the garage. He also said he was embarrassed that it took him so long to shake his paranoia and readjust, going from the submissive (Yes sir, Officer) back to normal pitch (Prove it, cop). He quit the chamber of commerce and joined the North End Business Association, which met in places like Cafe Mimo and Cafe Portugal to discuss parking regulations and Christmas decorations on the main drag. He also sponsored a kids' soccer team, as well as an adult version, both named the Mechanics.

According to Monk, booze is a necessary part of life and crucial to existence in New Bedford. Grapes grow in most North End backyards, and those arbors which remain pruned and weed-free signal a Portuguese islander still in residence. Monk's dad and Grampy-J were both semipro vintners and were able to sell as much as they liked. Growing up, Monk said, there was always wine at the table, while a pint of the hard stuff lived in Grampy-J's pocket. After he made First Communion, Monk was issued his own wineglass at family meals. While he still loves wine, he favors vodka, just like Grampy-J.

Typical of any boozehound, Monk considers himself a temperate man, nothing more than a social drinker. However, he once confided that his sipping briefly turned into guzzling when his marriage went to hell. He and Lisa were hooked together for sixteen months, but their relationship had soured well before then. Even so, when Lisa gave birth to a beautiful girl, Baby Rita, he stopped his bickering, willing to do anything to keep the family together. A proud dad, he'd leave the shop feeling ten feet tall knowing he was returning home to the most wonderful child in the world. Still on cloud nine two weeks after Baby Rita's birth, he entered the apartment and found a one-word note from Lisa on the back of the phone bill: SORRY. She had taken Rita and split to live with another man in the Azores. Eventually, the street gossip was verified by a Boston lab: Rita wasn't his kid. Monk rarely talks about it.

S-O-S, Sailor. Same old shit, Monk announces, walking into the garage with the latest news on the problem at the end of the block. The city crew packed up their pumps and left, the floodwater now less than an inch or two deep. As always, the sewage was sent in two directions, with some seeping into basements and most heading into the estuary. In a few more hours, he expects, Belleville will be bone dry, allowing the dregs to cook in the sun and cause a stink for a day or two. It depends on the thermometer and wind velocity.

Monk says the real damage from the flood is heading out to sea. In fact, he's willing to bet a million bucks that the coliform count in the estuary would redline any measuring device. In the mid-1970s, he remembers, the estuary was declared a dead zone by investigators hired by the EPA. Their study found only trace levels of oxygen in the water and no visible proof of marine life. Since then, the EPA has spent more than twenty years and over $200 million to dredge the so-called hot spots, areas in the harbor and estuary where PCBs and heavy metals had accumulated in killer proportions. It may take another twenty years and an additional $200 million to finish the harbor cleanup and shut down the SuperFund project originally budgeted at $120 million.

Although the effort was spectacularly costly and riddled with failed experiments and miscalculations, the EPA did improve water quality in the estuary. For the first time in his life, Monk saw a horseshoe crab there, in August 1995, and mussels and clams started appearing the next year. Even so, the ecosystem remains sick and large sections have yet to snap out of a chemically induced coma. Monk feels today's sewage spill will twist things the wrong damn way for the umpteenth time too many. Soon, maybe, he says, he'll see horseshoe crabs glowing in the dark.

He predicts more trouble ahead, as the *E. coli* rides the tide, exits the hurricane dike and takes up temporary residence in bivalves from New Bedford to Cuttyhunk Island. Much of the area is already closed to clammers and quahoggers, and Monk suspects that today's release of poison is just the sort of hopeless, never-right news that might send a shellman postal. He says those guys in the inshore quahog trade are going cuckoo from not working and not knowing when they'll work again, if ever. He thinks those men will especially appreciate his manual, *Tune-up for the Perfect Wreck.* Many of their boats haven't left the harbor in months, and the manual will put light back into the day for quahoggers.

A fresh breeze blows in off the sidewalk, arriving in the form of Alan. He carries a brown paper bag from R&B Liquors and greets Monk, saying, It's Saturday, fool, drink beer. Cans of suds are opened and a joint passed around. Everyone makes sure to exhale downwind from the shop door.

Alan is the first person I ever lied for in New Bedford, telling a cop in a cruiser, Nope, Officer, nobody ran this way. The runner was Alan—back in his slimmer and coke-fueled days—and he'd ducked down an alley at the mill. Once the cop left, Alan approached to both thank me and welcome me to the neighborhood. For you, brother, cheap, he said, offering to swap the Pioneer car stereo in his hands for twenty dollars. I had ten and change, so there was no deal, but the Welcome Wagon was still open and Alan decided to show me around. You'll love this fucking place, he promised, and led the way through backyards. The first stop was Monk's garage, to drop off the stereo. As Alan explained, You can't lie real good when shit's in your hands, ya-know.

Monk and Alan go back to the starting point, born days apart at St. Luke's Hospital and taken to homes sited within a five-minute walk of each other. Thereafter, the two kept pace in at least one direction, growing tall at the same rate, but Monk was always skinny and Alan usually chunky. Their identical height put them one in front of the other in class lineups throughout their stay at Immaculate Conception School, at the corner of Belleville and Davis. Other kids called the pair the (Fig) Newtons, because of Alan's pasty wrapper and Monk's deep, olive-brown skin tone. Today, Alan suffers in comparison to his best friend, his facial coloring a patchwork of bright reds from burst corpuscles, with a rummy's big-pored nose, and outfitted with clothes from the Big Man Shop at the mall. And while Alan is going bald, Monk's black hair is thick and heavily greased, as usual.

Alan is a Yvette, his family having settled in New Bedford after his grandfather left southern Quebec as a teen in 1922 and joined thousands of other Frenchies already working in the city's textile mills. From 1890 to 1925, they found life so utterly impossible in English Canada that a lousy job paying less than $3 a day could lead them away from home. Adept in the workplace, eager, and wanting to assimilate into American culture, the Francophones sped up the corporate ladder, many becoming foremen or meriting choice assignments as loom mechanics. They were also quick to depart tenement living, and by the late 1920s, the majority had either left the neighborhood for single-family homes in fancier parts of town or had left New Bedford for better-paying jobs elsewhere.

Alan's branch of the Yvette family dug in, buying the triple-decker which Gramps once shared with thirty-two other renters. Alan's dad held on to the property after Portuguese speakers started to flood the area, beginning in the late 1950s. Alan, an only child, inherited the house after his parents died in a freak accident while vacationing in Florida—a construction boom fell atop their car as they sat at a red light. He managed to keep the house through two bitter divorces, something he calls a miracle in the state of Missus-gets-to-choose-it.

He and Monk are among the six left of their old crowd who haven't died—AIDS, mostly—or haven't moved away from New Bedford either by choice or by court order. And they're the only two still living in the neighborhood. Inside Monk's desk drawer, there's a snapshot taken of guests at Maria Rebello's tenth birthday party. It shows twenty-seven kids crowding the frame, with Alan and Monk in the front row; it now sits atop a stack of fourteen mass cards, each bearing the name of someone at that party.

A shouting match erupts at the corner of North Front Street, about seventy-five yards away. Reflexively, Alan and Monk twist at the waist and lock eyes on long-handled tools before refocusing on the action. Last week a fender bender involving a Puerto Rican and a Dominican escalated into tribal warfare after a partisan crowd gathered and the two sides went at each other. By the time cops arrived, firemen had already extinguished two car fires and the crowd had vanished. Today, the dispute pits one drug dealer against another, each claiming exclusive rights to doing business at the corner and each determined to service a buyer idling in a red Pontiac Sunbird at the curb.

Monk, who speaks fluent Portuguese, says he also speaks Spic inside out, so he translates: Shithead One, see, is telling Shithead Two to back off or he'll kill the guy. Shithead Two is telling Shithead One to go ahead and try. And, well, you know: same old, same old, he concludes. The yelling, though, continues.

The would-be customer speeds away, leaving the drama makers to go at each other. They're woeful pugilists and no better at kicking; however, both men appear to be pro smokers, wheezing and too winded to continue brawling after an initial flurry of missed punches and kicks. As they walk in opposite directions, they issue identical parting shots: a pledge to kill the other with a bullet through the fucking head.

Monk can't decide what brand the dealers are riding for. Was it two Ricans? Two Dominicans? One of each? Alan hopes they're from the same tribe and intimate with each other's address and routines. Otherwise, he says, them dopes couldn't find tits on a cow. A few days ago, while he was putting out the trash, a lowrider cruised his block with three Spics inside. Two pointed automatics out the windows. He says the car stopped near him and one guy asked for directions: Where Pedro live, man? He gonna die. Alan pointed up the street, where, he says, every-fucking-body with a dick is named Pedro. Once the car pulled away, Alan ran for the door.

Gangs affiliated with the two ethnic groups (Puerto Rican and Dominican) have been fighting over franchise rights—who gets to sell what and where—ever since the first wave of Spanish speakers landed in New Bedford, in the early 1990s. Escalating rents around Boston forced the poor to find other, cheaper digs, and New Bedford tenements fit the bill. By 1999, with the gentrification of Beantown in full swing, rents never higher, Spanish replaced Portuguese as this neighborhood's lingua franca, a new majority in residence. Meanwhile, many Portuguese owner-occupants of triple-deckers began selling their homes to the same Boston-based landlords who had sent their Section Eight tenants packing in the first place.

As yuppies began displacing their clientele and crowding their old, well-defined turf, Boston-bred street gangs set up shop in New Bedford. They arrived well armed and well organized, putting the local cops on the defensive, and quickly took control of one rather small segment of the city's powder trade: street dealing. In a few years, good at their work, they established themselves as powder kingpins and turned New Bedford into a drug warehouse supplying product to cities from Bangor to Baltimore. But it may take several more years before they can agree among themselves on local turf ownership and a pecking order.

The influx of Hispanics gave the Portuguese a step up the social ladder, and Monk claims it's great to be out of the cellar. The rush of Spanish speakers also gave the Portuguese an opportunity to cash out of the neighborhood after years of watching their homes depreciate in value. Before the Spics washed up onshore, Monk says, the neighborhood was like a prison: nobody wanted in and nobody could get out.

The urge to cut anchor took hold of Monk's neighbors in the early 1980s. The glue bonding the Portuguese islander community was partly dissolved by the influence of maturing children born to parents who got green cards in the 1950s and 1960s. Monk, however, insists nothing changed people more than one very fucked-up night in 1983. It all happened atop a pool table at Big Dan's Bar on Belleville, when a woman from the neighborhood was gang-raped. He refers to that crime as the Horror on

Belleville, and says it and the hubbub surrounding the court verdict turned Portuguese heads like that kid in the movie *The
Exorcist*.

The cops arrested four neighborhood men on rape and
assault charges. Guided by a moral compass untrued for centuries, the Portuguese community was outraged, sure the men
were innocent, their actions merely the result of men being
men. It was all the woman's fault, they said, their reasoning
archaic: no good Portuguese girl would ever go unescorted to a
bar late at night; therefore, she was a bad girl asking for what
she got. Sadly, Monk recalls that what he and his family endured
because of Uncle Pete was nothing compared to the venom
spewed at the woman and her family. On March 17, 1984, the day
after a jury handed down a guilty verdict, eight thousand Portuguese speakers took to the street to cheer the guilty.

The demonstrators rallied at the Church of the Immaculate
Conception and then marched, chanting, Free the Four. They
believed the men were not only victims of a racist judicial system but also victims of a Jezebel. Clutching rosary beads and
carrying statues of the Virgin, the marchers wore black, and more
women than men walked the parade route down Belleville.
Their voices thundered as they passed the scene of the heinous
crime, now a Bunny Bread outlet store, which took over Big
Dan's space when the bar closed for good a few days after the
crime.

Monk recalls how TV coverage of the parade made the world
want to puke all over his neighborhood. The publicity prompted
the archbishop to muzzle local priests and nuns who'd helped
organize the rally. In turn, the state set up free, walk-in family
counseling clinics, while city hall, in its effort to effect change
among community leaders, dispatched health and building inspectors to comb through Portuguese-owned businesses. Meanwhile,
the city's very vocal and well-organized gay, lesbian and trans-

gender support groups starting outing big shots in the Portuguese orbit. They stapled pictures of closet homosexuals on
telephone poles, along with large lettering saying I AM A HOMO,
followed by pertinent testimony from partners.

Initially, Portuguese neighborhoods around town circled the
wagons and adopted a siege mentality. But that didn't last long;
the vast majority, Monk says, caved pretty damn quick. He
explains: The deny every-fucking-thing approach wasn't working. It couldn't. The problem was staring at folks in the mirror
and looking at them out of every puddle. The Portuguese had
to make a choice: Get with the program or get with the program. This was America, for Christ's sake. The island way was
no way no more. He doubts anyone was made happier by this
turn of events than he was, still bitter about the way the old system pummeled him and his family.

Fresh beers are opened and Alan toasts the neighborhood
majority. The more the merrier, he salutes. Monk issues a
quizzical look, but drinks anyway. For Alan, the rising tide of
Hispanics means he can charge higher rents and entertain ever
better offers to buy his triple-decker. During his last divorce, in
1993, the lawyer for his ex valued the property at $47,000, at least
ten grand over what the market would pay and grossly unfair,
he says. A month ago, though, the triple-decker at the end of his
block sold for $164,000, and he calls his place the Taj Mahal com-
pared to that dump. Realtors now approach him two or three
times a month with new offers, and sometime soon he expects
Joe Slick out of Boston to meet his magic number, $222,222.

Alan chugs what remains in the beer can, says he's hooked on
twos and belches loud enough to wake someone sleeping next
door. No matter what, he's ready to boogie, he says, and can't
wait to move. With the way shit's going around here, he doubts
there'll be a working-class family living on his street in another
year, two at the most. Instead, he predicts that every triple-

decker near his will be home to pissed-off people on the dole, the whole area a goddamn slum in the making. He says he can't see anything else happening and explains his view: There are no jobs. Period.

Alan steps into the street and points eastward, toward the former site of Pierce Mill, now a twenty-two-acre wasteland of rubble, weeds, litter and used syringes which separates Belleville from the estuary. For generations, the mill complex employed nearly a thousand people in the manufacture of cotton goods, only to end up as part of a string of mill fires attached to arsonists. They torched the mill in June 1993. The flames were seen as far away as Hyannis, while cops on Martha's Vineyard fielded reports of UFOs over the mainland, the callers unsure how else to explain trails of pulsing blue and yellow light in the air. In fact, the colors came out of blasts of superhot gases which zoomed skyward every time a mill window blew out with the force of an artillery round. More than one million square feet of flooring saturated in machine oil fueled the blaze, and firemen were on the scene through the night. Once the smoke cleared, cops ringed the 1,450-foot-long hulk with yellow tape saying CAUTION, and that's how things stayed for years.

Monk nods. Without the factories, he says, there'd be no neighborhood. Hell, he adds, the mills gave life and direction to the entire city and now that they're kaput, engine and rudder gone, it's the rocks for sure, and forever. Indeed, after watching Pierce Mill go up, he thinks the remaining empty mills in town could take down every neighborhood they built if they were torched. He says if the wind hadn't been out of the southwest and pushing all the hot stuff from Pierce Mill over the estuary, the whole North End would've lit up. He then gestures at the landscape of stick-built triple-deckers, all set cheek by jowl, and says, Matchsticks. It's the reason he never misses a payment on his fire insurance for the garage.

Alan was working the second shift at Titleist on the night of the big blaze, but he saw enough on TV to scare him half to death. Like his dad, he took a job making golf balls after graduating high school and says it was that or the army or a job in some other mill. He feels his choice, knock on wood, has kept him alive. He reasons: They shoot at you in the army and they shot the guts out of almost every other mill around. He lists some of the casualties: Chamberlain, Goodyear, Firestone, United Rubber, Atlas Tack, Morse Cutting Tools, Cliftex, Madewell, Justin-Shepherd, Cameo, Cornell Dubilier, Carol Cable, Continental Screw, Berkshire Hathaway, and Polaroid. He says he used to be 110 percent sure Titleist would never leave New Bedford, but now he wouldn't bet ten cents on that. Every time employees bitch about pay, bennies or whatever, he claims, the shits-in-suits just point to China on the map.

As Alan concentrates on draining another beer, a horn beeps aboard a sedan turning off Belleville and heading up the street. It's Mister Cuoto, Monk says, going for the peppermint Life Savers he keeps in his desk. Mr. Cuoto is a longtime customer, family friend and former neighbor, just the sort to tell his mom that her son was drinking in the morning. He owns the outboard set up in the test tank, and Monk wants to walk him through the repair process and explain why the bill is $13.60 over the original estimate. Mechanic and customer greet each other in Portuguese.

Which way you headed? Alan asks.

Down and over. I'm going home.

Hey, will you be able to stay in that mill much longer?

I shrug. It's for sale and has been for years. In the past, one glance at the estimate for building repairs and its yearly maintenance costs has chased away every tire kicker. The windows alone need a million-dollar fix (there are 290 of them and each is the size of a garage door) and the boiler eats 1.1 gallons of oil per minute. Recently, though, developers have been circling the mill and talking about demolishing it to make way for something new.

Alan says he heard a deal is an inch away from happening, with Home Depot about to call in the wrecker's ball. Believe me, brother, he says, the mills are coming down. Either fire or fat cats will flatten them, and soon. The machines are gone. The workers are gone. Industry in this whole damn town is pretty much gone. And what was just ain't-no-anymore. He lets that sink in, then adds, When she's dead, she's dead. The fighting's over, so's the shouting. Say, another beer for the road?

I head out but linger at the corner of Belleville, directly across from a sign erected by the city years ago that says FUTURE HOME OF PIERCE MILL PARK. It seems a good place to recall an earlier time, when the mills lining Belleville were filled with whirling machinery and the street crowded with shouters and fighters. The combatants were part of a fifth column that vitalized the American labor movement during its infancy and led the charge against the oligarchy. As a group, they were an unruly mix of socialists, Communists and anarchists, and Belleville was their home turf as well as their parade ground and battlefield. For a hundred years, starting in the 1870s, they helped shape the neighborhood, informing the conversation and molding character. And as spear-carriers in the war for workers' rights, they installed a fighter's tradition and a syndicalist's creed inside most triple-deckers: Fuck with me / Fuck with you / And double-fuck management lackeys, Pinkertons and cops.

Throughout the Industrial Age, New Bedford was a hard-core union town and, fittingly, the extremes, the North End and the South End, were bastions of radical unionism. During the mill strike of 1898, for instance, thousands of workers marched down Belleville and up the hill toward Millionaires' Row, on County Street. They intended to run all the rich people out of town and use their mansions for low-income housing and as headquarters for a battle ahead. Their plan: take over both city hall and the mills and put the proletariat in charge of the works. Remarkably, the revolution nearly started in New Bedford, the ranks of unskilled workers swelling by the minute, joined by members of the more conservative trade unions and the unemployed. However, their quest to destroy capitalism stalled a few blocks from Millionaires' Row, stopped by a phalanx of cops, state militia and Pinkertons. Afterward, there wasn't a bed available for months at any of the city's health clinics for the poor.

While the relatively tame unions affiliated with the AFL grew in size and power in other places, New Bedford workers steered leftward and stayed the course. The city was always a disappointment to headliners like Samuel Gompers, who drew a fraction of the crowd attending rallies hosted by Eugene Debs and his more lefty half, Daniel De Leon. But plenty of other local workers considered socialism a system of half measures, and by 1912 there were enough anarchists in town to pack four different meeting halls five days a week. Later, Nicola Sacco and Bartolomeo Vanzetti were regular visitors, arriving by train from Brockton, along with carloads of colleagues. Most likely, any plan to rob a bank and use the cash to finance the violent overthrow of government was hatched in the neighborhood.

Greetings from Comrade Lenin were read to city workers by Big Jim Larkin, who made repeated visits on business for the Second International. At one outdoor rally attended by nearly ten thousand people, Big Jim urged the crowd to retune the machine and junk all capitalist parts. It almost worked in 1898, and this time: success, he said. Within a year of his speech, more than a score were arrested while attempting to kidnap mill owners; as ransom, they were going to demand the transfer of factory ownership to the workers. Subsequent efforts to storm the jail and free the men also failed, further crowding the joint with revolutionaries. Their jailhouse chatter prompted one prison guard to ask a journalist, Who is this Marx prisoners talk about so much? And who's Bakunin?

In the 1920s, as the membership rolls of city unions surpassed the thirty thousand mark, the Communist Party gave rise to a new workers' group, The Mill Committee. In 1928, when factory owners threatened to cut wages by 10 percent, The Mill Committee called for a 20 percent wage hike, plus an equity stake for workers in all the factories. The owners went ahead with the wage cut and the strike of 1928 was on, and the battle continued from April to October. The city lost its hum, the machines silenced as thirty-three thousand workers walked picket lines.

Through a combination of tough talk, militant tactics and an open-door policy offering membership to women and immigrants barely able to speak English, The Mill Committee grew into the largest and loudest of all workers' mouthpieces. Almost as quickly, its star faded, blackened through the malicious and concerted efforts of other unions, the courts, clergy, cops, feds and, of course, mill owners and management. Even so, The Mill Committee kept up steam, its offices packed, until a few years after World War II, when Reds became as unwelcome as African-Americans in American industry. A court order outlawed The Mill Committee in the early 1950s, the feds seizing every chair, pencil and typewriter as instruments abetting a nest of Commie spies and seditious aliens.

The fight went out of the neighborhood in 1980, the year of the last strike by organized labor in New Bedford. Thereafter, the shouting eased to a whisper, and all went quiet when the last neighborhood union hall closed its doors, in 1997, unable to pay the rent.

———

Notes for Monk and his plans for the perfect wreck begin aboard a tug. There are three of us on station, and Garr stands at the controls. The tug is his baby. He watched her grow from a set of scaled lines on paper into sixty-eight feet of floating iron and muscle. She's triple-thick where most boats are single-ply and equipped with oversized hardware both welded and bolted in place. Powered by twin diesels, she's able to push around ships fifteen times her length and hundreds of times her weight.

The tug is the centerpiece of Garr's marine construction and towing business. Mostly, he bids on large-scale federal or municipal contracts, lengthy gigs which can utilize and pay for all his specialized equipment, including barges, seven-story cranes swinging three-yard buckets, pile drivers, small workboats, miles of hose and piping, jet pumps, regular pumps and more pumps. The tug puts everything into position, towing gear to the job and maneuvering each piece as work progresses; additionally, she's available for charter, and Garr says he'd tow whatever-the-fuck around the world for the right cheese.

Today, Garr is out to clean the slate. He owed a big favor to a man now dead, the owner of the *Conquest,* and when the family asked for help in sinking the old fishing boat before she fell apart and became an even bigger headache, he agreed. In fact, he welcomed the opportunity to erase his debt, imagining hell hard enough without getting dunned by a fellow resident. The mate signed on for the job at no pay because he wants to stay a mate on the tug. I'm aboard at the skipper's invitation. Neither of us has ever seen an offshore fishing boat sink and Garr thought burial duty would appeal to me.

The harbor bridge swings open, clearing the way to a sleepy inner harbor, and Garr lays into the throttle. The engines roar. Underfoot, the diamond plating shudders. Twin props big enough to lift an airplane whip the water into a froth off the stern. Coffee mugs on the navigation table come to life, their ceramic bottoms clicking like tap shoes. Slowly, as if she must raise herself from a chair she's sat in too long, the tug gathers momentum and picks up speed. As Garr says, Nothing much happens fast on tugs, except screwups.

Conquest is tied to a semisubmerged, 150-foot-long barge; it was commissioned by a navy at war with Nazis but launched after peace arrived and left to rot, unwanted and unused. Set back from the water, a Quonset hut carries black lettering inside its weather arch: MOBY DICK MARINA. The place was originally set up as a do-it-yourself boatyard, offering an alternative to the well-equipped and pricey shipyards in town. The operation went belly-up in the late 1980s, but the do-it-yourselfers kept coming. While many finished their projects and left, others gave up, drained of cash or desire, and abandoned their boats to rot. The junked craft attracted more junk, along with a new name for the place: the graveyard.

In the mid-1990s, the EPA measured heart-stopping amounts of toxins in the graveyard's muck and included the site in the harbor SuperFund program. That declaration, plus hefty fines attached to new Coast Guard rules on decommissioning fishing boats, made dumping risky business. But midnight deliveries continued, the packages arriving without return addresses— name boards and engine numbers scraped clean—and at the moment, more than thirty hulks are in view. All of them are woodies and most are over fifty feet in length, too big for long-term parking with the other derelicts near *Shell Shock* at the pier.

The tug comes abeam of *Conquest* with a slight tap and Garr gets his first up-close look at the unwanted boat. Yowsir, worm food, one hundred percent, he says, noting patches of rot and a deck riddled with holes where salvaged gear was sawed free of its moorings. He thinks she'll sink easy-deezy, bubble a bit and disappear. He predicts we'll be back by three p.m., leaving him plenty of time to drive to his kid's soccer game.

The hookup takes a few minutes, and with *Conquest* on a short leash, her rudder lashed amidships, the tug inches toward the channel, the props barely turning. One hand on the throttle, the other hand on the gear lever, a Marlboro between his teeth and both eyes on the depth sounder, Garr mutters a prayer: Sweet Jesus, please, a clear path. The tug draws twelve feet of water and he worries about the props getting fouled in this shallow stretch of the harbor hard by the estuary. Once, years ago, a coil of BX wire got wrapped in the propellers not far from here and he says the yard bill for repairs was like something from another planet made of cheese. His petition granted, the depth sounder showing ample water under the keel, Garr speeds up the channel.

This time the swing bridge opens to the main harbor, where the workday never stops. Scores of people go about their dockside business, including a panoply of hookers, dealers, boat crews and contractors. The South Terminal looks especially busy, every crane in use lifting product—scallops and groundfish—out of boat holds and depositing the goods into stainless chutes leading inside processing plants. A few people stop what they're doing to stare at the tow, but no one waves good-bye to the old lady headed to her grave.

With no traffic ahead, Garr increases speed. The faster he exits the harbor, the better he'll feel. Right now, as it is anytime he's flanked by fishing boats, he can't be sure what to expect other than a sensation of alarm. He says there are so many junkie-fishermen in the fleet that all bets are off and all rules of the road suspended. Of course, this makes him nervous, a prim among sinners, but he's glad the adrenaline is flowing. He might be forced to act in an instant, so he welcomes anything making him more aware than ever. He has seen fishermen nod out and slump over the wheel, their boats turned into battering rams. Other times, he has watched fishermen mistake port for starboard and reverse gear for forward gear, not realizing their mistake until they hit something. And sometimes, he adds, even when they smack into something, them piss-for-brains don't know it.

As proof, he recounts a recent incident involving a clammer which barreled into the bridge supports, rolled off and kept going. The boat was later found tied to the clam dock and showing a large dent on the starboard side. The captain was in his bunk, but too high to answer the simplest question: What's your name? The boat owner put a stop to further questioning and led the captain away before Coast Guard investigators arrived demanding a blood test.

As the tug and her tow pass through the gate in the hurricane dike and enter open water, Garr steps out of the wheelhouse to pump air while stretching his five-foot-seven frame. With his torso fully extended, arms reaching for the sky, his beer gut disappears and a man in his forties moans like a load-bearing timber approaching its limit. The exercise period ends in an equally long bout of coughing, and he spits the accumulated phlegm an impressive distance over the rail. No better medicine than ocean air, he reports.

Back at the controls, Garr opens a new pack of cigarettes, freshens his coffee mug and claims it's time for work. Flipping on the intercom, he blares orders to the mate at the bollard. He wants to lengthen the towline and put both boats, tug and *Conquest,* in sync, with each riding the crest of a wave at the same moment and in step out of every trough. This will minimize the slack-snap action on the load line. Tension, he says, constant fucking tension is what you want.

Conquest nears position. Slowly-slowly, Garr orders the mate paying out the line. A few seconds later, he barks, Snub 'er. He turns off the intercom, satisfied by the taut connection, and lets his eyes wander over the tow. For a dead lady, he says, *Conquest* is looking pretty sharp. At 250 feet astern, and awash in both direct sunshine and reflected light off the water, *Conquest* practically glows. From our angle, all her faults are lost in the glare or hidden behind her high nose and rail. Garr says if he didn't know better, he'd guess she was ready for another go at fishing.

Conquest was built at the Newbert & Wallace Shipyard in Thomaston, Maine, and launched in July 1966. Assembled with hand tools and sweat, and endowed with traditional lines that put a purposeful curve into every stick, she was made entirely of white oak. At sixty-eight feet long and nineteen feet wide amidships, she was treated as a member of the family by her original owner, who coaxed the best out of her, earning him high-line honors for landings several times a year. When he retired in 1977, ownership kept changing hands until, in the end, she was steered into trouble and forced by court order to sit at the dock, her license to fish revoked for five years. Rainwater eventually washed out the preserving effects of salt, and rot set in and spread. When her license was reinstated, the paper worth a considerable fortune, the hull was deemed worthless, too far gone to repair.

Garr pulls back on the throttle as the tug nears the cemetery, a rectangular patch of ocean twenty-one miles southwest of Gay Head. On nautical charts, the site is identified by a series of dotted lines boxing in the words DUMPING GROUNDS. For years, the Coast Guard has designated this place as the last stop for just about everything humans don't want anymore, including unexploded ordnance from conflicts dating back to the Spanish-American War.

It was right around here, somewhere, Garr says, gesturing at a markerless swath of Rhode Island Sound near Cox Ledge, where he saw a great white shark the size of a school bus. At the time (1986), he had a contract hauling garbage scows and remembers the area being thick with sharks. Sometimes there were so many sharks, he says, a man could've walked on their backs for a mile, maybe two. Last month, during a garbage run, he saw fewer than ten sharks and decides this can mean one of two things: either the garbage isn't as good or fish all the way up the food chain are getting hammered something fierce. His money, he says, is on fish be fucked.

The geographic coordinates double-checked, LORAN and GPS putting the tug in the middle of the dump, Garr sends the engines into neutral. *Conquest* rides up on the towline, her bulwarks a sail to the following southwest breeze. Moments later, with the boats rail to rail, the mate climbs aboard carrying a flashlight, Stillson and sledge. Aye-aye, he says, responding to Garr's command: Let 'er gush. Garr wants the boat to sink in minutes so he can be early for his kid's soccer game. He also says his debt to a dead man is clear as of right now. So far, the tug has swallowed nearly three hundred gallons of diesel; plus, he's out a day's charter rate.

The mate returns soaking wet and makes his report: She's Swiss cheese, bad with holes. He pulled each plug and smashed open every thru-hull fitting. He glances at the chronometer mounted on the wheelhouse bulkhead—1:32 p.m.—and predicts *Conquest* will be on the bottom before 2:00. He then tells Garr never to send him on a job like that again; it was superspooky, he says. Honest to God, he heard voices telling him to stop; once, he felt something push him just as he was coming down with the sledge and almost nailed a foot. More than freaky, really, he adds, was being below and hearing water gush into every compartment, along with the voices. He can't imagine what kinds of demons rise out of the bilge when a crewed boat goes down.

Helpless, *Conquest* goes broadsides to the wind and the three-foot waves it rakes up out of the ocean. Since dawn, the sky has remained cloudless, and it is just now starting to regain some of the color bleached out of it around noontime by an unblinkered sun at the peak of its arc. There's no land, boats or buoys in sight and, strangely, there's not a gull, shearwater or petrel to be seen. Our only obvious company is a lone shark, most likely a dogfish from the looks of its equipment: twin dorsal fins of nearly identical size set atop a five-foot-long cylindrical body. It circles *Conquest* a few times and vanishes, no doubt disappointed by the lack of garbage.

The gurgling of water inside *Conquest* draws us all to the tug's rail, an audience of gawkers since there's little to learn from a sinking ship in such wildly atypical conditions—relatively calm seas raised by a pleasant breeze, no screaming or injured crew-men, no clogged companionways, no sense of calamity and not an iota of chaos. Garr tries to put a finger on things, saying, It isn't Hollywood and isn't near the real deal, so it's more like PBS, eh?

No one changes the channel, all eyes on *Conquest* inhaling water as if in a race to fill her insides. Four inches of freeboard disappear each minute; within ten minutes, the deck is awash and water starts climbing up the wheelhouse and fo'c'sle. A mighty burp rises out of the main hold and sends water shoot-ing into the air. The spray looses dozens of tiny rainbows, none lasting more than a few seconds, but all point to pots of gold on the bow. With the deck underwater and the wheelhouse half-way there, *Conquest* broadcasts her misery, her timbers groaning as they twist on bronze fastenings and react to forces they were never designed to handle. More air vents, this time out of the galley, and the stern disappears in a snap, gone like some magic trick involving invisible thread, and the bow juts into the air, nose to the sky.

The tipping point reached, *Conquest* defies expectations and hangs in place, a portrait of defiance, refusing to sink any far-ther. Obviously, there's plenty of air trapped inside her, and that life force appears tightly contained by the effort and talent that went into her construction. The exposed planking up front, for instance, looks as snug as new, not a busted seam or blown piece of oakum in sight, and while her timbers continue to groan, the hull remains integral. Garr's impressed. He thinks the Down East shipwrights who built her should be congratulated for outstanding work. Too bad, he adds, they all lost their jobs wayback-like. He feels they're cut from the same cloth as those past generations who laid America's foundation and cemented it to bedrock. Without those hands around anymore, he says, he doesn't know what to think about the future, other than we're in for big trouble. He believes you can build shit as high as you want, but each new piece better be true, correctly plumbed every inch of the way, or watch out, everything will collapse.

More than an hour after reaching the tipping point, *Conquest* hasn't gone anywhere except sideways, drifting to the edge of the dumping grounds. His patience exhausted, Garr announces, That's it. He's tired of wasting diesel and he doesn't want to be fined by the Coasties for dumping outside the line. Hold on, he orders, and rams *Conquest* at quarter speed. The damage is slight, the tug merely denting the planking. He gives it another go, this time adding more speed, but the results are the same. Frustrated, he uses the tug like a bulldozer and pushes the fishing boat toward the middle of the cemetery until, at last, her oak splinters under the tug's iron. Air whistles through the gash and releases the smell of a nearly empty wine cask uncorked after years in a basement. The hull, however, only loses a few feet of freeboard. The stem and forepeak remain high above the water surface.

With the tug in neutral, Garr repeats, Never should've taken this job. Never should've taken . . . He now believes we were all wrong and mistook a sky-high repair estimate for a death certificate. Rot may riddle her bones, but it hasn't killed her. This boat was built the old way, now almost a forgotten way, Garr says, and made to weather repeated blows and serve generations of fishermen at hard work. We've been dopes, he concludes, absolute jerks thinking she'd go down easy.

In his opinion, *Conquest* has plenty of life left in her and we must respect every bit of it. Dammit, he signed on for transport and burial duty; there was nothing in the deal about killing and he's no executioner. He puts the tug into standby mode and puts us all on death watch. She goes when she sees fit, he commands, no longer concerned about how much diesel the tug eats. But, oh-God, there's one problem he must deal with: the missus. She expects him at the kid's soccer game and later at the dinner table. He calls his office on the ship-to-shore radio, asking for help. Would somebody, please, contact his wife and tell her he'll be home as soon as he can.

The sun sets and Garr trains the tug's spotlights on what's left to be seen of *Conquest:* her stem and half her forepeak. As if she had been waiting the entire time to exit under a spotlight while the rest of the stage went black, she fades as the western sky dims, going lower and lower in the water; she finally vanishes once darkness sets in. Garr leans over the rail and stretches for the froth and bubbles *Conquest* leaves behind. He pulls in air until there's nothing left of her dense, woody smell.

The tug makes dock at 10:45 p.m. Booked for a paying job starting at daybreak, Garr and the mate decide to sleep aboard. I leave as Garr dials his wife to explain things.

Sometime before dawn a Coast Guard cutter drops anchor outside the hurricane dike and puts an end to the free flow of local water traffic. Any fishing boat wanting in or out of the harbor must now first surrender to lawmen and allow them to poke, quiz, measure, weigh and scrutinize everybody and everything aboard ship. The feds call their action Operation Clean Harbor and promise that it's merely the start of a long campaign to rid the sea of rogues and outlaws. Fishermen call it Fucked-up Shit and start wishing out loud for a laser powerful enough to vaporize an enemy gunship. In a less public fashion, a small crew begins work on a torpedo.

Two fishing boats—one inbound, one outbound—are tagged before word circulates that this is no routine shakedown. The federal boarding parties include seasoned fishery officials and DEA agents on loan from the Florida office, plus Coasties wearing academy rings and carrying computers to run background checks on all crewmen. Reports from the scene are broadcast over the radio and piped through VHF sets in restaurants, fish houses and boats tied to the docks.

The heavy-handed action causes a ripple effect throughout the waterfront, all of it unwanted and bad for business. Nearly every outbound fishing trip is postponed by captains wanting to wait things out or needing time to muster a full crew with a clean record and no bad habits. Meanwhile, captains aboard inbound boats double-check their inventory, deep-sixing any illegal catch or stash, and some detour to Nantucket to offload crewmen fearing the results of a background check. Stevedores and fish processors warn employees of layoffs if the lawmen stick around much longer. Icehouses trim production, and fuel barges sit idle at the dock. Truckers begin lining up alternate work to keep their rigs rolling without fish aboard. And, of course, all smuggling activity is put on hold, affecting men and machinery as far away as Brazil, to the south, and Cabo Verde, to the east.

Monk welcomes me to his shop late that afternoon and gushes news of close calls and lucky timing. His adventures began three days ago, as he set out for Martha's Vineyard aboard *Shell Shock* to deliver weed. The transfer went smoothly, but minutes after clearing Vineyard Haven Harbor and steering for the clam beds off Hyannis, he confronted a flotilla of U.S. Navy ships about to set up positions in advance of a presidential visit. He says there was so much floating armor, it looked like an invasion, D-Day or something like that, on the TV. Men he describes as Rambos in wet suits boarded *Shell Shock,* checked his paperwork and left without a word. He's positive that if he had been fifteen minutes late delivering the weed, he'd be bunking with Uncle Pete right now.

He spent the next two days fishing on a one-day license and headed home, planning a predawn arrival to unload while it was still dark. Around three-thirty a.m., just as *Shell Shock* made the turn for the hurricane dike at the channel marker, he recognized the lights on his tail as a threat, either a large Coast Guard boat or an alien spaceship with a bow gun hovering close to the water. With the enemy one and a half miles astern and compatriots one and a half miles ahead, he says, he did what any fisherman would do: he opened the throttle, turned off the running lights and never looked back. The strategy worked. By the time the radio crackled orders to show his lights and stop for a boarding party, Monk was speeding through the gate at the hurricane dike.

Monk opens a fresh pint-sized bottle of cheap vodka and, as he bends his elbow, says, Fuck the sheriff. He worked hard, extra hard for every lobster, groundfish and clam he caught. Legal/illegal, to hell with that. His catch came out of honest labor. He didn't rip off nobody. There was no scam involved. No little old lady lost the farm. And he says there's neither mystery nor bad to what he did. He earned every bottom-feeder and swimmer which came up over the rail and he did it the Lopes way: by busting his balls. Look at these mitts, he orders, and claims a ton of hand cream couldn't soften his calluses. They're as thick as tire rubber, he adds. At sea, the only crooks he ever met wore badges, all of them feds and all of them dippers swiping cheese out of a fisherman's pocket.

He rehoists the vodka, takes a swig, makes the sign of the cross and says, Lucky, thank Christ, he's some lucky today. Before the next swallow, he salutes the less fortunate. Get out soon, he says, referring to the four men busted so far in the crackdown at the dike. He hopes all charges are dropped for technical reasons. Two men on the outbound vessel were arrested on possession charges, while aboard the inbound boat, one man was cuffed for outstanding warrants and another was snared on an immigration rap. The bottle goes back inside the liquor drawer, but the drawer stays open. Sustained by catnaps and black beauties over the last three days, he figures booze is the only thing which will guide him to sleep. If it's not medicine, he says, he doesn't know what is.

But, oh, man-oh-man, he doesn't look forward to waking from that deep sleep to what awaits him: an aching back, shoulder and legs. He says he'd be okay and maybe even start loving *Shell Shock* again if all he did was smuggle. But the weed delivery was a one-shot deal, a dollop of honey which appeared on his plate only because he's waiting on a part to finish fixing the motor to the regular dope ferry. He'd postpone delivery of the part if he didn't feel it would be a dead man's act. No kidding, he says, the regular courier would kill him if he ever found out.

Monk slumps in the swivel chair at his desk and points to a stack of mail. He calls it a heap-a-bills which only motor work can make disappear; fishing, he says, won't pay for his casket. If it's tough to make a living aboard a small boat today, he presumes it will be worse tomorrow, with new regs and more rules and fewer of everything to catch in the ocean. Perhaps if he owned a boat like the 80- to 110-footers he does engine work on, and if he owned a license instead of renting one, he could earn the cheese he once imagined waiting for him at sea. But nope, he grabbed on to the wrong damn boat and wished Grampy-J had been more specific in his description of the boat that would deliver him to a new world full of opportunity.

Burying the mail under a service manual for Detroit Diesel the size of an unabridged dictionary, Monk rubs his head while itemizing distress. His fifty hours of fishing netted a lousy $435. If he hadn't brought home some lobsters and groundfish, he would have cleared just $125 on clams. And by the time he finishes visiting the chiropractor, liquor store and pot dealer to erase the pain, he expects, he'll have lost money on the whole adventure, including the cheese he made from the weed delivery. The crazy part to it all, he says: If he doesn't land a big motor job before his wallet goes flat, he'll be forced, yes sir, forced to go fishing and poaching again just to keep breathing. The sooner he kills *Shell Shock,* the better. Then, and only then, with the weight of her bills and maintenance costs off his mind and chest, will he be able to start fresh and work on some other way to make his first million.

He reaches for the medicine bottle and urges the potion to make him sleepy. Normally, after a three-day fishing trip, he goes out like a light, but he says he got all wound up this afternoon doing research. He spent hours going through his stolen copy of Coast Guard postings and maneuvers, claiming to have read it forwards and backwards, sideways, too, and couldn't find any mention of Operation Clean Harbor; hell, he couldn't even find the name of the cutter stationed outside the dike. Equally disturbing, there wasn't one word about joint task forces, DEA agents or background checks. Like most people he knows, he has blown off court dates for traffic offenses and stupid minor stuff like that, he says, and reckons there are warrants out for his arrest. Plus, as a solo fisherman, he needs drugs aboard. A cup of coffee can keep him awake for ten minutes, while a black beauty can keep him alert, eyes roving, for hours.

Anyway, how can he pull off the perfect wreck if the Coasties won't follow their own playbook? he asks, and answers by shaping his hand into a gun aimed at his temple and pulling the trigger. There's no way he'll risk being rescued a second time before

Shell Shock is safely on the bottom. Once was too-too many and he doubts if it's possible to rebound mentally and financially from a repeat performance.

Frankly, he says, this Operation Clean Harbor thing baffles the hell out of him. Since many of the best and most experienced fishermen are users or have rap sheets and outstanding warrants, he's convinced boats will have to go out with an unsafe number of greenhorns aboard. And that, he asserts, means mistakes will be made and men will die. It reminds him of when those idiots capped days at sea, forcing boats to stay out in murderous weather when they should be in safe harbor. Like many others on the docks, he believes that rule caused the sinking of at least a half dozen boats and promises more destruction in the future.

While he and most independent fishermen, along with the service sector at the waterfront, trash Operation Clean Harbor, fleet owners and other big players cheer it on. At this point, they praise any anti-pirate action that doesn't adversely impact their bottom line. Having battled Washington for years, and having lost every skirmish, they're now eager to cut deals with the feds and pose as its dependable ally at sea and on land. In fact, they view the government as their only protection from lawyers representing environmental groups. And to further check the power of the courts, they've rechristened themselves as problem solvers, on the case figuring out ways to ensure the health of the fishery. Today, their message to the public: We care more than anyone; our livelihoods depend on a healthy ocean. Meanwhile, their flacks sit on various management councils and advisory boards, working with the feds to craft long-term policy.

Additionally, local fleet owners want drug-free boats and no ex-cons on the payroll. It would limit their liability in work-related lawsuits and, ultimately, lower their insurance premiums. Already, some fleet owners demand drug tests and background checks before hiring anyone; most likely, this will be routine in a few years. And perhaps most important to their agenda, the crackdown at the dike reinforces a message they want broadcast twenty-four/seven: the fuck-you era of fishermen and fishing is over; it's now the age of big business, with pencil pushers in charge. The old frontier mentality at sea is no longer acceptable; indeed, it has been criminalized and holdouts will be pursued until they either convert and renounce their old ways or go to jail and disappear. If this angers anyone and gets them to jump ship, the industry will gladly speed their departure. It will only help juice the pace of change and provide opportunity to replace their kind with foreign workers happy to make a few bucks over minimum wage.

How about some good news, Sailor, like *Conquest* sinking in a sec or two? Monk asks, and swallows some more medicine. He listens to the report of a seven-hour sink time and uncurls a length of swear words knotted at the end with a pledge to kill her, that damn boat, *Shell Shock*. He won't be deterred. Even if the insurance lapses on her and other woodies tomorrow, she's going down. It's me or her, he says.

It's eight-fifteen p.m. and dark out, so Monk walks me to the garage door. Someone has to work the triple locks at the jamb. The first dead bolt opens with a click. The second opens with news of Alan: a real estate agent offered to buy his triple-decker at the magic number and he's going to sell. The third lock opens with a warning: Don't take any shortcuts home. Last week Monk heard gunfire coming from somewhere near the water at the old Pierce Mill site, which now also hosts twice-a-week animal fights. Cocks are featured one night and pit bulls the next. He says gangbangers are betting thousands on each round and gringos aren't welcome.

There's only one streetlight on the way home and, as usual, it's busted. When I first moved to New Bedford, nobody ever thought about walking in the dark down Belleville Avenue. Every night for five generations, holidays and workers' strikes included, light spilling out of the factory windows kept the thoroughfare bright as day. Tonight, though, the only glow of industry rises out of the sodium-vapor lamps at the former address of Soule Mill and now home to the SuperFund dewatering plant, where PCB-laced muck is readied for shipment to a dump near Buffalo, New York. Also gone are the distinctive noises and ground vibrations issued by the machinery in each mill, which guided the blind for a century. Right now the only mechanical sounds come from cars either zipping down the straightaway or idling at the curb while dope and cash exchange hands. Over at the Pierce Mill lot, all is quiet, not even a cricket telling the temperature.

ACKNOWLEDGMENTS

NEW BEDFORD WAS MY HOMETOWN for seventeen years, and research for this book began early on, in 1988. That's when a friend called and told me to meet him at his boat. He and his crew had just pulled in with 23,600 pounds of scallops. They also caught lobsters and groundfish they intended to sell off the books for cash. He suggested that I bring along a notebook, because, he said, somebody or other should be documenting the way-so-good life on the docks. He then cautioned: Just remember to protect the guilty, you know, change names and enough stuff so nobody wants to kill-ya-like. Certainly, he'd rip out my lungs if the taxman nabbed him for cash sales.

When I weighed anchor, in 2004, the era of good times for the fishing business was over. My friend was still running a scallop boat, but he wasn't sure how long he'd have a job. Most of the men he started out with in the trade were either dead or banging nails. And with the way things are going in the fishery, he could be wearing a hammer holster tomorrow, he said, adding, There's not much left out there, except for feds, rules and headaches. To him and the other dock citizens who never flinched when a notebook opened, I say, Thanks. You offered me an insider's look at an industry as it went from crest to trough.

And to Dan Frank, I also say, Thanks. Your patience and skill as an editor invariably brought up the day. As well, I much appreciated the help of Dan's assistant and my boss, Fran Bigman. At home, Elizabeth McFadden gets a special nod for putting up with me all these years.

ABOUT THE AUTHOR

Rory Nugent is an accomplished mariner. His previous books include *The Search for the Pink-Headed Duck* and *Drums Along the Congo*.

A NOTE ON THE TYPE

This book was set in Monotype Dante, a typeface designed by Giovanni Mardersteig (1892–1977). Modeled on the Aldine type used for Pietro Cardinal Bembo's treatise *De Aetna* in 1495, Dante is a modern interpretation of the venerable face.

Composed by Creative Graphics,
Allentown, Pennsylvania

Printed and bound by R. R. Donnelley,
Harrisonburg, Virginia

Designed by M. Kristen Bearse